THE FAE KING'S ASSASSIN

Realm of Dragons and Fae

ALISHA KLAPHEKE

Cover Design by JV Arts

Hardback Case art by Julia Dea and Miblart

Editing by Laura Josephson

Map by Soraya Corcoran

Prophecy Graphic Design by Abide, Selah

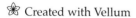 Created with Vellum

To Aidan and Amelia,
may all of your wild dreams come true

TWO RAVENS GATHERED IN THE SKY
ONE OF ICE, THE OTHER CAST IN DARKNESS
AROUND THE PEAKS THEY FLEW AND FLEW

BODIES COURSING
TALONS LASHING
BEAKS BREAKING

WIND THEIR CLEAVER,
NIGHT THEIR BALM

AT DAWN, THEIR HEARTS SOARED
ON AND ON.

A CROWN IS BROKEN
ANOTHER MADE
WHAT CURSES CUT,
OATHS OFTEN SAVE.

-THE DRUID'S PROPHECY
AGE OF ILLANIUS

REVNA

Assassinations and spying had never been my preferred missions. Fights with fists and teeth and steel were refreshingly honest when compared to plotting seduction or slipping herbs into drinks. Which was why I was thankful that my current assignment had nothing to do with gold-hemmed dresses and everything to do with stalking an Unseelie gargoyle through the forest alongside my dragon familiar. I had lost the Unseelie in the heavy underbrush, but the snap of a twig behind me stilled my breath.

I spun and sliced my iron and adamant blade across the gargoyle's abdomen, loosing a stream of smoking black blood. The monster's ratty wings flared wide as he leaped from the brush, lashing a clawed paw at my head. I rolled under his arm, but the Unseelie still clipped my shoulder and I let out a hiss. Pain slithered over the injury. Springing up behind the gargoyle, I gritted my teeth and rammed my sword into its back. The monster fell to the blood-soaked ground.

Steely clouds billowed beside the autumn sun as I stepped over the dead Unseelie monster. Another day, another assignment. And while I might have preferred one mission over another, my master didn't care about my opinion. He owned me in every sense of the word, the curse rune on the back of my neck ensuring my obedience. With one ancient word, he could kill me even from afar. I wiped the gargoyle's stench from my blade and surveyed the skies, seeking a particular pair of dragon wings.

"Where are you, terrible beast?" My dragon, Arkyn, had grown impatient waiting for the gargoyle to show and had flown off to survey the area. Lucky for him, he'd missed the fight. "If you're lolling about in a field of blueberries, I'm going to roast you for my dinner."

Arkyn was a good companion, but he had one weakness. Food.

A shadow blocked the sun, then Arkyn was landing beside me, his color the same hue as the surrounding oak trunks, his eyes as bright as torches, and his wings buffeting me with wind. The dragon was roughly the size of three horses, and when he nudged my stomach, I widened my stance to keep from toppling backward. I rubbed the smooth scales of his head, my heart warming.

"You're lucky I'm still alive." Maneuvering my

round shield onto my back, I found a patch of dark moss. I dragged my dirtied sword along the ground to clean it, then I tucked a leg into one of Arkyn's stirrups and hauled my tired arse onto the dragon's back. "No one else would sneak Cook's scraps to your nest. She values those scraps more than all the lives at Isernwyrd."

Arkyn sniffed as if he didn't agree that he had only me to find his favored meal. He spread his bat-like wings and ran over the rocky ground, and we took off. Leaves brushed my boots, and branches tried to snag my cloak as we drove up and away from the forest floor in uneven bursts of forward movement. Above the broken canopy of green, the coming storm blew a chilly wind across my face.

Below, a drumstone's deep blue surface flickered with emerald light and I turned my face toward home. Hopefully, that stone was finished causing trouble for a while. At least long enough for my nap and a meal. I didn't mind the drumstones and the way they spit out Unseelie monsters from hidden realms—killing off things like the gargoyle paid for my keep and gave me coin to save for my ultimate goal. But I needed a day off.

Arkyn flew over the toothlike walls of Isernwyrd. Black pennants snapped from the five towers, the color denoting the Hunters' collective grief over losing the crown princess. The shouts of my fellow Hunters rose as Arkyn landed in the courtyard. Ignoring the other Hunters' kind calls to Arkyn, I slid out of the saddle and ran both hands down the dragon's body, checking for wounds.

"So tell me, was it blueberries or a lady friend?" I made it to his snout and picked a dark blue bit from one of his viciously long canines. Holding it up for him to see, I raised an eyebrow. "Really? I mean, I had guessed… But you truly left me to die for a snack?"

He exhaled a heavy, damp breath into my face, blowing my brown braids back, then bumped me with his snout.

I flicked his nose gently. "You might not believe one gargoyle could have taken me down, but you underestimate my need for a nap."

Wishing the other Hunters would leave us be, I glared at our audience.

"Ah, come off it, Revna." The newest of the Hunters, Cuthnor, a recruit with far more brawn than brains, stalked around Arkyn. His swagger and smirk said he didn't know the story of my dragon and the last arsehat who'd tried his patience. "Let someone else take this beast into the skies. Someone whose strength matches his."

I sighed. I wanted ale and to sit the hells down. "Fine. Let's get this over with." I motioned to Cuthnor. "Take me down and I'll ask Arkyn nicely if he'll take you on a mission. Which he won't."

Cuthnor snorted and tugged at his ragged beard. Inside and out, the man was as ugly as they came. He lunged at me, then went left, trying to take my back. I put out one boot and tripped the fool. With a grace that showed why Master had recruited him this late in life, he caught himself. Normally, we started here as children. Easier to manipulate that way.

Cuthnor grabbed my hair and laughed as he attempted to wrap an arm around my exposed throat. I took hold of the fist tangled in my thick, messy braids, pressed it down onto my scalp to hold him there, and donkey-kicked the moron in the stones. He howled as everyone else guffawed.

"Want another one or are you finished?" I kept both my hands on his fist on the top of my head, not allowing him to use the hold to his advantage.

He let out a few garbled words and spat on the toe of my boot. Fire simmered in my blood.

"These are my favorite boots." I twisted, skipped closer a step, then slammed my heel onto his instep.

He roared and released me to the cackling of the other Hunters.

"It's not the dragon you need on your next job, Cuthnor," the gangly Tynin called out as I used a rag from my pouch to clean spittle from my finely stitched gray leather boots.

Cuthnor stood, still cupping his man bits. "Berserker bitch."

The slur had always pleased me because I took pride in my Berserker blood. I didn't know how many folk still possessed the battle rage magic of my people, but the gift had to be rare. *The king had seen to that,* I thought darkly.

"That's right," I said to Cuthnor. "Don't forget it."

Cuthnor stalked away toward the horse stables as the rest of the Hunters gave me space. I smoothed my hands down Arkyn's belly and unbuckled the saddle. Drawing it over him, I was careful not to clip his wing. Sure, he could handle the pain of a scratched wing, but those lovely appendages were sensitive. I handed the saddle off to a stable boy, then walked alongside Arkyn across the mud-slick cobblestones of the courtyard.

In the sanded square near the entrance to the mess hall, Raulian fought Vi bare-knuckled. Raulian's gaze flicked to me as we passed. Vi knocked him hard with a nice right cross.

"Better focus on the training, Raul." I snorted a laugh.

He came back at Vi with a series of expert strikes. Raulian wasn't the sharpest fellow, but he was a good person and the nearest thing to a friend aside from Arkyn.

Servants in crisp linen aprons and tunics carried baskets of dirtied laundry from the arched doorways of the barracks and into the servants' hall near the chandler's workshop. I'd always thought it ridiculous that Master insisted the servants remain so tidy when he didn't give a rat's foot about what we Hunters looked like.

A shudder rippled through my bones and I

swallowed a familiar sour taste on the back of my tongue. Arkyn nudged my shoulder and his tongue darted out to touch my cheek.

"Stop, you little beastie. You know I hate that."

With the sleeve of my tunic, I wiped dragon drool from my face. Though Arkyn's concern over my longstanding full-on fear of Master was sweet, I had no space for it in my life. Hunters had to be cold and show no trepidation—even in front of the man who beat us when we failed in a mission and who controlled the death curse runes inked at the back of our necks.

When we reached the corner of the lower kitchens building, Arkyn lifted his head and sniffed loudly right next to my ear. I shoved him away a step as the scent of freshly baked bread and venison stew filled my nose.

"Don't worry. I'll get you some later." Master would pay me well for killing that monster so quickly. I'd have enough to feed us both for at least two days.

Wide stone steps led up to the abandoned scriptorium, which was now Arkyn's nest. Master had ordered the entrance torn down and a new one crafted of roughly hewn wood, wide enough to permit Arkyn easily. Three slender windows let in some of the approaching storm's metallic breeze and a portion of the day's weak light. Fresh hay sat in a large circle in the back corner of the empty room, along with a trough I filled with water every day before sunrise. Beside that, a wide copper bowl showed the remnants of Arkyn's squirrel and crabapple breakfast, cores and small bones discarded neatly into two piles.

I grabbed the dish and dumped the contents into the rubbish bin that the servants would discard for me later. They did it for free because Master ordered them to keep Arkyn's nest clean. Master didn't give food freely to people, but he did provide a portion for the only dragon Isernwyrd had housed as a Hunter's familiar in two centuries.

A knock sounded behind me and I turned toward the entrance to see Raulian.

"You look even paler than usual." The man was as fair as a summer's day. Though I hailed from Fjordbok, I wasn't as light-skinned as him.

Raulian pushed his curly white-blond hair away from his face and swallowed. "Master calls for you. The king is here and asking for you."

I dropped the copper dish and it clanged against the flagstone floor, making Arkyn draw back and hiss.

"What? Now?" I hadn't even washed the gargoyle muck off my hands.

"Immediately. Need me to get Arkyn some grub?"

I scratched the only soft spot on my dragon's body— a tiny square of hide behind his ears—then left him with a lazy fist-to-the-chest salute. Starting out of the room, I clapped Raulian on the shoulder.

"Yeah, that would be good. Thanks, Raul. But watch your fingers."

I grinned wickedly and Arkyn took his cue, bristling

so that the spear-sharp spikes on his tail fanned out and upward.

"Good dragon," Raul murmured as I left them to it.

I enjoyed teasing Raul, but it was only a weak distraction from the buzzing in my head and the tingling of my fingers. Why was the king here and asking for me? I had never met our ruler. The king always gave his assignments to Master, who then passed them on to whichever Hunter fit the job best.

Hurrying across the courtyard, I eyed the cut on my arm. It wasn't deep, but I needed to clean it soon to avoid infection. Gargoyles were nasty beasts.

Two guards stopped me at the door to Master's chambers. One pointed to my forehead. "You've got Unseelie blood on your face."

"All the better to show him I've been hard at work." I gave the man a nod and he opened the door.

Standing in a pool of sunlight that was as gold as spilled dragon blood, Master spoke in quick whispers to the king. Road dust caked the hem of King Darrew's ruby-red cloak and made his salt-and-pepper hair look brown. He turned as I walked in, his eyes already studying every inch of me.

I didn't know which one I'd rather run through. Both, if my dreams ever came true. I laughed silently at myself and sank into a low bow, my fist against my shoulder in the Hunter fashion, waiting until they spoke to me.

"The dragon Huntress with Berserker blood." The

king's voice slid across the chamber's dark stone floor like a snake. His boots sounded his approach while the slap of Master's bare feet marked his movement. "Rise," King Darrew said.

I did so but kept my eyes cast downward. "As you order, my king."

Master poked my ribs with his walking stick. "Show him your ice eyes, Huntress Revna."

Standing perfectly still, I looked at the king, whose eyes flickered with interest. But what kind of interest? A man's lust? A rich man's desire for that which is rare? Or was he only here for a job and my pale blue eyes— the mark of Berserker blood—meant I could do what he needed done?

The king's gaze left my face and found Master's. "Will she do it?"

Master set a heavily ringed hand on his stomach and raised a thick eyebrow. "If you order it so."

"This job will require an especially strong focus to complete successfully and with grace."

"If she doesn't complete this mission, she dies." Master shrugged.

The king smiled and he crossed his arms. "I like the way you work, Master of the Hunters. It's simple. Clean."

"Effective," I said.

Both men's eyes momentarily widened, but respect shone in the king's look. I guessed he would like a show of my bold nature. If he wanted a Berserker, he wanted the death of someone difficult to kill. And he'd come here in the flesh instead of sending a missive. Whatever this job was, it sure wouldn't be a walk down the flowered lane.

"I am your servant, my king." I bowed again. Groveling to these monsters was disgusting, but I had no desire for a beating before my nap and meal.

The tip of Master's stick found my chin and he lifted my head. "Shall I tell her, my king, or do you want to?"

King Darrew's smile turned my stomach. He met my gaze. "You, my rare Huntress, are to kill the King of the Fae."

My mouth fell open and cold swept through me like winter had fallen on Isernwyrd with that one sentence.

My life was over.

2

REVNA

I schooled my features, keeping my face blank so as not to show my horror at the king's words. "As you wish, my king."

The king paced Master's chamber. "I'm sure you are aware the crown princess's death was not natural. Someone murdered her."

I could hardly concentrate on his words. Killing the Fae king was impossible. They were sending me to my death. Was it a political move to show a failed assassination? What was their plan? If I died, I'd never fulfill my mother's dying wish. I had to stay alive. Even if I survived the Fae forest of Gwerhune and all of its dangerous creatures, the moment I entered that castle, I'd be living my last moments.

"A thousand condolences, my king." I bowed again. When men were grieving, they often struck out at the nearest person.

Master padded closer and lifted my chin with his thick thumb. "Enough groveling. Listen."

"Aye, Master."

"When my retinue found her and her guards…" The king's gravelly voice trailed off and he coughed.

I'd seen the crown princess while on a job at Earl Finton's estate. She had been dancing with cousins, her light brown skin and long black hair so similar to the late queen's.

When the king turned at the base of the three steps that led away from this greeting section of the chamber and into the bedroom quarters, the sun showed his eyes and his unshed tears. His cheeks drew in tightly, shifting his beard so that it brushed his gold-hemmed cloak and the bronze clasp at his throat. "My men found… Near her body, they found a sigil ring."

My ears perked up. I hadn't heard about this. I was aware that she had been killed with a blade to the throat and that the killer had burned her body, perhaps in some attempt at a magic ritual.

The king removed a circle of pale gold from the plum and black leather pouch at his belt. He held up the sigil ring and Master hurried over to look closely.

"A hare and a fern…" Master squinted. He was losing his sight in his old age. "What else is on the ring, my king?" he asked, his voice more humble than I'd ever heard it. He sounded like a stranger instead of the man who had raised me.

"There is also a mace and a drumstone."

Master let out a small gasp.

"Yes, this is the sigil ring of the Fae king." The king's lips twisted into a grimace. He was holding back tears. My heart pinched and I wanted to say something. But what? I had no comforting role to play here or anywhere. Clearing his throat, the king continued, "He had his assassins kill our kingdom's most treasured daughter and he left his ring here as a warning."

Master motioned to a one-eyed servant named Rori, who had once helped me sneak back into Isernwyrd after a night out drinking with Raulian. Master mouthed the words *Bring wine* to Rori before facing the king again.

"What do you believe this horrifying act warned us of?" Master asked.

The king rubbed a hand through his hair and exhaled roughly. "To remain on our side of the Veil. They will continue to trade with us because it benefits them, but the Fae king wants us to remember our place beneath his boot. He has flat-out refused my attempts to draw up a proper treaty to protect resources on both sides of the Veil. Fae are haughty creatures. Deceitful animals. All they care to trade away is their Fae gold."

The way he spat gold made it seem like it was worthless. The gold had worked just fine to buy King Darrew the lumber, sails, and men to build a new fleet of ships designed by the Deigs people. He was currently using said fleet to attack the western kingdoms beyond the White Sea.

Regardless of the strange way the king denied his need and past use of Fae gold, he certainly had a good reason for hating the Fae king, the Ruler of the Realm of Lights. His own daughter had been slain by our new neighbors. Not that the Seelie Fae were actually new to the world; they had been behind the Veil and had recently thinned it enough to engage in trade.

"I will have revenge." Lifting his fist, the king squeezed his fingers until his knuckles were white. "We all will." He whirled on me, his grief giving way to rage. "You will kill him in the most painful way possible."

The image of a four-pronged leaf flashed through my mind. "With cherubium root." It was the worst way to die. Painful. Slow. And the victim couldn't cry out for help or thrash about. No antidotes either. It didn't matter though. I was not going. Not a chance. I would escape Master's network and get away from him for good. Maybe Raulian would come with me.

But only if we could cut out our curse runes.

Everyone who had tried that—two that I knew of personally—had died from self-inflicted wounds or by Master's stick. But I wasn't just anyone... A memory of Oolard's broken legs and his corpse left to rot in the wasteland blinked across my mind's eye.

Sick glee poured across the king's features and more tears glistened in his gaze. "Cherubium root. Yes." He turned to Master. "She is the best choice. I can tell by the look of her."

He had no idea I was plotting escape rather than his impossible task.

Master nodded, tapping his stick on the floor like he always did when thinking. "I will take care of the details. Unless you wanted to, my king?"

"No, I leave it to the experts." He pocketed the sigil ring, his own ring flashing briefly in the sunlight. "Do not fail me, Wacian. You will not live to tell the story."

I had known Master had a name, but never, not once, had I heard anyone speak it. Master gave me a quick warning glance and I forgot the name as best I could.

Master bowed low and set his fisted hand against his shoulder. "As you will it, my king."

The king left, the sound of boots in the hallway outside Master's chamber door fading.

"Sit and listen." Master pointed to the usual three-legged wooden stool near the bookshelves.

I did so, keeping my back straight and my hands on my thighs. Master insisted on seeing our hands—a show of being unarmed, he always said.

He stood in front of me, closer than the average person would do naturally. This was his habit. Tapping his stick on the glistening floor, he stared at me. "The strategy is to infiltrate the Fae court during the three-day Brezhoneg Branle disguised as one of the Fae females that are hoping to snag the king's interest. They don't care about the potential mate being from a certain house as we do. The Fae are animalistic. Their goal is simply to continue the royal line because his Fae magic is the most powerful of all their people."

I was to seduce the Fae king. A thousand outcomes flurried through my mind, a cold death at the end of each of them. My death. If the stories were true, the Fae wouldn't be as easily tricked as a human target. "No matter how good my disguise, they will catch my scent immediately."

Master pursed his lips and shook his head. "The Witch is concocting a potion for you. It will cast a thick illusion over you and mask your scent as well."

I blinked. The Witch? Of course. I pictured the hag with her owl eyes and sharp teeth and fisted my hands. Aside from creating our death runes, she mostly stuck to working during great wars.

Master crossed his arms, his stick tucked against him. "Tell me your thoughts on the plan."

"I assume it's the usual *get close enough to be trusted so that I can poison his drink without his taster present*." It didn't matter what I thought. No plan would succeed against the Fae. The Fae king could strangle me with one hand. In his sleep. They were unbeatable in battle. I knew because I fought one once.

A Fae female had left her lands and been adopted into a border family. She had battled the greedy marsh lords—horrible men I'd been working for at the time due to an agreement between them and Master. I had nearly died that day and the Fae hadn't broken a sweat. Nightmares about her accuracy with a javelin and the way she bashed in skulls with a bejeweled mace haunted me. And she had probably only been half-Fae. Arkyn had saved me and I accepted the beating for my failure without a word of protest. Bruises were better than a grave. Granted, I had been younger and my training incomplete, but still. The Fae were no joke in a fight. I couldn't fathom how deadly their full-blooded king would be.

Master had been going on about where to get cherubium this time of year. "…meet me at the gates at sunrise. We'll go to the Witch and get your mission underway." He flicked a hand in dismissal.

I bowed to his back—he was already shuffling scrolls and slips of old parchment on his desk—then strode toward the door.

"Revna," he said, stopping me, "don't be late." His eyes were flat and cold, a promise of death in the worst way he could think up.

Shivering slightly, I bowed again, then slipped away as quickly as my legs would carry me.

It was time to get the hells out of this living nightmare, and I had a plan to do just that.

3

LYSANAEL

King Lysanael of the Fae opened his door to see the slim, quick-eyed messenger he'd sent to the Shrouded Mountains months ago.

"No sign of your brother, my king. But I do have this message from your contacts there."

Lysanael swallowed and clenched his jaw, attempting to hide his grief at the news. Though his body had never been found, his younger brother had been reported as dead, lost in an avalanche during his winter trip to watch the Mist Knights at their work. Neither Lysanael or his brother's wife had given up searching for him.

He accepted the small scroll from the messenger and dismissed him. "Find food in the kitchens. Celin will see to it that your rooms are ready if you wish to rest here for the night."

Lysanael took a sack of gold coins from his desk and

handed it over. The messenger bowed and slipped down the dim corridor.

Aragael couldn't truly be gone. His half-brother should have been the one on the throne, not Lysanael. Even if Lysanael was the eldest, Aragael was the one born of the last king. But of course, no one could find out that terrible fact. Not if Lysanael wanted to remain alive and holding the throne until Aragael's daughter grew ready.

The seal on the messenger's scroll cracked with a pop and he unrolled it.

Alas, King Lysanael, we have not found anything further with regard to your late brother's demise. No bodies have been found at the avalanche site. We nearly lost one of our team in the continued search and had to call off the mission due to increasingly dangerous weather. The snow and ice are here in force now in these altitudes. Condolences once more on your loss. Neeria proved herself a powerful warrior while she was with us. She should return to you shortly, as she left before I penned this note.

Your Servant,
Lord Melianst

At the side table near the flickering hearth, Lysanael poured himself a goblet of firemead, pushed his black hair away from his face, and downed the drink. He shook his head and savored the burn of the firemead in his throat.

His niece came to mind. Little Gwyn... She deserved better than this life at court, this life of deceit and grasping nobles. He'd searched for her father for over a year, then returned at the demand of the council, who had said if he didn't resume the duties of the crown bestowed to him, they would give the throne to Gwyn. His niece didn't have any magic yet, her training against thralls wasn't nearly complete, and she still knew next to nothing about politics. She was but a littleling and would have been their puppet if he'd failed to return.

The council wouldn't allow his brother's wife, Neeria, to take the throne because her blood was tainted by ancestors of a shamed house—plus she'd not been raised to rule. Neeria was a warrior without the gilded tongue necessary to run a kingdom.

He served himself another drink and sat by the fire. Neeria would return soon and they'd both have to give up hope for Aragael.

It was over.

His fingers tightened on the goblet and his eyes burned.

"You would have made a great king, Aragael," he said to the empty room, to the imagined presence of his younger brother. "I should have told you my secret. I thought we had so much time still... I thought it would all somehow work out and I could leave this place where I don't belong and spend my days in the Gwerhune."

He held up the goblet and eyed the chestnut-hued liquid through the goblet's crystal surface as he recalled a long-ago trip to the forest.

"Do you remember the time we camped by the salt lick and found the old caves?" A laugh rumbled from his chest, surprising him. "You should have left me there, Brother. I'd have caused less trouble seeking trolls."

He had to tell Neeria his secret. Perhaps the three of them could simply leave here and never return. They could disappear into the mountains or the woods. But then the kingdom would be left to fight between potential heirs. There would be war. His people would suffer. No, that wasn't right either. He had to remain, at least until he figured out a way to solve this.

Fisting his free hand, he studied the veins running down his forearm and the blood shushing through those pathways.

"Why, Mother?" he whispered despite the fact that she was gone too. "What made you so evil? Didn't you realize this was a possibility when you made your dark deal? Did you know the truth when I was born and just denied it? Or was that the true reason you took me to the Gwerhune's deepest meadow that day?"

He stared at his fist, and for a moment, he saw his mother's blood on his fingers. The vision disappeared, and he blinked and set his head back against the chair.

His mother had wanted the throne all to herself. Perhaps she had seen Father's health failing and eyed Lysanael as a threat to her power. She had feared being replaced and that's why she had tried to kill Lysanael. If she'd only known that Father would manage to hang on to life for years, things might have been different. Or she might have known Lysanael's secret the entire time and she'd simply longed to undo the past.

Lysanael should have exposed his secret right away and urged the council to crown Aragael before there was a chance to lose him.

But *should haves* would only tear him apart. He had to focus on moving forward.

Starting tomorrow, the council would demand that Lysanael take a wife and beget an heir to retain the power of Fae magic. But no matter what, he could never allow that.

4

REVNA

Thunder pounded like an active drumstone as I stood at the entrance to Arkyn's room. I touched the dragon's cool, scaled snout and looked into his fire-bright eyes. "If anyone is even close, let me know." I snapped three times—his trained signal for keeping watch. Most of the time I didn't bother with signals because Arkyn seemed to know my mind and the way I worked. But I wasn't taking any chances right now.

Lightning washed the stone chamber in white as I left him at the door and joined Raulian near the hay nest.

Raul eyed Arkyn's tail as it dragged over the flagstones. "What is this about? I have to get back to sparring. I signed up for four rounds tonight."

"Good." His night vision was atrocious. "Are you taking the nightlet herbs?" I worked to keep my words steady as fear about the mission attempted to shake every syllable.

He nodded. "Every afternoon."

Now for the true reason I needed to speak with him…

Raul had an aunt who knew of the old magic, and he had answers to questions I had always been too afraid to ask. But it was long past time. I had to see what he knew about the death rune. The Witch worked them into our skin soon after we arrived here as children. With just a word, Master could use the spelled ink in our skin to kill us—slowly or quickly, as he saw fit—no matter how far away we were from Isernwyrd. Just one little word and we dropped dead under the curse of the rune.

My palms were slick. "What do you know about getting rid of the death rune?"

His throat moved in a swallow and he grabbed my forearm. "Have you lost your mind? Where is the real Revna, my friend, who has a brain in her skull?"

I jerked away from him. "The king and Master have ordered me to infiltrate the Fae court."

Raul's eyes went wide as moons. "No."

"I have been instructed to assassinate the Fae king."

Stuttering out a few unintelligible sounds, Raul dropped back a step. A lesser person would have tripped over the clump of hay there, but he was a Hunter too and grace came even when shock tried to seize it away. "You can't travel beyond the Veil. The monsters there… The Fae… You'll die."

"So now you get why I'm asking what I'm asking." I glanced toward the entrance and at Arkyn. He eyed me, huffed quietly, then turned back to keep watch.

Raul just kept shaking his head. "There's no way to get rid of the rune. You know that. Remember the eastern child last season?"

"How could I forget?" There had been so much blood, as if even trying to cut the rune from the back of his neck had activated the curse. "Now, stop telling me it's impossible and help me think."

"Only the Witch can remove the death rune." Raul's gaze went to the floor.

"Please stop parroting what we were taught when we were knee-high. What about your aunt? Didn't she tell you something about some Old Ones' spell?"

He glared, his dark eyes fierce. "Don't."

"I have no choice. I can't die. Not yet." My mind brought forth the memory of Mother's face, bloodied and caked in filth… *Swear that you will stay alive. You will find a place for our people and gather them together once more.*

Closing his hands around mine, Raul took a slow breath. "I'll request to go with you to the Fae court."

"Absolutely not." I lowered my voice to the barest of whispers. "What happens to your son and wife when the money stops coming?"

His lips fell into a straight line. He knew as well as I

did that even though they had never had the opportunity to wed properly, Elena was his wife. He managed to see her a few times a year and they'd just had a son last moon. He also knew they would starve without the money he sent to them secretly. Elena was incredibly skilled at weaving on a loom, but she had worked as a prostitute for years and no one with good money would buy her textiles for fear of her reputation. The world was a shameful place sometimes. Most of the time. Creatures like Arkyn and people like Raulian kept hope flickering in my heart.

"What was the spell?" I asked. "I swear on my mother's unmarked grave that I will never reveal where I heard it. Your aunt is safe. You are safe. From me, at the least."

He exhaled and shut his eyes, letting his head fall back. "I know."

"Tell me. I have no time. I'm to meet Master at the gates at sunrise. I'm guessing this…solution will take hours to complete."

"It will." He gave me a resigned look, then opened his hand before me, showing his palm. "Draw blood from your first finger and trace your life line here."

To memorize his instructions, I mimicked his movement on my own hand.

"Then, when you're ready, you draw the death rune exactly as it is on your neck. Yours has a cross mark at the base."

I would do this in my room. "And a flourish on the

right fork." I would have to get rid of any servants fussing about, but then…

"Exactly."

I knew his rune as well as I knew mine. We used to study one another's when we were children, right after the Witch visited to dole them out like dark gifts.

"What comes next?" I asked.

"You speak in the tongue of the Old Ones. Accuruttalai akarru." *Remove the threat.* Raul sniffed and his eyes narrowed. "Caktiyaik kalaikka." *Dispel the power.* "Ennutaiya arralai nan mattum vaittirukkiren." *I retain the energy that is mine alone.*

We had learned the old language secretly, Raul and I, from a scroll I found on my very first mission. It was still buried under a loose stone below Arkyn's nest. Never once had a spell worked for either of us. But we didn't know the blood rune work that had to accompany spells. The knowledge had been beaten out of the populace a century ago by the king's great-grandfather. Raul's great-aunt was the single person I had ever heard of who knew a few of the spells still. When he had been taken by Master to become a Hunter, she had visited under the guise of a trader and told him the runes and the words.

We had tried it one time. Together. I had blacked out for four days. Raul had been out for a sennight. The curse runes had remained, and once we were well again, Master had beaten us to within an inch of our lives. *Do not speak of it,* Master had said, his face blank and chilling. *If I hear even a whisper or see a drop of blood on either of your palms, your lives are over.*

"If this works… Do you want to leave with me?" My voice cracked and I cleared my throat, forcing my emotions into that dark box at the back of my mind. "We could bring Elena and your boy."

"They wouldn't survive it. Master will hunt us until the end of our days. You know this."

"I have no choice, but I understand that you do." I rolled his fingers and fisted his hand, cupping it with my own. I squeezed his hand and fought back the press of emotion trying to surge out of me. It touched the edges of my Berserker blood and I shut my eyes for a moment to control myself. When I opened them, Raul was staring at the entrance.

Master's scent of marula oil hit my nose and my stomach caved in on itself. Nausea swamped me. I dropped Raul's hand and struggled to remain standing.

Holding a spear to Arkyn's scaly throat, Master stood at the steps. "We are leaving now." Master must have made use of some potion from the Witch; otherwise, Arkyn would have scented him. Master had so many secrets and tucked-away advantages. It's what made him so frightening.

I shut my eyes briefly and silently repeated, *Master didn't hear Raul and I speaking.* I said it to myself to make it true. It had to be true. He didn't know about the spell. He already would've run Arkyn through if he had.

Arkyn trembled with a blend of fear and rage, his form shimmering and nearly invisible.

Thunder boomed and lightning cracked. My Berserker blood rose hot in my veins, ready for battle. If he hurt Arkyn, I would lose control. Consequences be damned.

"Come." Master drew the spear's point away from Arkyn, eyes softening in that manipulative way that had tricked me as a child. "Now."

I traded a look with Raul, then joined Master, Arkyn following us as we made our way down the wide steps and toward the courtyard. Rain whipped through the open corridor and stuck my tunic to my chest and my braids to my neck. It was colder than it should have been this time of year.

My mind raced as Master laid out our travel plans. We were to see the Witch within the hour. Arkyn would fly both of us there.

"Will I need to take the potion immediately?"

"No. The potion will not remain potent for long. Wait until you are in the trees of the Gwerhune or, better yet, very close to Caer Du."

Caer Du. The Fae king's castle.

Well, great. So every Fae creature would scent me on my way through the forest. No, if I did this, I would be taking that potion the moment I reached the Fae woods.

With the servants' help, we were up in the skies in minutes. The ragged remnants of the storm clouds floated over the setting sun in the west and the distant green of the Gwerhune to the east. Not only had I missed out on my nap, I was on my way to meet the Witch. But if they weren't dosing me with the potion right away, maybe I still had a chance to get rid of the death rune and get out.

I won't fail you, Mother. I won't fail our people.

My life had been a rough one, but I wasn't ready to give it all up as lost. Not yet.

Master twisted in the saddle to regard me. Wind tore at his bound gray hair and made his cloak flutter wildly around the both of us. "The Witch can read your mind, you know."

Arkyn dipped suddenly as if he had felt the knowledge like a blow as well as I had. My stomach rolled and I gripped the back of the saddle with shaking fingers.

"Interesting. Is that why the king won't be meeting us there?"

Master chuckled and turned back around. "Careful now, Revna. Watch that tongue of yours tonight or the Witch might decide to see how it looks on her mantelpiece."

"It would be difficult to seduce a Fae king with no tongue."

Master shrugged. "You have other attributes he'll enjoy, I'm sure."

I swallowed bile and forced myself to look away from the back of his head. The clouds shifted below us and the last of the sun painted them the color of fire and ash. Memories flooded my mind. My home going up in flames. The scarlet cloaks of the king's men who had thrown their torches on the thatched roofs before cutting down anyone who dared to rise against them. I could still feel the grip Mother had on my arms the night they'd torn me away for my Berserker blood. They'd brought me to Master when I was eight years old.

Arkyn's head moved and his gaze found me. He blinked at me and my blood rang with outrage for him, for my people, for Mother, for Raul and his little family. Someday I would let my blood sing the death of those who deserved a vicious end. Someday.

A cluster of blackened trees made me think for a second that my memories had summoned fire. The dead trees surrounded a towering stone structure topped with slate tiles and ringed in drumstones.

We had arrived at the Witch's abode.

5

REVNA

Arkyn wisely landed several feet away from the stones.

As we slid off Arkyn's back, Master glanced my way. I lifted my eyebrows, reluctantly impressed that the Witch used the presence of the portal stones as a defense. She knew how to take down monsters as well as I did apparently. But the real question was—

"What is worse than what comes out of the stones?" I asked as we walked through two of the largest ones to rap on an iron and walnut door.

Master set one end of his stick on the ground and fiddled with the other end. I licked my lips, feeling sick in so many ways. When Master was nervous, the world should be nervous. "When you have won wars over the span of centuries," he said, "you have countless enemies with endless resources."

"Do the Fae have something against her too?"

He shrugged. "Not that I know of, but it wouldn't surprise me." His gaze went from my face to his fidgeting fingers and he ceased the telling movement in favor of glaring at the door.

The door's ironwork began moving. The scrolling loops became black snakes that slithered over the carved leaves in the wood under the ironwork. A raven spread detailed wings and opened its beak before landing at the bottom of the intricate entrance. Insects with glittering black shells scattered across the door's uneven surface, their movements eerily silent.

Then the door swung open to reveal a chamber unlike anything I'd ever seen.

Emerald light similar in shade to the drumstones' luminescence flickered from sconces placed here and there around the stone walls. A tapestry hung on the nearest wall, and the farmers in straw hats and the maids leading geese moved as if alive. In the same scene's background, Unseelie creatures with glimmering teeth grinned at the peasants.

The smell of the place was nearly overwhelming. A metallic scent similar to the stench of a gargoyle's blood and the bitter tang of dangerous herbs filled the air.

Standing before a cauldron at the center of the room, the Witch stirred a steaming pot over the fire. No smoke rose from the fire. No scent of wood lingered.

I swallowed and followed Master farther inside.

He bowed and lifted a hand in a more casual greeting. "My lady, we thank you for your summons."

"Don't bother with false niceties. You loathe me. I loathe you. We both must do for the king what we must do or suffer the consequences. Now, come, Huntress, and I will give you what you need to stay alive for as long as it takes for you to play your part with those of pointed ears and eyes that see the night as day."

I put my hand on the hilt of my sword, feeling the worn edges of the bronze dragon wing inlay that the smithy had pressed into the pommel.

The Witch's owl eyes shifted until she was staring. Her gaze slid over my very soul. "Easy, Berserker."

My hand had gone to my sword as a reaction to Fae. No way I would enact violence here. The Witch rightly scared everyone on this side of the Veil. The Witch nodded as if she'd heard my thoughts. So perhaps Master hadn't been kicking the hive of my mind with his earlier comment. If she could…

I thought of white space and focused on her and her steaming cauldron. She turned and took a dark glass vial from a table near her elbow. Dipping the vial into the cauldron, she whispered words of the Old Ones. The hairs on the back of my neck stood on end. In my periphery, Master shifted his weight from one foot to the other. The Witch lifted the vial high and a humming sound issued from her throat as one of her many necklaces—this one a circle marked with three blue swirls—glowed and illuminated her deep wrinkles and the tangled lengths of her loose hair. The scent of pine, crushed green oak leaves, and lemon-scented herbs filtered into the air.

Was that what Fae smelled like? I hadn't noticed the Fae female warrior's scent when I'd fought her, but I had been a little busy trying to keep my head on my shoulders and my guts on the inside.

It was a lovely scent. The Fae were designed to lure both one another and other creatures, so it made sense their scent was pleasing. I didn't like to think that I could be swayed by a pretty smell though. My thoughts began churning again, and I once more summoned a mental image of solid white glistening like the surface of a bowl of milk. White. White. White. I had to keep my mind free of anything just in case.

The Witch corked the vial and wrapped it in leather before handing it to me. I tucked the potion into the pouch at my belt. She reached for my arm. I began to pull back before I realized she was only checking the wound the gargoyle had given me earlier. Her cool fingers drifted over the dried blood and she whispered the language of the Old Ones. A popping sensation covered the entire injured area, and when she lifted her fingers, the wound looked days old. My skin was nearly mended.

"How quickly does the potion take effect?" I asked, giving her a nod of thanks for the healing. "Will I see the illusion as well? And how long will it last once taken?"

Master nodded in approval of my questions as the

Witch braced both hands on the cauldron and seemed to study its depths for the answers, her gaze darting here and there over the bubbling contents.

"The potion will function like a mintbane poison," the Witch said.

Twenty minutes to full potency. So it wouldn't take even a half hour for this particular potion to make me look and smell like a Fae female.

"You will see the differences set over your true form. It will be disorienting at first but you will grow used to it. The effects should last for ten days. Maybe not as long with your magical blood."

As a part of Hunter training, Master had forced me to dose myself with nearly every potion and poison available in the human world, and my Berserker blood did indeed tend to fight the influence of foreign substances. The strongest concoctions still worked on me, but not as quickly and thoroughly as they did on others.

"Don't you believe we should test it?"

The Witch's white eyebrows drew close together. "This is no simple dram to bring forth, child."

I nodded in understanding. I had one shot and if this failed, I'd be dead. I shut down my imaginings there. White space. Milk. Cold and plain and unmarred.

If she knew what I was hiding, she would tell Master and the king as well. The king's respect of her was the only reason she continued to live as she had for centuries. She was the only one permitted to practice spell work. For that, she remained fully loyal to the king.

Master bowed, his fist on his shoulder and the fabric of his cloak bunched at his elbow. "Thank you for your work tonight, Witch."

I gave the Witch a bow as well, and Master and I left the cottage.

The stars glittered above Arkyn, whose focus remained on the door. His gaze flicked to me and I gave him a grim smile.

Master mounted Arkyn and arranged his cloak around his legs, tucking the thick fabric under his knees and calves. "A moonless night. Perfect for such a mission as this."

Arkyn grunted as he took off into the night sky. I couldn't formulate an answer. I was too full of plots that had nothing to do with Fae.

REVNA

The moment we returned to Isernwyrd, Master was hailing servants to bathe me and give me a sleeping draught. "Sleep. You leave in four hours." He handed me a scroll that I guessed was my briefing on Fae culture, magic, and so forth. For each mission, he gave information via a scroll that we could take with us and study along our route.

I unrolled the brief and scanned its contents. "I don't need a draught."

"You know the risk. You won't rest until it's forced on you. And it wasn't a suggestion." Master faced two servants who cowered and showed fresh bruises. "Watch her take the draught then report to me. You stay with her while she sleeps. Wake her at the third bell if she doesn't rise on her own."

I was to have no time by myself. He knew what I would attempt.

Glaring at the ground and crushing the brief in one hand, I stormed to my room in the barracks. I was one of two Hunters who had the privacy of a single occupancy bunk room. Fat lot of good it was doing me at the moment. I read over the brief. It gave details I hadn't known, but most of it had been part of our training.

The day the Fae thinned the Veil and began trading with humans, Master had brought every Hunter back to Isernwyrd. Hunters on missions of assassination and spy work had been called to return. He'd discussed how even though the Fae couldn't lie, they were exemplary deceivers. We weren't ever to tell them our true names and Master ordered us to always use the same false name. The training we endured to be certain our minds refused to give up our true name at the request of a Fae had been… Well, I recalled a red haze similar to when my Berserker blood would take over when I was young. But this haze had to do with Master's brainwashing and his stick. *Resaynia,* Master had repeated over and over and over again. *When a Fae asks, Resaynia is your name.*

Shaking off the foul memory, I began packing my bag with trembling hands, shooing the servants out of my way.

"Just eat that and take a break." I pointed at the tray of bread, boiled oats, and baked chicken the cook's men had brought. It would come out of my pay, but I couldn't eat it now and the Old Ones knew the poor servants didn't get enough to fill their bellies.

"Thank you, Huntress Revna." One of the servants did as I suggested and gobbled down a portion of the chicken while the other just stood there, looking like he was about to weep.

I crammed thick woolen stockings into my bag beside a pair of dark green court slippers. "Pull yourself together, man. You'll get no sympathy at Isernwyrd and the sooner you learn to grab what you can, the longer you'll live."

There was a knock at the door and the dry-eyed, full-bellied servant rushed to greet whoever was bothering me.

"I came to wish you well." Raul stepped into the room.

"Leave us," I said to the servants.

"But Master said…" They both looked ready to weep now.

"Fine. But go into the bathing chamber." I shut them in the small room with the tub and rejoined Raul on the far side of my bunk. "He has them watching me," I said, keeping my voice to the barest of whispers. "I'll give the…" I glanced at the door where the servants were certainly listening as best they could, already spying for Master. "I'll give that new technique a try once I'm beyond the border."

"So you can bleed to death in the Gwerhune?" He huffed and shook his head. "No, Revna. Don't. Just do this thing and do it well. If anyone can, you can."

Not wanting to argue considering this was probably

the last time I'd see Raul, I pulled him into a hug. "If I die, you know what to do." I'd told him where I buried the vast majority of my earned money and how to get it north to my people.

His arms held me tightly. "I'll see to it. I swear on my father's tomb."

The word *father* cut me. I didn't remember much about my father before my mother rightly ran him through. Meaty fists. The stench of old ale. A cold wall against my cheek as he held me there and Mother warned him that death was coming.

My Berserker-blooded mother had known how to solve that problem—darkness, a blade, and a hole in the summer earth.

Berserker magic flowed in some born in Fjordbok. The power it lent when roused gave incredible strength, speed, and agility. Some believed it aided in healing as well, but it wasn't dramatically different—at least from my experience. But the magic was unwieldy and it always wanted to be unleashed. Too many times I had lost control of that raging power and I did my best to hold it carefully these days.

I gave Raul one more hard squeeze then released him. "You're my only friend," I whispered. My heart cinched as I memorized his face.

He shook me a little. "Nah, don't start that. I have a good feeling tonight. The stars are with you. The Old Ones shine blessings down. When you return, I'll give you a turn with my new mace."

My blood simmered, quietly dangerous. A mace was primarily a Fae weapon but since the trading of late, more and more of us were using them.

Raul swallowed and his gaze darted around my face. "Go on, now. Get some sleep."

And then he was gone. I took a deep breath, threw my pack on the ground, and crawled into my bunk. "Come out, you two."

The servants scrambled out of the bathing chamber and administered the sleeping draught. I took it, not wanting to get them in trouble.

A dream stole me away so quickly that, at first, I didn't realize it was a dream. Arkyn and I were flying over rolling hills. But then I was in a candlelit room and a man stood at the far side, facing away from me. His black hair was knotted at the nape of his neck and he stood as if I'd surprised him, his arms loose at his sides, his body still and alert. He twisted a fraction.

One pointed ear showed.

I bolted upright and the dream shattered, leaving me in my bed at Isernwyrd, confused and panting. The dream had felt too real. I'd never been one to see visions—I didn't personally know anyone who did except for the Witch. Squeezing my blankets in my damp hands, I pulled my thoughts to the present, to reality.

The servants assigned to me backed up, their

wooden clogs knocking on the floor and their gazes wary.

"Sorry, Huntress Revna," one said. "They told us to wake you at the third bell."

The high window near the ceiling beams showed only the darkness. Shaking off the dream, I let them dress me in my fighting leathers and tie on my gauntlets and boots. One presented me with a new dress and cloak.

"This is to be for the mission," the braver of the two said. "Master says the wool won't wrinkle too badly if rolled properly. He showed me what to do."

The dress and matching cloak were lovely. Dresses were a form of disguise, a way to fit in, sometimes a way to disappear or stand out. This one was simple, woven of indigo and deep green wool. I rubbed the embroidered hem between my fingers. This was the highest quality wool from Gourton. The designs showed a leaf I wasn't familiar with and a swirling pattern that brought water to mind. Shrugging, I let the servant roll it and then placed it into my bag.

The other servant shook out my regular black cloak and helped me clasp it at my neck. I didn't need their help, but it was better for them to be busy here than busy with some other foul duty set on them by Master. A tray arrived so I could break my short fast. I did eat then, only saving a half roll for the servants. I would be traveling quickly with no market or town for who knew how long. I would be scavenging from the Gwerhune if

I finished the dried meats and hard bread stashed in my bag.

I rubbed Arkyn down to wake him and saddled him carefully. Sturdy buckled straps held the water skins, blanket, and bag behind the saddle.

I didn't look back at Isernwyrd as we flew toward the jeweled night sky. The only one I cared about was surely asleep. Arkyn flew quite high and soared on an easy wind. Thank the Old Ones that the storms had passed. That was one blessing at least. I smiled sadly, thinking of Raul and his persistent optimism in the face of the life we had.

Once we were free of Isernwyrd lands, I tapped Arkyn's neck and he began soaring toward the ground.

It was time to try removing the death rune.

The starlight limned his outstretched wings, and the sound of the wind fluttering across the soft membranes comforted me despite what I was about to attempt.

I'd most likely die and leave Arkyn alone. But he'd be fine without me. Yes, we were bound in some unspoken, hidden way, but there were dragons in the forests, albeit they were somewhat rare. Plenty of game lived in the wilder areas between towns. He would thrive. Maybe have a family of his own, a possibility that had never been imaginable while he was enslaved beside me at Isernwyrd.

We landed and I hopped off. While Arkyn munched on a few dandelions, I unbuckled the saddle's girth and removed my bag and blanket from his back. I ran my hands down his side, the scales smooth and warm. He was healthy. Strong. Not yet old at all. He'd be fine without me if this went wrong. If it went right, well, then, he could choose his future. I'd welcome him into my new life if he chose to come along. We'd dig up what I'd saved and head north to find what remained of my people.

I made my way to Arkyn's front, cupped my hands on the sides of his snout, and looked into his fire-bright eyes. "I love you, Arkyn."

His eyes shuttered closed and he set his head against my torso. He blew out a hot breath and I scratched his soft spots. After a short while, I forced him to look me in the eye again.

"I'm going to do something painful." I made a fist and held it up. "But I'll be all right. And if I'm not, you go." I pointed to myself then gestured to him and the sky. Raul never believed that Arkyn understood everything I said, but he did. Recognition of my words showed somehow in the dragon's eyes. He blinked and snuffed into my arm, which I knew meant *Be careful*. I nodded then stepped away to begin Raul's great-aunt's spell.

I made a tiny cut on my first finger as Raul had instructed and drew my death rune on my palm. As the old language left my lips, a prickling danced over my skin and the scent of sage rose in my nostrils. Ancient magic. My heart pounded in my temples. My blood froze.

And I fell to the ground, emptying my stomach and unable to see.

Arkyn danced around me, making terrible snorting and wailing sounds, his terror evident. His tail lashed around me as if he could chase off what I had done to myself.

Once my stomach finished turning itself inside out, I lay on my back.

Whimpering, he leaned over me and I squinted at his face. The stars and his eyes melded into one blur of light.

"Go," I said to him, my voice rasping and weak. "Live your life, my friend."

He threw back his head and wailed.

Then I knew no more.

7

REVNA

I woke up feeling like I'd been dropped from a cliff and run over by a herd of Arkyns. Rubbing my eyes, I squinted and focused on his face. He sniffed my hair, mouth, neck, and then the rest of my body. I pushed him away gently and sat up. Groaning, I reached to the back of my neck, trying so hard not to hope that the spell work had destroyed the death rune and that my life was my own.

The tingle of dark magic brushed my fingertips.

I slammed a fist into the ground.

The rune and its dark magic remained intact.

Rising to my feet, I fought the intense weight of desperation. Master had trapped me entirely. I would never break free. I would be his killing machine until my last breath unless I made enough money to buy my freedom. But when would that happen? Would he ever even allow it to happen? What was his motivation to permit such a thing? He'd never given me an exact amount. Probably because that amount of coin didn't exist.

I wiped my hand across my mouth and found dried blood at the corners. I touched my nose as Arkyn whined softly and there too were lines of dried blood. If I hadn't had Berserker blood, I probably would have died trying to remove the rune. I wrapped my arms around Arkyn's neck and just stayed with him for a while, savoring his warmth and comforting him with the fact that despite my efforts, I was indeed alive. For now.

Until I tangled with a Fae king. Then I would surely meet my death.

"If I go, you have to move on," I whispered to Arkyn. "Don't mourn me. Live your life."

He shifted forward, bumping me back a step as if to say *No*.

I rolled my burning eyes and gave him one last rub before striding to a nearby creek to wash. I would just have to do this job and live through it. No other choices here. Kill the Fae king, cash in on what had to be a massive payout, and maybe Master would let me go. No Hunters had ever bought their freedom, but perhaps I could be the first.

My body buzzed with energy, my Berserker blood rising to the challenge Master had set on me. I didn't precisely have hope, but determination blazed through me because I wasn't one to do anything half-arsed once

I'd decided to get it done. If I died at the hands of the Fae king, so be it. If Master took my life with the use of the death rune, there was nothing to do about it. But I could control my own efforts in this mission. I was the best assassin at Isernwyrd, and by the Old Ones, I wasn't leaving this life without a fight.

Arkyn's saddle creaked as I tightened the girth buckle. I packed us up and then we were off toward the Gwerhune.

After two hours of flight, farmlands and tended human forests gave way to a worn stretch of land where bare earth showed beside a river. The rising sun glinted off an arching bridge made of pale wood.

"Now." I pressed myself against his neck as he dove and the wind tore at my braids.

The scales under my hand faded from view and then I could only feel the heat of Arkyn under me. His body had faded into complete invisibility. All forest dragons wielded this special talent. And as an added bonus—he made me invisible as well as long as I stayed within wing's reach.

The Fae forest—darker than any human woodland—stretched from the other side of the bridge into the distant horizon with no break in sight. The trees were as tall as several Isernwyrd castle keeps stacked on top of one another. Lights the same indigo hue as the dress in my pack glittered among the massive boughs of thick leaves. My heart raced. The Berserker magic in me was more than ready to turn me into a monster to match the ones who surely lived and hunted there.

Hitting the ground hard just beyond the bridge, Arkyn raised his head. He let out a low growl and his usual clicking sound.

"Hush," I whispered, sliding off his back. "We don't want to announce our presence."

There were dragons like Arkyn in that forest, true, but not many humans, unless they were slaves or were someone's dinner.

I took the potion from my bag and drank it down.

My body shook. A sweat broke over my forehead and back as the potion took effect. I stared at my hands. My rather short fingers showed beneath a pair of slender hands. I felt the shell of my ear, but also the point of a Fae ear crowned the ear set on top. I swallowed as my stomach turned. I looked like a Fae now. My clothing remained the same and my body held the same dimensions. The potion only altered my face, ears, and hands. Interesting. My hands were very scarred up so it made sense to mask those. I did hope that the nausea would fade quickly. I didn't care to be puking in a bush while trekking through the dangers of the Gwerhune.

I looked up at Arkyn, well, I eyed the spot where he should have been, though I couldn't see him. We had an hour maybe of his invisibility. Arkyn couldn't keep it up continuously for longer than that.

We walked toward the line of towering trees and I

looked up and up and up. The Veil wasn't visible, but we were approaching it. Its presence gave off a feeling akin to someone watching, to eyes trained on my back. Arkyn's breath heated the air beside my shoulder. I reached for him. His sides heaved in a deep, scenting inhale. The only other noises were the wind shuffling the leaves and some far-off melodic keening.

A sudden prickling ran from my feet to my scalp, like I'd been struck by a thousand miniature lightning bolts.

The Veil.

I had to force myself to keep striding forward and Arkyn's body jerked in surprise as we passed through. A cool breeze blew over my face and a slightly sweet scent—almost like honey but with a tartness to it—wafted in the air beyond the Veil. I inhaled deeply and sighed.

Could the air fog my mind like goblinbloom? No, Master would have warned me of that. He wanted me to succeed so he'd get the king's gold and the king's favor.

Moss in every shade of yellow, white, and green carpeted the forest floor. Ivy dressed in black and blue leaves stretched between the sky-high oaks that dominated the landscape.

A tingling sensation crossed the side of my face.

I turned. Nothing.

But something lurked here. My pulse thumped and I took a slow, deliberate breath, lowering my heart rate.

Between all the lush growth and shifting shadows, those indigo lights floated. They were almost like hand-sized soap bubbles but even less substantial. I could hardly focus on them, seeing everything through them clearly. A pathway of cobblestone stretched from the Veil and into the sun-dappled forest.

I led Arkyn away from the path and into the thicker brush where ferns grew in tight clusters and plants with flowers like fist-sized bells hung from a fallen, half-rotted pine. I walked the way Master had trained me, between dry-looking twigs and last year's leaves. We were nearly silent, Arkyn and I, as we kept to the shadows.

Every time we had a mission that called for quiet in a woodland, Arkyn impressed me by keeping his tail and wings from tearing limbs from saplings or crushing lower shrubs. Such a graceful creature. The Old Ones had blessed me by sending him my way. I reached back and rubbed his snout. He sniffed my fingers and snorted, obviously not approving of my new scent. Despite the fact that something Other was most likely about to rip our heads off and chomp on our entrails, I choked back a dark chuckle.

The keening I'd heard when we first landed started up again. The ethereal sound chimed down from the canopy that stretched far, far above. The music was barely audible. Pale blue wings flitted from one branch to another. Pixies. I grimaced, hoping the tales of their predilection for nibbling human flesh was wrong.

We continued on and the forest opened up to show expansive room between the gorgeous massive oaks and some sort of indigo-hued pine species.

I touched Arkyn's invisible side twice. His scales were very hot, a sure sign he had been using his magic for too long after a night of no sleep. "Let's give your invisibility a break."

He shimmered into view, both of us now fully visible to anyone—or anything—that cared to look. I crawled onto his back and nudged him with my heels. He galloped into a run then took off. The golden green of the canopy showed more pixies zipping this way and that. Their wings splintered the beams of sunlight and cast an array of colors on the surrounding green growth.

"Let's fly a little lower and stay clear of those fellas." Leaning forward, I motioned with a flat palm.

The ground below went by in a blur, but I could make out a large shadow near a bank of shrubbery dotted with berries. The shadowy creature looked like a black bear with the horns of a mountain ram. We gave that fella plenty of space. Later, a beautiful moss stag bounded over a rippling river below our aerial route. His Fae-beast coat boasted bright green and yellow moss and his antlers stretched impossibly wide.

As we flew, the sunlight waned and stars began to peek through the canopy. I was not excited about sleeping in the Gwerhune, but we both needed rest and a meal.

Motioning for Arkyn to begin a slow descent, I

watched for any activity below. Arkyn tipped his wings and tail and we began soaring toward a rocky clearing near another river.

We couldn't be too far from Caer Du, the Fae king's castle. The maps we had of the Realm of Lights were limited, so I had to guess on distance, but we were no more than a day's flight away surely. Once we reached the last of the Gwerhune, we would go invisible and fly over the castle so I could plan out a strategy. I didn't want to use Master's plan of attending the Branle. Sneaking in and finishing the job under the cover of night was far preferable. Arkyn and I could set up a hideout camp and prepare to infiltrate the keep. The Fae king would die by poison in his sleep and we'd disappear into the Gwerhune again before the sun rose.

Before we landed, a smear of darkness flew from our right and hit my shoulder. Arkyn roared, shaking me. I gripped his sides with my legs to keep from falling off and slashed out with my sword, catching the edge of what appeared to be a bat as big as a royal's bathtub. The bat shrieked in pain; I had sliced through its leg. It came at us again as Arkyn continued toward the forest floor. Arkyn swiped at the bat with his spiked tail, but the bat was fast, despite being injured. It flew high, then dropped onto my back. I thrust my sword over my shoulder and felt the blade strike its body. The creature wailed in my ear, and pain lanced my back and my eardrums, but the bat fell away. Its body landed with a thud just before we alighted on the ground.

With my shield out and ready, I wiped my sword clean on a cluster of thick, low grasses by the river. I wasn't badly wounded—just a cut on my back that I could feel wasn't freely bleeding and a deep scrape on my forearm. The bat hadn't hit Arkyn at all. The stars winked through the breaks in the canopy and threw salt on the rippling surface of the water.

Eyeing the surrounding area, I led Arkyn away from the body of the Fae bat until we found a small clearing sheltered by a ring of man-sized ferns and tall pink flowers that trailed blooms like a bride's veil. Arkyn settled onto a spot nearest the water while I rummaged in our bags for the dried meat and waterskins.

"Don't drink that water," I said in a whisper as I washed my cuts with the chilly contents of one of our skins.

Arkyn blinked his glowing eyes at me in understanding.

I poured out a portion of our water into the crockery bowl I'd brought from his nest, then I sat with my back against his tucked wing to eat. Now and then, Arkyn clicked his tongue happily as he took the dried meat I'd set out for him and gobbled it down. I kept my sword out and sitting beside me even as Arkyn's light snoring filled the air. Rubbing my eyes, I fought to stay alert until he had rested for about an hour. My eyelids were so heavy. Blinking, I bit my cheek and pinched my leg. Despite the incredible danger that lurked here, the air was so lovely with its perfumed scent and soft breeze.

The glittering indigo spheres floated above us and went gliding down the river like they were sentient and enjoyed the ride. I shouldn't have felt peaceful here, but I did.

I woke up surrounded by Fae males.

8

REVNA

My heart hammered my ribs and my Berserker blood simmered like fire in my veins.

The dark shrouded the details of the Fae males' faces and bodies. All were fairly tall and well built. Pointed ears showed here and there. They wore daggers at their belts and tangles knotted their hair. Their tunics and trousers were stained and ripped along elbows and knees. The most disconcerting thing was how their eyes reflected the light like an animal's.

One of them stood in front of Arkyn, a sparkling rose-colored cloud pouring from his palm. "What is a little female like you doing out here alone?" he asked, his voice smooth and accented. The Fae spoke the same tongue as humans, but their vowels were rounded in odd places and their tone was far more melodic.

My shield remained on my arm, but I reached for my

sword only to find it missing. I hadn't made this big of a mistake in ages. "I have a dragon. I'm not alone."

"He is fatigued," the Fae who had been casting a spell over Arkyn said. He dusted his hands off and joined his co-conspirators.

Getting to my feet slowly, I smiled at them. "I'm not."

The males glanced to one another, chuckling and looking very pleased with themselves. "Well, then," the tallest of the bunch said, "how about we give you a running start."

"And what happens if I lose?"

"If," the one at the far end said, a laugh in his voice.

The tallest ignored him. "You become our female."

"For breeding?" I would die defending myself before that ever happened. I eyed the group, looking for the shine of my sword's pommel. Which one had grabbed it?

They laughed. "No," the same Fae said. "You are too scrawny for proper Gwerhune tribe breeding. You'll be our slave. Cooking. Cleaning. To take the beatings for our mates when we deem it necessary."

"I hate to disappoint you, but I'm not running." I shrugged as I focused on my Berserker power and stoked it like one would yesterday's fire. A push of rage here, a pull of need there... It slithered through my body, faster and faster until every inch of me sparked with power.

I lunged for the tallest, pulled his dagger from his

belt, and sliced his throat before any of them even realized what was happening. The cut had taken three times the strength as normal.

Two of them reached for me with Fae hands that I knew could choke the air from my throat easily. My blood whipping through my body like living fire, I spun, dropped low, and sliced through the first one's thigh. Blood soaked his trousers immediately and I rose up quickly and slammed the knife between the second one's ribs.

Three down, two to go.

They drew their blades as Arkyn dreamed under the Fae spell. One had double swords, short and curved. The longer-haired one had a jagged-edged dagger the size of my arm.

I leaped away from them, stacking them instead of staying between them. As they lurched forward, I moved with the lightning-fast power of my mother's blood, getting behind them. Surprise glimmered in their eyes, eyes that glowed in the night like Arkyn's. I went for the long-haired Fae's face, but he shifted away and I only managed to cut his shoulder open. He turned and struck out at the same time his fellow did the same. My Berserker blood fine-tuned my vision momentarily. I deflected their hits with my shield, their strength blasting pain down the bones of my arm. I ducked low and they did too, following the pattern I'd shown earlier, doing exactly as I'd predicted they would.

I leaped high and rammed my shield across both

their heads, my movements blurred with speed. Landing in a crouch, I plunged my stolen steel into the long-haired Fae's throat. Blood ran down my arm as I forced myself up again to slice a diagonal line across the last Fae's body. He growled, far more animal than human despite his looks, and whipped that jagged blade toward me with a speed I'd never seen. The blade glanced across my chest as I slid backward, raising my shield, feeling the heat of the wound. As fast as my blood would allow, I angled myself and shoved my nicked dagger into his lower back. He dropped, snarling. I grabbed his hair, pulled his head back, and finished him.

Panting, I hurried to our bags and retrieved another waterskin. I poured it over Arkyn's head, the water like silver running down the hexagonal pattern of his scales.

"Wake, friend. We need to move."

He blinked those big eyes open and shook himself, spraying me with water. I exhaled in relief and braced myself on my knees as my Berserker blood settled back into the center of my heart. Lightheaded, I gave Arkyn a pat then began searching for my sword. I found it tossed into the brush, no worse for the treatment. Though I worried about environmental poisoning, I washed in the Fae river. I had to get at least some of this blood off of me and clean the shallow cut below my collarbone. I doubted the Witch's potion could completely mask the scent of blood. Once we were packed and ready, we took off again.

Except for the spell they worked on Arkyn—a magic Master had detailed in his brief—the scenario with the Fae males had gone rather well. I grinned into the cool wind of the Fae forest as Arkyn flew us closer to the heart of the Fae, their king's dark castle, Caer Du. My Berserker blood had risen quickly and I'd been able to settle it. That wasn't always the case.

My mind threw memories at me like Fae javelins.

A blur of blood and shouting and a body—someone I knew at my feet, someone outside of the politics that drove my life's work. Tawnia hadn't deserved the death I'd given her. She'd been an innocent between my target and me. But sometimes my Berserker blood didn't take time to distinguish friend from foe.

I shook off the bad memory and the others stacked high behind it, then sheathed my sword and flexed my blood-stained fingers. I'd washed most of the blood away, but the dark red always stuck under my nails.

Arkyn flew us on and on and I checked my compass regularly, squinting to see its shining bonestone needle. My regular compass was of no use here because of the magnetic fields on which the Veil sat. This kingdom, often deemed the Realm of Lights, didn't truly exist in our world. Thankfully, bonestones always pointed north and could therefore be used for navigation purposes.

The sun rose. We stopped and slept for several hours, waking covered in thorned ivy that took far too long to untangle from Arkyn's wings. The ivy fought our efforts like it had a mind of its own. We traveled until the light dulled and went blue.

The sky eased into night as we went invisible again and cleared the forest.

On a plateau overlooking a deep valley and a large body of raucous water, two curtain walls circled Castle Caer Du and the most powerful of the Fae.

A shiver of excitement and terror ran through me.

The wiser side of me signaled terror. Excitement was birthed by the side of me that leaned toward recklessness—the element of myself that longed for a thrill, danger, a challenge. I wished I could cut that portion out forever. It had only led to pain for myself and for others.

The outer wall of the castle was newer, the five towers peaked and finely outfitted in bright banners of silver and indigo. That wall would house a bevy of guardsmen and would be a town in and of itself. Inside the outer wall, a city with two-story shops, homes, and businesses slept. Very few candles were lit in windows.

I nudged Arkyn's sides, urging him higher.

The older, inner wall possessed squared-off battlements and a tattered keep standing three stories high. Left in ruins, the stone appeared soft and almost hazy. Part of that wall, there on the eastern side, had likewise been left to crumble into the earth.

But at the back of that inner wall was King Lysanael's castle keep. It was no dusty ruin. The newer keep stood silent—a dark, hooded god in the moonlight.

Three main towers made up the bulk of the structure, each with peaked slate roofs and silver, gold, and indigo banners. I had a map of the enormous place, given to me by Master. But even with that map and my extensive training, it would be no easy task to slip in and not get lost in the array of corridors, false alcoves that were actually secret passages, and numerous private balconies.

I had Arkyn land in a cluster of scrub pines where the forest's river split into two. Covered by night and the trees, I had him relax, eat, and drink. I might end up needing him tonight beyond dropping me off at the correct balcony. Being invisible inside the keep would be great, if, and that was a big if, there was room enough for a dragon in the bedchamber.

Once Arkyn had eaten, I snapped three times quietly to get him to keep an eye out. Then I spread the map on the mossy ground and used the scant moonlight to go over my route for this evening. If I could slip in and kill the Fae king tonight, all the better. I had no desire to pretend to be Fae any longer than necessary. With my plan in mind, I pulled out a black scarf and tied it around my head and the lower half of my face. I tucked the map into one of the many pockets on my fighting leathers and strapped on my thigh sheath. The sheath had a multitude of pockets and loops that held everything from poisons and tiny blades to antidotes and my dagger. I checked that the cherubium remained in its waxed and folded piece of parchment inside one of the sheath's pockets. Yet more knives went into the sides of my favorite gray boots.

I was ready. Well, as ready as I could be to do the impossible.

My heart chilled in preparation as it always did before a mission. I dropped my features into a flat expression. Raul had told me that my battle face scared the shite out of him. I couldn't deny I was proud of that fact.

I flexed my gloved hands and climbed into Arkyn's saddle.

We went invisible as we left the sheltered area, then he flew me toward the Fae king's private balcony on the eastern side of the keep. Small fires flickered in the inner bailey, guards on watch at the two sets of gates. They didn't so much as flinch as we flew over. The potion worked to mask my scent, and Arkyn's invisibility shielded us from view.

So far, so good.

The balcony wasn't large enough for Arkyn to land, so I leaped from his back, landing with no sound. Two large doors made of black wood led into the chamber. Crafty hands had carved the silhouette of a great bird into the wood, and a piece of golden glass served as the bird's large eye. I peered through the glass to see a dark room lit by faint moonbeams coming from somewhere above the four-poster bed. In the bed, a large form lay still aside from the shifting of regular, slow breathing.

Did the Fae king not have any guards at his balcony at all? Had I read the map wrong?

Though I couldn't see Arkyn, I knew he hovered above the balcony. The wind from his wings tossed the ends of my scarf. I motioned for him to circle the keep, then I removed the cherubium from my pocket. A little smear on his lips and his life was over.

Checking one more time through the glass that no one waited behind this sliding door, I entered the bedchamber of the most dangerous king alive.

The chamber smelled of woodsmoke, sandalwood, crisp cedar, and fresh water. A fountain bubbled in one corner and smooth-carved wood beams stretched over the high ceiling. I wasted no more time gawking at the beauty and hurried to the sleeping king.

He lay on his side, facing away, his nightshirt stretching tightly over his broad shoulders.

A chill pierced my chest. One wrong move, and I would be letting my people down, forever unable to do as I had vowed.

A pointed ear—its tip pierced with a golden loop—showed through shoulder-length obsidian hair that fell over his smooth forehead and closed eyes. His eyelashes were impossibly thick. That chiseled jawline alone had probably lured countless lovers. A golden torc with a snake and raven pattern circled his neck, the metal reflecting the room's scant light between locks of his sleep-mussed hair. I swallowed. He was painfully handsome. This murderer would make a lovely corpse.

I slid one gloved finger into the fold of cherubium and gathered a small amount. Holding my breath and leaning over his face, I set my finger against his full bottom lip. Lips tended to absorb cherubium more quickly than other expanses of flesh. A fang showed at the edge of his mouth, dagger-sharp and ivory white, and I made an effort to stop imagining it piercing my jugular. Dragging my finger a fraction of an inch across his lip, I poisoned the Fae king.

Suddenly, I was shoved against the wall.

The Fae king pressed his body against mine and I could feel every lovely line and angle of his. His eyes were slitted like a cat's, and he narrowed them as he pinned my arms above my head. His grip was vicious.

Forcing every emotion into that imaginary box in the back of my mind, I shut my eyes to hide the only visible part of me. I had Fae eyes from the potion, but if this all went south—which it seemed to be doing rather quickly —I might have to visit the king in his court. I had to remain anonymous.

"Who sent you?" His voice was a deep purr, the heat of his breath passing through the scarf to warm my neck.

If his lips touched my flesh, the cherubium would kill me too.

I jerked one hand free and slipped my dagger from its hiding spot. I held it against his thigh where the cut would bleed him dry. Even though Fae were more animal than human, they had the same system of veins and arteries.

Keeping my voice pitched low, I whispered, "Release me and I won't kill you."

Of course, that was a lie. I'd already killed him. No magic or concoction could save him now.

The heat of his mouth left my neck and his intake of breath meant he was about to speak.

A roar sounded. My eyes flew open as an invisible Arkyn blasted through the balcony doors, sending cracked wood and crumbled stone across the floorboards. The Fae king's grip went slack. I jerked away, rushed through the swirling dust to Arkyn, then felt my way with shaking hands until I could leap onto his back. We lunged for the broken balcony and fell into the open air.

My stomach crawled up my throat. Diving and diving, too fast...

"Up, Arkyn. You can do this."

He hadn't had time to take off properly—plus, what felt like a large splinter was stuck in his right flank, the wood possibly a shred of the balcony door's remains.

The air stung my eyes and ripped the scarf from my head. "Up, you fantastic animal, up!"

The tangled rose bushes and dark ivy on the ground below the king's window came closer and closer. Groaning, Arkyn worked his wings against the harsh air and drew up right at the last moment. We shot into the night sky, invisible and soaring away from the castle.

In a matter of minutes, our makeshift hideout beyond the outer castle wall enveloped us.

Once I had Arkyn's wound treated, we settled down to wait. If the Fae changed the banners to black, I would know we had succeeded.

❧ 9 ❧

LYSANAEL

Lysanael lunged for the assassin but she was already leaping from the destroyed balcony and toward some invisible force. And that roaring sound… What in the name of the nine hills?

Panting, stomach turning, Lysanael set a shaking hand on the ruins of the balcony door. The night wind blew his hair into his eyes as he searched for any sign of the assassin. She had simply disappeared. He'd had encounters with a few killers since his coronation, but never one with that kind of explosive and unique magic. He couldn't understand what he had seen. Or not seen. Who had sent her? And why did he feel so…

He dropped to his knees and the view of the annihilated wall spun.

His bedroom door burst open and guards stormed inside.

"Your Majesty! Are you hurt?" Celin led the group.

He had no mace or sword of his own, but everyone behind him was armed to the teeth.

Lysanael braced himself on a chunk of the demolished wall and stood on shaking legs. "I'm fine. There was an attempt on my life, but the assassin has fled."

The guards and Celin gasped and began asking questions, but the room tilted and Lysanael waved off their inquiries. "Get a healer and meet me in the Maple chamber."

He made his way out of his room and down the corridor. Two guards came up beside him and offered help. Placing an arm around each, he permitted them to aid him.

Celin's sharp voice sounded over the guards and servants now crowding around the door behind them. "Healers. To Maple. Now. Go, fetch them. Don't just stand there gawking!"

In the Maple chamber, starlight bled through the colored glass of the large window on the northern wall. Lysanael crawled into bed as aches and a gnawing pain slid through him. The world grew blurry, the canopy of the bed faded, and his mind wandered to the assassin— to the way she had moved with such grace and speed. Her lithe but curved body had pressed against his in a way that had he not been under attack would have been incredibly enticing despite his stance on mating. Her voice had held a spark of arrogance. Her eyes had been a simple brown, but the rest of that night he dreamed of a gaze as cold as the ice of deep winter.

At some point, healers applied concoctions to his forehead and chest. Gentle hands washed his face and helped him sip sour potions. Hours of blurred dreams passed and he imagined the assassin waiting in the shadows to see if he would die from whatever she had used to poison him. The knife had been a mere distraction.

A swirling darkness beckoned, offering warmth and a release from pain. But he summoned the thought of Gwyn's sweet little face and he fought the alluring dark, pushing back at the numbness and tuning into the pain to stay present, to stay alive.

REVNA

Unable to sit still, I waited for the rest of the day, staring at the snapping banners that the Fae would change out to show their king had died. King Lysanael's voice echoed through my mind. I could still hear his dark whisper in the Fae accent, feel the heat of his breath on my neck, recall the exact sensation of his powerful body pressed against mine…

Arkyn sat up from where he'd been napping and huffed at me.

"Go back to sleep. I'm fine. Just being a female human fool."

Snorting at me once more, Arkyn settled back down. Soon, snores echoed from the dragon's mouth.

I was a fool. Or at least, my body was. The Fae king would rip me to shreds if given the chance. He was not a creature to be attracted to.

I prayed I wouldn't have to deal with seducing him. *Please just be dead, Fae king.*

Leaning on a pine, I went back over the events. The important events. He hadn't seen me. I was sure of that. He might have glimpsed my eyes before I'd closed them, but surely Master had thought of a color for the potion that blended in. Neither he nor the Witch were idiots. Blending in would be good for Master's plan and a basic eye color wouldn't hinder my ability to seduce.

After years of working in various houses and courts around the world, I'd learned firsthand that seduction had little to do with looks and everything to do with confidence of speech and posture. Small and deliberate movements drew the eye here and there. Leading questions lured the mind into shadowed corners.

In my true form, I was no slouch in the great arena of human attractiveness, but I also wasn't some legendary beauty. And yet, I had thrown many a man and woman under a metaphorical spell using what I'd learned about what people desire in a potential mate.

King Lysanael was my prey. I was the lure. Though I preferred a nice, simple stabbing, seduction with a side of poison was acceptable.

But I put off heading back inside to give it another try, still hoping to see black banners flying.

When the moon reached its zenith, Arkyn bumped me viciously, persuading me to sleep while he kept watch.

Sleep took me hard and fast.

I woke to see the banners the same colors they had been since we arrived. I couldn't deny the truth any longer. The heaviness of failure sat on my back and kept me from standing. Rubbing my face with my hands, I tried to shake off the defeat. How in the name of the Old Ones had he survived cherubium? How hard would it be to kill a person who withstood such a poison?

Struggling to my feet, I eyed Arkyn, who stretched his wings. "Well, friend, this Fae king is exactly as difficult a target as I'd imagined."

Arkyn trotted over and nuzzled my stomach with his snout. The sun through the trees that hid us glimmered over his dagger-length teeth and the brown-black of his scales. Consoling my wounded pride while a multitude of fears roiled inside me, I petted my dragon and set my mind back on track. I had failed and it was past time to get more information about his status so I could plan my next move. Time to head onto the castle grounds and listen to the gossip. This mission had failure written all over it, but I wasn't a quitter. I'd go down fighting to stay alive for myself and for my mother and her final wish.

Leaving Arkyn shadowed from the morning sun by our thick cover, I entered the outer castle walls with a small reed basket. A normal Fae female on her way to market. I had dressed in one of the simple hooded Fae dresses the servants had packed for me. The pale cream-colored dress hung loose around me, flowing along my ankles like shallow water. Green embroidery ran from

the shoulder all the way to the hem. The common Fae
pattern showed the three circles of their Mother,
Maiden, and Crone gods.

The guards at the gate didn't give me a second look
as I walked alongside a farmer. The male shouted at his
two sons about how they were driving the cart of wool.
His sons—one had a tail and the other's skin was a dark
blue—elbowed one another and laughed, apparently
used to their grouch of a father and knowing they
weren't in danger from him.

I pushed away thoughts of my own father's fists. His
shouting. Shaking my head, I pulled my hood closer
around my face and kept my eyes mostly on the ground.
Even though the potion masked my eyes, I feared
somehow the ice blue of them would show through. Fae
didn't have eyes like me. For starters, their pupils were
vertically slitted. Also, the pale color of my eyes wasn't
seen here or even in the human world unless one was
from Fjordbok. I usually wore special glass shields over
my eyes during open missions when my targets and
their retinue would see me—the Witch always provided
what Master needed.

A table laden with spices of dandelion yellow, ocean
blue, and root brown stood between a leather worker's
cart and a baker. Listening to the chatter of two middle-
aged—well, they looked that age, but who knew with
Fae—females near the bubbling fountain in the center of
the wide road, I inhaled a sweet, spicy aroma. It wafted
from buns shaped like hydrangeas with intricately

looped and layered flakes of bread like the petals of the Fae's favorite flower. One of the chatting women had ivy for hair and the one standing beside her possessed hooves in place of feet. I eyed the buns, trying not to show my curiosity, acting as though all was normal. They were talking about a hunting accident with their cousins. Hmm. Not helpful. I needed to find the gossipmongers in this place.

The stall beyond the baker's held an array of gold, silver, and beaded jewelry. I picked up a silver bangle and turned it this way and that. Heavy and expertly crafted, the two metal circles linked in a way I couldn't quite figure out.

"How much is this?" I asked, making use of the Fae accent I'd learned from Master.

The merchant's silver-bright hair gleamed in the sunlight, her wrinkles deeper than I'd seen yet on a Fae. She had slitted eyes like all of them, but one was brown and the other green.

"Two gladecoins and a copper," she said. "But you'd look better in this and I'll give it to you for the same price." She held up a silver torc with a wolf and spiral pattern. It resembled the one King Lysanael wore.

"No chance that is the same cost as the bangle." The torc held twice as much silver and had hours of work in it with all that engraving. What was the old female's angle here?

Her smile widened, her pointed ears sticking out from her loosely braided hair. "I like the way you beheld that bangle like it was a fine piece of art. You appreciate my work."

"You're a master craftsfae."

She gave me a low nod in the manner they had of accepting praise. Master's brief had gone over that mannerism.

I hadn't planned on spending money, but this activity did help me blend in. "I'll take it," I said.

As I handed over the gladecoins plus an extra copper, she took a mirror out of a cabinet behind her and set it on the table.

She smiled. "See how you look with it on."

I slipped the torc onto my neck, feeling the cool touch of the metal, then I looked at myself. I bit back a gasp.

"Is something wrong?" the jeweler asked.

"No, no. I just…the torc is lovely."

I had underestimated how odd it would be to see myself with pointed ears, slitted eyes, and those sharp, angled features the Fae had. It was me, but…not. My coloring remained the same—fair, slightly tanned at the cheeks, forehead, and chin from training in the sun. My hair held the same brown shade as always, but the potion lengthened the single braid over my shoulder so that it hung five inches longer than it truly was. My eyes were brown. Only a pale ring around the edges gave a hint at the icy Berserker blue hiding below, and I breathed a sigh of relief. No one would notice that.

I turned away from the reflection as a large male and

his petite partner walked up to the jeweler and greeted her with a nod. Fine wool and silk draped over their light green skin, and the shoulders of both their cloaks boasted copper embroidery.

"We are looking for something special for the Brezhoneg Branle," the male said.

Finally, some Fae talking about what I needed to know. During the Brezhoneg Branle, a three-day event, a member of the royal house would attempt to choose a mate. This was the whole reason Master had sent me on my mission so quickly. Well, that and the human king's distress.

The jeweler paused in lifting a necklace of raw emeralds and fine gold. "The Branle is back on, is it?"

The female raised her eyebrows, her gaze shifting toward the inner bailey gates. "They say King Lysanael had a simple ague. The humans he met for trading at the coast gave it to him."

An ague? I almost whistled, impressed that cherubium only doled out ague-like symptoms to the Fae king. What gave him a stuffy nose turned humans into corpses. But perhaps the court had spread a lie to dispel any worry. They certainly hadn't shared the fact that I'd been in his chamber. Fae couldn't lie exactly, but they were masters at twisting words to suit them. I'd heard more than one trader vent about that problem.

I also wondered if the Fae here knew about the murder of the human crown princess? Were they aware of their ruler's involvement?

Fiddling with the lovely torc, I stalled to keep listening. "Dirty beasts, those humans."

"Indeed." The female sniffed and eyed me.

I bet she wondered if I'd show up at the Branle. Her gaze hung on my hips.

I gave her a look. "Find anything you like?"

She huffed and turned away, pulling her friend away from the booth and down the road.

"Sorry that I scared them off," I said to the jeweler.

Waving a hand, she made a dismissive sound like an exhale through her nose. "They weren't the type of customers I enjoy."

I stared at her a moment too long. I had expected Fae like those two who had just left, haughty and eternally in the prime of life. This jeweler was neither and I had to admit I liked her.

Luckily, I didn't like the king whom I would succeed in killing today.

S tanding behind three Fae females dressed to drop jaws, I waited my turn to see if the event leader—a Fae male with hair like the sun and a body that didn't disappoint—would invite me into the keep at Caer Du for the Branle. I kept my newly pointed ears open for more gossip regarding the king's condition.

I was not disappointed in that either.

"...and I heard that he nearly died," one of the females said, raising her dark eyebrows. Her eyelashes were more like whiskers, long and thin.

The one beside her whipped her head around, her looped braids shifting with the movement. "Who?"

The third gave the clueless one a glare and put a blue hand on her shapely hip. "King Lysanael Oakthorn. Heard of him?"

The first female snorted a laugh. "I wonder if he likes those too simple-minded to trick him."

The event leader examined the females' faces, lifting their chins and looking into their eyes. Perhaps he was checking for health, seeing as Fae mating and marriages were for heirs first and foremost. He glanced at each of their waists and even put a finger to the pulse points at their wrists. My stomach turned. The females seemed fine with being studied like cattle at an auction.

Now it was my turn to pretend I was good with a male deciding my worth. I stifled the growl that tried to crawl up my throat. My fingers itched to grab the iron and adamant dagger hiding in my thigh sheath.

"A bit lean, aren't you?" the male said as he looked down his nose at me.

Whisking my flowing dress to the side so he would see my bejeweled slippers and the curve of my leg, I lowered my eyes, then peered up at him. I slicked a sly grin over my lips.

"The females in my family bear at least five littlelings with each pairing," I lied. It was nice to be a human masquerading as a Fae. They thought I couldn't lie, but I most assuredly could.

The male's eyes widened, desire flashing through them. He checked my pulse, nodded, then extended a hand, encouraging me to walk through the keep's doors.

I was in.

The doors led into a wide entry foyer where sconces flickered along stone walls. Deep green tapestries showing the Gwerhune ran the length of the back wall, ancient oaks woven into a scene with three drumstones and an owl flying overhead. At the center of the tapestry's scene, a Seelie Fae warrior with a flashing sword fought off an army of Unseelie monsters.

Lush carpets in obsidian, emerald, and ruby lay on the worn and polished wood floors. Beams the width of two men held up the ceiling, and chandeliers stocked with glowing beeswax candles hung over a long dark table to the right. A cluster of cushioned chairs huddled in front of the crackling hearth on the left. Stacks of books and piles of scrolls crowded a ceiling-high set of shelves. A human skull sat atop one set of yellowed parchment.

The place bustled with activity. Blue, green, fair, tan, and dark-skinned courtiers in all manner of loose dresses, tunics, and open-front shirts drank and whispered. The black wools and jewel-toned silks they favored exposed the males' well-muscled chests and the females' chests almost to the point of nudity.

My dress did not plunge quite that far, but it was the flimsiest dress I'd ever worn. I'd put gold sparkling cosmetics on my eyelids and over the tips of my Fae ears—not an easy task with the illusion. I could feel the points there, but not as firmly as I did my own flesh.

The Fae talked in groups, pewter goblets in their elegant fingers as they waited. Possibly, they were waiting on the king. Nearly every one of them was beautiful and tall, and every last one had those vicious canines at the edges of their dangerous smiles.

Some gazes flicked to me, but I made little fuss as I crossed the foyer and headed under a very wide black wood archway into what appeared to be a throne room. No one stopped me; the whole affair seemed rather casual.

The throne room did indeed house a massive chair for the king. The Fae had carved it from the same black wood as the archway. Expertly crafted oak leaves and acorns decorated the back and the arms. The seat was empty.

Where was my victim? Still recuperating?

A servant held out a tray of goblets and I took one with a nod. The wine had the sweet taste of fully ripe raspberries and the spice of warm cinnamon—much like the air here beyond the Veil.

Two of the king's men walked through a side door and raised one hand each. They wore King Lysanael's livery, their surcoats showing the same drumstone, mace, hare, and fern design as the sigil ring left beside the murdered princess.

"The king arrives!" they said in unison.

The courtiers quickly lined up along the walls of the throne room and I fell into a spot beside the females who had entered the keep just before me.

Everyone lowered their heads, and they curtseyed and bowed. I did likewise and watched Lysanael's black knee-high boots approach.

"Rise," he said in that deep, accented voice of his. That voice like smoke, like drums.

He had stopped right in front of me. In my early days of spying and assassinating, I panicked easily, my blood pushing me to start a fight. But after years of work, I was quite good at breathing deliberately, slowing my pulse, feigning ease when I truly wanted to destroy or escape.

I lifted my eyes to his face and my mouth fell open.

Sunlight streamed from the high windows to illuminate his finely sculpted face, high cheekbones, and aristocratic nose. When I'd seen him in the dark of his bedchamber, I hadn't fully experienced the beauty of him. An adamant crown sparkled on his brow, skystones decorating the metallic peaks. He'd pulled his hair into a low knot as if to keep it off his wide shoulders and show off his torc. His dusky gray tunic boasted gold and silver spirals of embroidery and the ends dragged the floor. The front lay fully open, showing the proud muscles of his chest and stomach. Below a wide black leather belt that held a sheathed sword and a Fae mace, black trousers hugged his small waist and powerful-looking thighs. His gaze went to my torc and his lips parted slightly like he might say something. His slitted eyes were the color of the Fae forest at twilight, deeply green and dark with specks of gold like a diadem around his black pupil.

His gaze flicked to the thin Fae-style ceremonial dagger I'd attached to my woven belt, and his smile showed two long fangs, the vicious teeth of a Fae with strong, royal blood.

"You should consider masking your want, little viper." With one finger under my chin, he closed my mouth and his eyes turned bedroom soft. "Because this beast enjoys the hunt."

Heat flooded my cheeks. My thighs clenched together as a fine shiver rode through me. The arrogant arsehead. I couldn't wait to trap him, to have a knife at his throat, to see the shock on his face when he realized he had lost and I had fooled him. It would be glorious.

As my mind and body warred, he moved on to speak to another female. The blue Fae female at my elbow gave me an impressive glare. Lysanael's hand moved as he talked to the other female. A sigil ring circled his pointer finger. It was a twin to the one King Darrew had shown to Master and me at Isernwyrd. Had he ordered a new one made? Most likely.

Lysanael climbed the three steps of the dais, flipped his long tunic aside, and sat gracefully on his throne. Legs wide, he leaned back and perched one elbow on the throne's arm. He toyed with an amethyst ring beside his sigil ring and the light bounced off the raw stone.

His gaze went to a spot hidden by the lined-up courtiers. "Music," he commanded.

And it was so. A lyre's light sound echoed through the room and a piper joined in. The courtiers began grouping up once more, most of them staying near the throne and vying for their king's attention but some wandering back into the hall, where more music now flowed and the sound of dancing began.

I drank another goblet of wine while the male who had been at the door introduced females to Lysanael. I heard his name mentioned—Gyrion. Lysanael came down from his throne and danced with each female, but his mouth never moved. He didn't say a single word to any of them. It was as if he weren't even really there. Perhaps the cherubium fogged his mind. But he'd seemed fine earlier...

Standing beside a sage green female dressed in white and indigo, her embroidery nearly as fine as the king's, I finished my goblet of spicy wine. It was quite good and I'd built up a solid tolerance to alcohol, so I didn't need to worry about losing my head.

"He certainly doesn't seem like he's been ill," I said to the female, fishing for information.

The female's gaze alighted on Lysanael and dragged its way up and down his body. "Certainly not."

"What happened to him? Have you heard?"

She shrugged one exposed leaf-hued shoulder. "Supposedly, he dropped into a deep sleep and none could wake him."

I ran a finger over the rim of my goblet. A lock of Lysanael's black hair had escaped the knot at the back of his head, and the loop of gold in the tip of his ear and the torc around his neck glittered under the flickering light of the chandelier above. The way he moved... The muscles of his exposed forearms twisted as he took his dance partner's hand. He spun the fair-skinned female slowly. He was grace incarnate. My pulse increased as I fought my body's idiotic response to his good looks.

"All that royal blood helps," I said.

The female nodded. "They say he is a direct descendant of an Old One's tryst with a Fae princess."

"I haven't heard that tale yet."

"The story has resurfaced because of his quick healing from the mysterious illness."

Lysanael was part god? Could he even be killed? Stones, did I have a chance at all in this mission? I'd have to strike fast and true if I got close enough to use my dagger. Straight to the heart.

Gyrion approached us. We curtseyed, our dresses swishing along the wood floor.

"The king would like a dance with you," he said, eyeing me like he had at the door.

Time to throw the dice. "I'd be delighted." To stab him.

The female I'd been chatting with raised her eyebrows and smiled. "Old Ones' luck to you."

A servant took my empty goblet.

"And to you." I gave the female a grin and set off with the male.

When we reached Lysanael, he turned away from his dance partner and gave me a shallow nod. I curtseyed very low, angling my body so the tops of my breasts were on full display. The king took my hand. Sparks as hot as a candle's flame danced up my arm. I swallowed and attempted to pull back on my emotions as he looked into my eyes. His broad shoulders blocked the other side of the room from view and I felt oddly protected by his sheer size and proximity. Because of the magic in my blood, his power and virility drew me to him. But the fighter in me knew well how dangerous he was and how he could snap my neck with little effort.

This was not going to be easy.

His eyes bored into mine and warmth curled across my chest, hips, and lower. I shoved those feelings into my mental lockbox and willed my blood to cool. Fawning over him would not end well. I had to keep the image of his death foremost in my mind and remain detached.

His fingers were warm and calloused—most likely from the sword and bow. He led me toward two lines of courtiers as the music for the Starleaf reel flowed through the room.

Arranged opposite of me, he narrowed his slitted eyes. The corner of his lips lifted to show a fang. "What is your name and who gave you that torc?"

I touched the thick metal that wrapped my neck, then I set a finger between the end points to draw his gaze to the hollow of my throat.

"I'm Resaynia," I said, using the Fae name Master

had beaten into my mind. "I bought the torc at the market from a lovely female merchant."

The suspicion in his eyes cleared and a smile graced his beautiful mouth. "From Alaina?"

"I don't know her name."

"But I know her work. She is a friend," he said.

He considered a common old merchant female a friend? That was incredibly unusual for a Fae royal or any royal for that matter.

Once the line had bowed and curtseyed, each pair taking their own moment to do so, we both stepped forward, our bodies almost touching. He lifted a hand and I placed mine against his. Another flurry of tingling sensation spread through me. We turned in a slow circle, and I held my dress up slightly so the side slit would show off my leg. His gaze slid down my body like a caress. I fought a shiver of pleasure at the attention from this full-blooded male Fae whose veins held the magic of the Old Ones. I could only imagine what it would be like to have those hands on me...

I shut my eyes and silently berated myself as I crammed all that lust into the box in my mind. The imagined lock clicked shut and my head cleared

"How did you meet Alaina?" I asked.

His eyes narrowed again as his hands wrapped around my waist. He lifted me and spun me around. As he lowered me to the floor, my body brushed against his. His breath came faster now. I hid my victorious grin by turning my head as if to look for more wine.

"She knew me when I was a littleling," he replied. "I used to... Never mind."

The music drew to a close.

"Have a lovely evening," he said curtly. Then he walked away.

Wait. What had I missed?

I clapped for the musicians and strode casually in the same direction that Lysanael had gone. Acting as though the bundles of ivy and pine decorating the sconces were the most amazing thing ever, I eased my way through the crowd only to see him slip through a hidden door behind another tapestry.

I grabbed a random male's goblet and apologized, slurring my words. He rolled his eyes and went back to his female and another tray of drinks and fruit a servant carried. I glanced around the room to make certain no one watched me, then I trailed Lysanael through the hidden door. The door clicked shut behind me. One flickering sconce lit a corridor where low voices echoed off the dark wood paneling of the walls.

I kept my goblet and hurried toward a corner. Pressing myself against the wall, I held my breath. Fae hearing was far better than a human's, so even with the music and partygoers, they might have been able to hear me in this quieter, hidden area.

"You must wed immediately. Your brother is not coming back. You have to stop encouraging her wild goose chases." The voice belonged to what sounded like an elderly male. "There is no time to waste. You must beget an heir to carry on your bloodline. If you die without one, you know what will happen."

Beget. These Fae really held on to ancient words. Now, what was this about a brother? His brother had died in an avalanche. At least, that was what Master's brief had detailed.

"I am attending the Branle, aren't I?" Lysanael answered, his tone sharp.

The elder made a grumbling noise in that way even old human men had. "You're not meeting any females hiding here in the dark."

"Bornien, I like you. I do." The sounds of someone pacing knocked through the floor. Lysanael, perhaps? "But if you start hounding me like the others," the Fae king continued, "I cannot be held accountable for my actions."

Bornien made a dismissive sound.

Lysanael's indulgent chuckle made me pause. He was joking about with an elder of his council as if the fellow were his kindly grandfather. Strange. Seemed out of character for a murdering Fae king.

They both went quiet.

Suffering sacred stones. They must have heard my footsteps.

I straightened and wheeled around the corner, grinning the grin of the tipsy. "Greeeetingssss. I found you." I lifted my goblet in Lysanael's general direction, allowing the contents to splash over and onto the floor.

Bornien put himself between Lysanael and me. Interesting.

Lysanael gently pushed the elder back and stepped close. "Resaynia? Alaina's customer?"

He'd remembered my name. I tapped my new torc with a finger. "'Tis I."

The king glanced at the elder. "Leave, Bornien."

"But, Your Majesty, I—"

A growl built in the back of Lysanael's throat and despite all my training, my knees wobbled. Those green eyes stared into my false Fae ones as the elder made his way out of the chamber. The secret door closed with a quiet click and then the Fae king and I were alone.

REVNA

His scent of cedar, woodsmoke, and some spice that was him and him alone roused images of hands splayed over skin in the midst of pleasure. My tongue tasted the salt of sweat. What would bedding a Fae king be like? I took a slow breath and reined in my wild thoughts and ran a hand over my leg to feel the strap of my thigh sheath. I could have my dagger out and at his painfully lickable throat in a breath. Old Ones save me, I had to stop thinking like that. I was a professional.

"Why are you here?" His nostrils flared. He was studying my scent.

I sent up a prayer that the Witch's potion would hold, then I shrugged like I wasn't about one step away from either killing or being killed. "I saw you slip in here and thought maybe you wanted company."

Towering over me, he looked down his aristocratic

nose, his nostrils still flaring slightly and his head cocked to one side as if he was considering my offer. "I don't bed drunkards. Be gone and don't let anyone see you leave this secret chamber or I'll have you fed to my mountain lions."

"To your…"

"Go."

I pressed into him, trying not to enjoy the feel of his hard body. My lips found the warm skin of his chest. "I'm not that inebriated." I bent to set my goblet on the floor, making sure to brush my cheek over his thigh as I did so. Then I rose up on my tiptoes and lifted my face to his. "I only feigned drunkenness so you wouldn't bite my head off. I've heard the tales."

His gaze smoothed across my cheeks and forehead. "I don't know which of the council folk is paying you, but I'm not interested in marriage or bonding. With anyone."

"Why?" The question was real. I was truly curious and it never hurt to let a dash of honesty enrich a ruse. "You know what will happen if you don't." I had no clue what would happen to the Fae folk if he didn't produce an heir and continue his bloodline, but he surely did and perhaps he would reveal a measure of that information.

He grabbed my upper arm firmly but not hard enough to cause me pain. As he dragged me toward the secret door, he said, "Biting your head off would be better than what I could truly accomplish if given the opportunity." His voice remained eerily calm despite the rough handling.

With the speed and power of a royal-blooded Fae, he pushed me out of the door and had shut the secret entrance before I could utter a word. I stood in front of the tapestry, blinking. Dancers dressed in every color of the Gwerhune and the mountains—indigo being the most favored hue—filled the floor. Laughter rose from the crowd and no one seemed to notice the king wasn't there finding a mate. Wine flushed most cheeks and several couples of varying types had wandered into alcoves to enjoy themselves.

Questions flooded my mind. He didn't want a mate. He had mountain lions? How was this brother—the one the older Fae male had mentioned—involved?

I joined in the dancing that spread across both rooms, taking the arm of a male with long blond hair and brown eyes. He wasn't a pleasant fellow, all scowls and looking down his nose at me, but at least he didn't step on my toes like many human males did in these circumstances. His gaze said he admired my appearance even if he was doing his level best not to.

"Say," I murmured as we turned a circle around one another, "if the king waits too long to find a mate, what happens?" I had found that many Hunters on the job took the long way around to gaining information and often it wasn't necessary. Sometimes, a direct question worked well. And yes, other times a direct query ended with a knife at one's throat.

The male's brow furrowed. "Our magic dies with him, of course. Do you live in a cave? How do you not know that?" He broke away from me, looking my dress up and down.

"I live on a farm," I said shyly.

"I didn't realize farm females had access to such finery." Sniffing haughtily, he left me.

I fought a grin and made my way to a table of food they'd just set up near the hearth in the great hall. Popping a sliced cherry into my mouth, I watched the room of Fae spinning and chatting for a while.

So these uppity folk lost their powers if the crowned ruler—Lysanael—died with no heir? Now that was a piece of information worth another sack of gladecoins from Master. The king would be thrilled to hear it.

A littleling with honey-colored curls sprang from a side door across the room to the table. She flashed a smile at me, grabbed a handful of bright pink sweet rolls, then ran back the way she'd come. I chuckled, then I paused in taking a roll myself.

What would happen to that littleling when I killed her king and the Fae lost their magic? What did their magic do for them? Perhaps it would only level the human-Fae playing field, so to speak. If they had a similar life span, no sleeping spell, and could be injured as seriously as easily as we could, then perhaps the Fae would be more inclined to work fairly with us humans. Would the Unseelie also lose their magic? No, the Seelie weren't tied to them. Hmm. I almost hated to strip power from an ally against such Unseelie monsters as the gargoyles, goblins, and the rest that came through the drumstones seeking blood and terror to feed their dark souls. If the drumstones ever activated all at once, humans would need all the help they could get. But that was a ridiculous worry. That had never happened.

A shout went up from the throne room, and I gathered the hem of my dress and rushed over to see what was going on. All dancing had halted and everyone's gazes locked on two guards in Lysanael's livery. They held a Fae male dressed in dark blue. Blood ran from the Fae's nose and from a gash in his cheek as well.

Lysanael sat on his throne.

"I didn't do it," he said to Lysanael.

The king left his throne and walked down the steps. "You were seen. There is no use in arguing." He unsheathed his sword. "What is your wish before death?"

I'd heard that the Fae honored death wishes as highly as my people of Fjordbok, but still, the respectful tone in his voice surprised me. In Saxonion—the human kingdom where Isernwyrd was—no one cared for the tradition.

"I..." the accused Fae stuttered. "No, I have no wish."

Lysanael's eyes narrowed. "That tells me you are guilty more than anything else could."

He swung his sword and the accused male fell. The

servants hurried to clean the mess and dispose of the body as the Fae king gestured for Gyrion. The male brought Lysanael a cloth and the king cleaned his sword, then sheathed the weapon at his belt before returning to his throne.

The brutality of the Fae wasn't a surprise, but seeing it with my own eyes did shock me.

"What did he do?" I asked a Fae male beside me.

The Fae glanced at me and then returned to staring at the blood staining the floor. The liquid seeped into the rug and ran along the lines of the floorboards. "He spied on the king for the Unseelie. Something about a scheduled appearance and the location of one of the king's personal lodgings outside of the lands of Caer Du."

Not showing an ounce of regret for the killing, Lysanael rolled his amethyst ring around his finger. I understood a measure of what he had to be feeling right now—first, the numbness rose, but then the details of the deed flooded in. Even after all these years, I always smelled the blood as if I were breathing it. My stomach turned. The voice of the one killed echoed, screaming and shouting inside my head. I didn't shake anymore after killing, but that had been a tough battle to win. The taking of a life wasn't without cost to the wielder of death. Every death marked me deeply, and the unseen scars helped me build that box to shield my feelings and to clear my mind like an empty landscape. I studied Lysanael's flat gaze. Yes, in this moment, I understood

him. We were required to kill and we had the coldness
to go on with our work when others would have
stumbled.

Eventually, Lysanael rose from his throne to wander
through the crowd with Gyrion at his side. Two females
at the far end of the room had their heads together, their
gazes on Lysanael. The males in the room made way for
him, bowed heads acknowledging his dominance as he
passed by. His features held no emotion; he could have
given my battle face a run for its money. He glanced
toward my side of the room and his heavy gaze snagged
on me. His eyebrows drew together as if he couldn't
quite figure me out. Several courtiers eyed me
enviously. I took my time walking through the gathering
as I slowly but surely followed the king.

Gyrion left his side, and the king disappeared
through a stone archway beside a set of winding stairs
from which great ferns grew, their leaves cascading over
each step and giving the archway below a shielded view
of the dancing.

I strode under the arch, keeping my hand ready to
whip out my dagger and my body coiled with the
ability to respond if anyone should attack.

"I scent that you fear me, which is wise," Lysanael said from a dark corner. Of course he scented my fear. I would rather him have called it readiness for a fight, but... "But I've ordered you from my sight and here you are again. I feel your mind is muddled. Be gone."

As I neared, I realized he sat in a wooden chair that had wide arms and feet like a bear's. He steepled his fingers.

I lifted an eyebrow and stopped in front of him. He didn't want a mate. I didn't want to be one. It was time for a change in tactics. "I have an idea."

He cocked his head and his gaze slid up my body. He might be ordering me away, but a part of him desired me in the basest sense.

"Do tell." His tone flattened out, but interest flashed in his eyes.

I glanced at the archway to be certain no one was around to listen. The revelry had only grown louder and we were very deep into this large chamber.

"Court me as if you wish to mate with me," I said. "It will be a farce, but your council will leave you alone."

He leaned forward and set his elbows on his knees. A loose lock of hair fell over one of his eyes. His slitted eyes were mesmerizing—like a green loch where a treasure of gold had been dropped into the depths.

"What do you get out of this bargain?" he whispered, his deep voice raspy.

I swallowed. Bargains with Fae were never, ever a nice way to do business. "Status. I am but a farm female, used to tending geese. I could get used to those courtiers kissing my arse."

A laugh came from him as he leaned back. "That, I did not expect."

"I would of course want gold. And perhaps a stretch of land to call my own? My father isn't the pleasant sort."

"If I agree, the bargain will be as such. You will accept my offer of courting but will not press to mate with me. You will keep our arrangement to yourself. Once our wedding ritual is complete—"

"Wedding?"

"Courting leads to a wedding. I will, of course, never expect you to act as my mate. The bond will be in words only, not in our hearts or souls. You will be free to do as you wish. Once my...situation is settled here, you can leave, then I will terminate the marriage on grounds of your disappearance and carry on as I see fit."

My mind whirred, trying to untangle all the dangers here. Should I do this? Or change the wording?

He went on, keeping his deep voice to the quietest of whispers. "Once our wedding is complete, I will gift you a stretch of land."

"Four hundred acres." I had to appear motivated by gaining Fae lands. In fact, I had no desire to remain here any longer than I had to. It was gorgeous, but deadly.

"I will gift you four hundred acres and a measure of gold to equal your performance."

"Hmm. And how will you measure that?" I asked.

He stood swiftly and ran the tip of his nose over the line of my jaw. I fought a surge of desire as hot as flame. "React exactly like that in front of our onlookers and you will find yourself a very wealthy female." Smirking in a way that made me very eager to start stabbing, he strode across the room and looked out of the archway.

It would work. I could get him alone this way and then end him. The Fae would be forever weakened. My quarry dead. My reward and life secured. I wished I knew more about his *situation*, as he called it, but as it stood, he'd suggested a solid bargain.

I cleared my throat. "I agree."

Returning to me, he took my hand and met my gaze. "I agree," he said darkly.

A cool breeze wrapped around our joined hands. I

had agreed to a Fae bargain, a deed Master had warned me against time and time again. But this bargain was an opportunity I could manage. I was no springtime lamb. Deception was to me like paint was to an artist.

"Come," he said, "we'll dance together again. Afterward, you will have your first lesson with me."

He led me out of the room and into the crowd. The courtiers and attendees parted neatly for us, glares of envy piercing me like arrows and gazes of appreciation showing on some of the Fae's faces.

"A lesson in what?" I asked quietly.

Glancing down, he murmured, "Do farm Fae learn how to resist a thrall?"

My heart dropped into my knees. Master had said that thralls were only the stuff of stories. What should I answer here? Well, I was either in this with him or I wasn't. "We have brief instruction."

"Not enough. It is the most dangerous aspect of our…" His eyes shifted as he watched the room. "Of our relationship."

He didn't speak another word about thralls, but instead danced with me expertly, a slight smile on his face. Every brush of his fingers on my wrist, each squeeze of his hand on my waist, and all the moments of our gazes meeting left me breathless in a way I hadn't experienced. I had loved once before. But it had been a simple love. Young. Rushed. And Master had beaten us both bloody when he'd found us kissing by the stables.

That boy had died a year later in a sparring match gone wrong.

But the way my body responded to this terrible Fae king was something else altogether.

I had to get my emotions under control before this Huntress became the prey.

LYSANAEL

All night long, Lysanael had dreamed of Resaynia. Her confident gaze, the way she looked at everyone as if they couldn't possibly bother her, how she'd touched his hand and a feeling like fire had branched up his fingers and arm…

Like every morning for the last decade, Celin entered Lysanael's bedchamber. Celin smiled and the scar that crossed his lips tugged at his skin. Lysanael's valet had survived an Unseelie troll attack with no training at all. He was a multi-talented Fae.

A new servant entered behind Celin; Celin must have been training this new fellow. The servant worked on the banked coals of the fire while Celin readied Lysanael's riding clothes.

Lysanael strode into the bathing chamber and washed his face in the cool water waiting in the basin. He eyed himself in the mirror propped against the wall, then ran a hand through his tangled hair. He tied it back into his preferred style for travel. Today, he would ride alongside his partner in crime, Resaynia.

A sensation like lightning flashed through him.

Who was this Resaynia? She had walked into his throne room like she owned the castle and yet she was a farmer's daughter? Lysanael had met many farmers, and though he respected them for their practicality, work ethic, and knowledge, none of them would have looked like Resaynia had, all grace and confidence.

Well, he wouldn't look a gift horse in the mouth and all of that. She was a gift, the perfect female for his ruse. He could easily pay her off and she seemed more than willing to feign attraction. The simplicity of the ruse pleased him. He hadn't thought finding a female willing and able to play the part was even possible. Every other Fae wanted more than lands or coin. The desire for a piece of his royal life, a place at court higher than all but him, had been obvious in every other possible female. They wanted to be his consort and eventually his partner, crown and all. But Resaynia genuinely seemed to hold the same view of court life as he did—at least she displayed that attitude. She wasn't huddling in corners plotting and twisting gossip to suit her nor was she throwing herself at him. He would watch her carefully and see if his first impression was false.

"You are distracted this morning, my king." Celin helped Lysanael out of his sleeping shift. "It couldn't be that sultry female taking up space in your mind, hmm?"

Not even Celin could know about the agreement, about the ruse. Lysanael pulled his trousers on, then slipped on a tunic bearing the scent of the soap the laundress preferred to use this time of year. So much cinnamon. "I smell like a pastry. Can you ask her to ease off the spices with regard to my clothing?"

A grin pulled at Celin's mouth. "I will do that, my king."

Lysanael accepted a tray to break his fast, tucking in by the hearth and ruminating over Resaynia as he sipped mulled wine and enjoyed fresh bread with pixie honey—the tart flavor waking him up. Celin and the other servant bowed themselves out and he was left in peace.

There was something odd about the female, but he couldn't put his finger on it.

She had stalked him into private chambers and sought his ear, but that was understandable. In fact, trying to speak with him in such a manner was the only action that pointed to a rural upbringing. She didn't know the court's inherent rules. Her curiosity had bested her good sense and she had trailed him to where Bornien had been berating him for the thousandth time.

Finishing his food, he set the tray on the table, then pulled on his boots. Time at the vineyard would tell him more about this stranger who had entered his life at seemingly the perfect time. He would be watchful, but also, he might have a wonderful time with a companion so unlike the usual schemers at court. A rapid knock sounded at the door.

Lysanael stood. "Enter." He grabbed his cloak, ready to leave.

Celin peered in, eyes worried and a sheen of sweat on his forehead. "Lady Resaynia is missing."

Lysanael's heart iced over. Had the court wolves already attacked?

I spent the night in the keep. Lysanael had ordered a bedchamber provided for me—as well as for numerous members of his court and a few other females he pretended to be interested in. The servants had set me up with a sleeping shift made of the softest silk and four dresses in varying degrees of formality. Two were split-leg dresses of green and brown for riding and hunting. They came accompanied by riding boots that miraculously fit me perfectly. The third outfit was a fine night-blue gown that was quite nearly transparent to the waist, where it then turned into large feathers made of silk that dragged the floor dramatically. The fourth was made almost entirely of gold embroidery. They were gorgeous but terrible for hiding daggers.

Two hours before sunrise, I put last night's dress back on, left a vague note for Lysanael on the tasseled pillow I'd slept on, then slipped past my sleeping guard. I exited the castle with a mind to check on Arkyn.

Wings slightly extended, he jogged up as soon as I entered the sheltered spot on the edge of the forest. I rubbed the sides of his snout and he stretched his wings farther. The sunrise peered through the canopy and painted his wings with golden light.

"How have you been?" I noticed a pile of bones and a set of antlers. "Any nasty Fae creatures bothering you out here? I see you've had a nice meal."

He bumped my stomach with his head and I held him, savoring our quiet moment. Arkyn had never once betrayed me. He had only protected me, aided me, and been a true companion for the five years I'd had him with me. Dragons were so much better than humans or Fae.

As I picked mud from Arkyn's scales and checked his right eye—sometimes it grew irritated from an old injury—I recalled the day I'd found him in the fighting pits. I still wondered if I should have tried harder to set him free before giving up and bringing him with me back to Isernwyrd. Like he could sense my thoughts, he sniffed into the bend of my arm and made a low clicking sound like a fussing hen.

"You could still go, you know. You could stay here after this job. Live in the Gwerhune. It seems to suit you fine. Maybe you could have a family."

He lurched forward and grunted.

"Don't get angry. I would be crushed if I didn't have

you. But I feel terrible keeping you by my side in this bloody life of mine."

The dragon reached out a wing and cocooned me. The soft membrane filtered the early morning light, turning it pink. I leaned against his lukewarm scales and shut my eyes. Arkyn knew leaving me would kill me more surely than the death rune. I would be a husk of a person without him.

I patted his side and he moved his wing. "It's time for me to go. Feel free to find some adventure in the forest. I don't know when I'll be back."

He grunted and bared his teeth.

"I wish you could come too, believe me. But I have to do this bit on my own." I gave him another scratch, then left our hideout and headed back to the castle.

When I reached the doors of the keep, a guard approached me, ignoring the Fae lined up for entry.

"Come with me, my lady."

Lady? This had to be the Fae king's doing. He must have noticed my absence. "All right."

The guard escorted me through the crowded gates, then another guard joined us. They shepherded me quickly to the inner bailey, through the streets, and into the keep. We walked up the wide main stairs at the side of the entry foyer and hurried down a corridor decorated in a dark tapestry that showed a tall menhir with a circular hole in the top. Flickering sconces lit our way.

"Where are we headed?" Maybe Lysanael was onto me.

We reached a tall set of doors with gilded carvings of oaks and maples. One of the guards knocked. These weren't Lysanael's personal chambers; Arkyn and I had pretty much destroyed his balcony, so he would have moved to a new location. Perhaps this was it.

"Enter," a deep voice said.

They pushed the doors open and there stood Lysanael, his hair still mussed from sleep and his eyes narrowed. Once again he wore a tunic that draped open in front to display his fine chest, finer abdomen, and trim waist. I gritted my teeth. These outfits truly made it easy to stop drooling over him. I fought an eye roll at my own sarcasm.

After shoving my desire for him into that imaginary lockbox in the back of my mind, I slammed the lid shut. This was a job. It was my life or his and I knew my choice. I would live to help my people and do as my mother asked on her deathbed. If I didn't kill Lysanael, Master would enact the Witch's rune.

The floor-to-ceiling colored-glass windows behind Lysanael made him look like an Old One, the light like power glowing around his silhouette. He swept forward and took my hand.

Looking up at me through his thick lashes, he whispered, "Lovely Resaynia. I sent a message to your chamber only to find you missing. I worried that one of your rivals had taken action against you."

Was he actually fretting over my disappearance or was this part of our ruse? "Apologies, Your Majesty. I didn't intend to cause panic. I merely wanted a morning walk in the woods."

The tense—and most likely feigned—fear in his face dissolved in a look of quick surprise that had to be genuine with the way it pulled at his features. He truly wanted to know why I had gone to the Gwerhune before dawn like a madwoman. Not a bad question really, but much could be put off with the suggestion of eccentricity or ignorance. I was a farm gal here anyway…

"Was that not a good idea?" I said, keeping my voice sweet and young.

During my training, Master had taught me how to appear younger than my years. It was all about voice and the way you looked around a room or at a person. I kept an element of faked wonder in my gaze.

"The woods at my father's farm are safe enough when you know what to watch for. Pixies, moss stags in rutting season…" I shrugged. "I know how to take care in the wilds."

A smile tugged at one corner of Lysanael's lips and a dimple appeared in his cheek. I swallowed and took a slow, deliberate breath.

"Of course, you do, wood nymph." He lifted my hand to his mouth, turned my palm up, and set a kiss at the base of my thumb. My pulse increased in pace and heat spiraled down my arm to gather low in my body. He looked around me at the guards who had stepped back to await orders. "Have the kitchen bring us a tray and some hot cider."

The guards bowed low and left. Lysanael dropped my hand gently and went back to the fire.

I blew out a breath and crossed my arms. "I have never once been accused of being something as dainty as a wood nymph."

A chuckle came from him as he leaned on the hearth's mantel. "As crafty as you are, pretending to be drunk and following me into secret corridors that none but Bornien and I know about, well, the nickname of viper fits more than nymph certainly."

I smiled. I liked that the Fae king believed me to be a dangerous serpent. But my pleasure over my new nickname worried me. I shouldn't care. Acting as a clever snake in the grass and hiding the fact that I was prepared to strike was a challenging role to play even without the complications of true attraction.

Now was as good a time as any to finish this ordeal.

I sauntered over and stood at his back. His backside brushed my stomach as I slid a hand over his spine and up to the base of his neck. I tangled my fingers in his hair, and through the thin layers of our wispy Fae garments, I pressed my chest flush against the muscles of his back. He moved with a slow breath and I heard his lips part. My body responded hotly despite knowing full well this was a ruse.

Honestly, I was amazed he permitted this, considering our agreement. Maybe I roused his blood the way he woke my desire...

My other hand slipped through the cut I'd made in my dress and I had the dagger at the murderer's ribs, poised to drive upward through his back and into his heart in a blink.

Unfortunately, he reached around and his fingers circled my wrist, keeping the thrust from doing more than causing a shallow cut. His strength was maddening. Impossible.

My heart hammered blood into my pulse points.

Now, how to play this...

"Tired of our courtship already, my viper?" He kept his hold on my wrist and pulled me to him, my face now pressed to the space between his shoulder blades, my lips catching on the thin fabric of his tunic.

"I just wanted to see what you would do."

"I've never met a farmer who wields a dagger so expertly."

"Then you forget that we too are hunters. I learned to skin a doe at age eight."

"So are you pleased to see that your king isn't so easily knifed in the back by beautiful females?"

He thought I was beautiful. Or at least, the Fae version of myself. So I hadn't imagined the way his breath caught at my nearness. "I am pleased."'

"Why aren't you worried I'm going to end your life immediately for this treasonous act?" His voice echoed in his body, vibrating against my cheek. His fingers bit into my skin.

"I've heard the stories of your games. How you enjoy vicious partners who like to argue with you."

"A lovely debate is one thing. A knife to the heart is quite another."

He released me, snatched my blade, spun to face me, then flipped the dagger so that the hilt stuck out of his grip. He rapped my backside with the hilt and focused his narrowed eyes on me. My heart stuttered and my palms went slick.

"No more games with sharp objects." He tossed the dagger onto a desk littered with scrolls, books, and quills.

Well, I was still alive. Unfortunately, so was he. He wasn't even trying to punish me. I would have thought he'd have me killed for the attempt. Was it because my slow human efforts were a joke to him? Our deal must truly be important. It made no sense, but I'd keep playing along to see if it worked for me.

"Where are we headed, darling?" I said with a smirk.

He raised an eyebrow. "My vineyards. We'll work alongside the folk there for a while. It's good for them to see me get my hands dirty."

I imagined the human king doing such a thing and nearly laughed.

"What is it?" he asked.

"Nothing. I was just…I didn't realize you did lowly jobs just to please your subjects."

Someone knocked and the scent of hot apple cider wafted under the door.

"Come in," Lysanael said.

A servant hurried inside, set a tray on the table near the hearth, then left with a quick bow.

Nodding to the tray, Lysanael lifted one of the papers on his desk and cocked his head at the writing. "Tending to the grapes is not lowly. Now, eat."

True. "What job is?" I was curious. This murdering king didn't behave the way I'd imagined he would. I gobbled down a slice of bread and a portion of roasted chicken. The cider burned my tongue, but I finished it anyway.

"Exactly," Lysanael said. "No jobs are low. We all have our parts to play. Granted, my role is in many ways far more pleasant than a maidservant's or a stable lad's."

"But stable lads don't have as many powerful old grouches demanding they bear fruit." I spoke of Bornien.

He huffed a laugh and bent to sign the parchment he'd been studying. "I would prefer a life in the stables, honestly. I have done that work myself enough times to know the hard labor of it. I would love to live without politics being present in every moment of every day. Horses can be exhausting but it's a joyful fatigue mostly, if one has the food to remain strong. Court life is a unique drain on a soul." He turned and the truth of his words flickered brightly in his fine green eyes.

How could someone like him kill a little girl? Maybe he hadn't. It was certainly within the realm of possibility that King Darrew had fabricated the evidence, but it didn't matter. My mission called for the Fae king's death and I had to complete the job. I shook off the momentary lapse in professionalism and forced a smile.

"Never would I have guessed I'd hear the Fae king wishing he could brush out mares and scoop manure."

My stomach rolled. I shouldn't have said Fae. Of course he was the Fae king. To my false identity, there should have been no other king to refer to. Farmers didn't visit the human kingdom. They knew little of the world beyond their land.

His gaze fell on my face, then slid down my neck to my chest. I slowed my breathing and smiled. "Guards," he called out.

I stopped breathing entirely.

The guards opened the doors. This was it. The end of me. I hoped Arkyn would find happiness in the Fae woods.

"Take her to her chamber. It is time we ready to leave."

So I wasn't being dragged to a dungeon or thrown to the Fae wolves. I tried not to show surprise and gave Lysanael a bored look.

I curtseyed to the king and left before I could make another stupid mistake.

She had tried to kill him. Resaynia was the assassin who had fled from his balcony.

A laugh crawled out of Lysanael's throat, surprising him. Many had attempted assassination over his lifetime—a dark thought, but the truth nonetheless. But something about Resaynia's betrayal was... expected? Entertaining? Exciting? He wasn't certain. A part of him must have realized she was more than she claimed to be, more dangerous than a farm Fae from the rural lands. How had she accomplished her escape the other night? He wouldn't ask her. Keeping one's tongue and waiting for the subject of interest to speak first worked wonders.

Did she have an array of magical capabilities like the Druid? The Druid supposedly had an apprentice now that could work the spells of the Old Ones, and magical artifacts certainly existed here and there. Perhaps she had some rare power that he had not yet seen?

Now that he had this assassination attempt on her with no doubt of what she had done between them, he could control this ruse further. One wrong move and he would have her head on a platter. His mind brought the memory of her chest against his back and his breaths grew shallow. Swallowing, he turned to find Celin asking him a question, wonder in his eyes. Lysanael didn't recall the fellow entering the room.

"Apologies, Celin. What did you ask me?" Lysanael set his simple coronet on his brow and grabbed his leather gloves from his desk.

"Are you unwell?"

"No, I don't believe so." He raised an eyebrow at Celin.

"Should we research the female's background or are you only having a bit of fun?"

Lysanael tilted his head and gave Celin a look. "Since when have I indulged in *a bit of fun*?" He pulled on his gloves, the soft, familiar leather molding around his fingers.

"I can hope."

Lysanael grinned and patted Celin's chest. "All is well. Now, mind your own business, my friend."

"As you wish, my king." Celin bowed, a smile tugging at his mouth.

Lysanael left for the stables, dodging two diplomats from distant territories and one courtier who seemed to believe Lysanael wished to discuss hunting hounds in painfully dull detail every time they met.

Celin would have lost his mind if he knew Resaynia had poisoned him. Granted, Lysanael knew he was being a madman forgiving her and carrying on with the ruse. But he felt more alive than he had in ages and it had everything to do with that blade-happy and beautiful female. He wasn't about to give up this ruse for such a simple thing as a possible injury. She wouldn't be able to kill him. No one had succeeded yet and those who had tried had far more murder in their eyes than Resaynia possessed. No, he somehow knew she didn't actually wish to enact his demise. And he was determined now to learn her story.

18

REVNA

As our horses galloped out of the Gwerhune's dark cover and toward the royal vineyards, I worked on a new plan for killing the king. We crossed a lush meadow and the land opened up further, a vast array of emerald and amethyst vines decorating the sloping hills like Yuletide garlands.

A direct strike wasn't going to happen. He was too fast. Too smart. Too strong. It would have to be poison once more. Sadly, I had very little cherubium left, but something else would do the job. I could place a portion into his tea, weaken him, then end him in his sleep. But to do that, I needed more alone time with him. Since the deadly cherubium hadn't killed him or even set him off his kingly schedule for more than a few hours, I would need to experiment with a few doses of various poisons I had tucked into the hidden pocket of my thigh sheath.

I didn't have a dagger any longer, but the sheath itself had many uses.

Lysanael's dark hair broke free of its knot and flew behind him as he rode ahead of me by a few paces. His black cloak fluttered as he pulled to a stop. "This is the area where we grow our reds for the winter wine." He pointed to another hill beyond a row of stacked stone buildings with thatched roofs. "Just there you can see the rose blend my vintner treats like his child." His lips lifted into a half grin. "I like to visit often to show him my support of his efforts. In addition, bringing you here will affirm the fact that I am courting you because this place is known to be a favorite spot of mine."

Curiosity burned a hole in my chest. This king spoke so highly of his subjects, all the way to the lowest rung of status. He didn't seem like the murderer of an innocent. Why had he killed the human crown princess? But there was no careful way to ask that I could think of. After my flub in saying *Fae* when referring to him, I couldn't possibly mention humans at all. Hmm. Maybe I'd just poke around his head.

"Why don't you want to mate and produce an heir?" I'd asked him about this earlier and he'd evaded giving an answer.

He urged his horse to a trot and I did likewise, coming up alongside him as we neared a two-story building with fresh thatch on its roof and a line of bright yellow flowers out front. The indigo spheres of light that

I'd seen in the Fae forest floated around the building and danced on the early autumn breeze.

Lys—because that was what he was now in my head —glanced at me as he reined his horse in at the post beside the front door. He didn't answer and instead pretended as if I hadn't spoken. Maybe he was simply young and didn't care to tie himself down yet. He appeared twenty-five or so, but one never knew with Fae. But that was a terribly selfish reason to ruin magic for all the Fae. And it would ruin his power too, wouldn't it?

"You're just putting off your royal duties?"

"I don't look forward to a life at court under everyone's greedy, prying eyes. A marriage will begin that life in full, with whomever I drag to the altar suffering with me."

"What if your chosen ends up enjoying court?" The fact that he hadn't truly answered my question didn't escape me.

"I could never choose someone who would," he said quietly.

I was out of my depth. Master had taught me about Fae, leading me to believe they were like animals in fine clothing, every last one desperate to outmatch the other and always thirsty for dominance and blood. The Fae I'd interacted with at the market and during the first day of the Branle had been much the same as humans. Granted, they were more graceful and far more lethal creatures, but Master's lessons had definitely been incomplete if not terribly erroneous.

As we dismounted near the vineyard's two-story stone building, I studied Lys. His pointed ears, the way he spoke quietly to our horses, who munched happily on the short grass by the front door, the confidence with which he went about with his bare chest exposed.

Lysanael lifted his head and inhaled.

At my side in an instant, he glared at the pines darkening the far end of the structure's garden.

"Stay beside me," he whispered. "Do not speak."

It was only then I realized the birds had gone silent. Our horses stomped and huffed, their eyes rolling. We released them and they galloped around the building and out of sight.

I stilled myself, readying to fight.

Anything that set a Fae this strong on edge would be an impressive danger. My thoughts flew to Arkyn. I hoped he was all right with his holiday in the Gwerhune.

Four twelve-foot-tall goblins stalked out of the pines, their fingers so long that they bent the decorative grasses planted at the garden's border. Their heads were humanlike but so much broader and only one eye graced each of their gray-skinned faces. The green light of Unseelie magic flickered across their chests, a match to the lights of a drumstone.

Lys shoved my adamant dagger into my hand. "Try to resist using this on me."

I hadn't seen him remove the blade from wherever he had stashed it.

The goblins shot toward us and veins of emerald light flashed across Lys's forehead. But no, they weren't there. I had imagined that or it had reflected off the monsters.

One goblin roared, the sound staccato and reminiscent of the first battle I'd fought alongside Raulian. I'd nearly lost a leg that day.

Lys moved like the wind, leaping high to slice the head clean off the closest monster. He then raised his Fae mace in his other hand, spun, and smashed the knee of the next. I aimed for the one angling to my right. A dagger wasn't great for this work, but it would have to do because Lys was quite busy with his second attacker. That goblin knew his way around a fight. I ran at the third goblin, then rushed to the side to slice my blade across the back of the beast's leg. My adamant and iron cut true and the goblin dropped down on that knee, halfway crumpling to the ground and smashing a nice cluster of orange squash. The goblin swiped his long fingers in my direction and I spun out of reach. He lurched sideways and snagged my cloak. The fabric choked me and I fell backward into the muddy garden.

Out of the corner of my eye, I saw Lysanael jump onto his foe's back and plunge his sword into the goblin's neck. They fell together as my attacker reared up above me. His gray lips stretched into a smile that showed knife-sharp teeth. His roar sounded like a mountain lion being dragged over cobblestones.

I shot to my feet. "Impressive that you can stand on that leg, you filthy thing." As I passed under his wide-set legs, I embedded my dagger in his nether regions—a nasty business, but it got the job done.

Wailing, the goblin fell and then Lys was flying through my periphery to lop my monster's head from its rickety shoulders. More goblins lay dead behind him —two I hadn't even noticed him fighting. Stones, Fae were fast.

I panted, catching my breath and trying to get my heart to calm down as I wiped my dagger on the wooly leaves of a plant beyond some cabbages.

Lys eyed me like a man with a debt to collect.

The cat was out of the bag.

No farm gal knew how to fight like I just had.

19

REVNA

He kicked my dagger out of my hand and gripped the back of my neck, his palm hot on my death rune as he marched to the stone building. He pressed my cheek against the cold structure, pinning me there with his body behind me.

He snarled in my ear. "Tell me everything."

"My brother fought in the last war," I lied.

When I was very young, a war broke out over trade routes and territory between the kingdom where I lived, Saxonion, and Deigs, the kingdom to the west over the White Sea. The war had ended with a treaty that was tenuous at best.

"Your brother lives still?" Doubt laced his words and his breath dusted over my cheek.

I forced an uncomfortable swallow and eyed the front door of the vineyard's stone building. Was anyone listening to us right now?

"He does," I said. I fought a wicked grin, loving the fact that he didn't know I was human and I could therefore lie my arse off. "But he lost an arm and he never wanted me to be helpless if I ran up against an Unseelie."

Releasing me, Lys stepped back as I turned around. His eyes said he didn't trust me at all; he was probably rolling my words around in his head to make sure no Fae trickery hid in the phrasing.

I brushed a clump of mud from my elbow and straightened my cloak. "I've never seen those creatures though. Only a gargoyle once near our back acreage. Do you have many active drumstones around here?"

"Many drumstones hide in the earth near Caer Du, but they are more active of late than they have ever been." He handed back my dagger but kept eyeing me.

A bump sounded and the front door opened to show a male Fae with bushy eyebrows and fair skin. "Is it safe now? Are the demons gone?" The door flew wide open to show a low-ceilinged room from which countless dried herbs hung. "Oh." The male bowed to Lys. He appeared middle-aged with lines around his eyes and mouth and two stripes of white over his otherwise brown hair. "Your Majesty. I had no idea."

Lys gave the male a smile. "The goblins are dead."

The male nodded, eyes severe. "Unseelie. Such filth." He fisted his hand and held it to his throat to ward off the evil of the Unseelie. I'd seen that action performed by traders who must have picked up the warding behavior when interacting with the Fae at the Veil. Everyone loathed the foul, demonic Unseelie.

Looking fatigued, Lys nodded.

"I'll have my folk clear the mess." The male surveyed his garden, his lips pinching.

I curtseyed. "I don't think your lovely squash survived."

He leaned around us to peer at the dead goblins. "A tragedy. But I suppose your safety is an adequate consolation prize."

I laughed, surprised by his cheek, and Lys chuckled.

"I don't know," I said. "I've had squash tarts I would gladly die for." I had not enjoyed such a meal, but Master's brief had detailed Fae cuisine—both upper class and lower. Squash tarts were something of a middle to lower class treat.

As we followed the male inside, Lys said, "I sent a message, but you know how Gyrion can be."

The male gestured to a long table and four empty chairs, his gaze sliding to me. "Too focused on the court gossip to remember he is in charge of your house."

Nodding, Lys stood close, his thigh brushing mine. "It's too much work for him, I'm afraid." He lifted my hand and kissed it, the warmth in his green and gold eyes incredibly convincing. "Master Waith, meet Resaynia. I am courting her."

I curtseyed to Waith. "Greetings."

Lys continued to hold my hand, tucking it over his arm. His bare forearm shifted under my fingers. His skin was so smooth but there were scars there too, evidence of battles and training. "Master Waith is the head winemaker here."

Waith urged us to sit and soon enough we were tucking into a meal of hot stew, cheese, and mead. Another male made an appearance, telling us that our horses had been secured and set up in the stables. During the casual meal, I made sure to keep glancing at Lys to make my false adoration of him obvious to his winemaker. Plus, I figured I'd better enjoy the look of him now because I'd be killing him shortly.

I tried to feel pleased at what I'd accomplished thus far. I was here, close to my target, with opportunities to strike and flee fairly easily now that we were outside the castle walls. But the lockbox at the back of my mind shook as if everything I'd shoved inside wanted out. It was a new, unsettling experience.

In a private room Master Waith provided, I removed my riding clothes, my thigh sheath, and my dagger. Flipping the sheath, I lifted the leather flap that covered an array of tiny pockets. Each one held a square of waxed parchment and a poison.

I didn't want to try the cherubium again even though it had incapacitated Lys for a time. If he experienced the same symptoms now on this little adventure with me, he'd know me for the poisoner. Plus I had very little left. No, it had to be a different poison.

The second pocket held belladonna berries and two of the deadly plant's leaves. All had been rather terribly crushed inside their parchment, but they would still work. I smashed them further, using the waxed square to protect my skin, then dropped the mash into the crockery mug Waith had given me. I kept hold of the corner of the parchment and stirred the mashed belladonna in the red wine.

If a human drank this, they would be dead in two hours or less. For a Fae king... Who knew? Hopefully, it would at least hinder his coordination and strength enough so that my next effort to pierce his heart would end with my victory.

But my attack would need to wait for the perfect moment.

20

LYSANAEL

In the room Master Waith had given him, Lysanael's mind buzzed like a hive of angry bees. Shucking his riding boots off with rougher movements than was probably necessary, he replaced them with a pair of farm boots. Resaynia was not a farmer's daughter. He'd suspected as much already, but the way she'd fought at his side against the monsters... Such grace and precision. No hesitation at all. Her body moved nearly as quickly as his did, which was remarkable considering his bloodline. Her leaps were astounding and her strength pointed to far more than what one would gain as a farmer's daughter.

This female had magic in her blood, but nothing like any type of power he'd run across in his long life thus far. Was she some curse-touched Fae creature? Some odd mix of selkie and Fae or perhaps pixie?

He tugged off his cloak and tunic to replace them

with farm clothing more suitable to the task at hand. But his mind was far, far away from the vineyard and the peace he usually found at this place. What was he going to do about her? Try a thrall to get answers? She said she hadn't been trained, but she'd managed deceit already so what was one more trick? Not that it surprised him. Deceit was on level with breathing at the Fae court. But it had been a direct statement, so it had to be true. His tongue tapped his right fang as he pondered the problem of the beautiful, dangerous female.

Finally, he left the vineyard house and joined Waith and the other workers in the rows of glistening fruit. The sun warmed his shoulders and cheeks, easing his soul a measure.

"She is stunning, my king," Waith said, his gaze on Resaynia as she walked from the side door toward them.

Lysanael's body warmed at the swing of her hips and the cool regard in her eyes. She flexed her murderous little hands at her sides. "Frightfully so."

In the vineyard, yellow birds swept this way and that catching gnats, and the sun, halfway to its zenith, glowed through a ribbon of clouds.

Though Lys had dressed as a peasant farmer, he retained his regal posture and aloof expression. Lys had left the court, but the court survivor behavior remained with him even in this gorgeous rural landscape.

He'd tied all of his shoulder-length hair back with a leather strip, and his sharp cheekbones and pointed ears caught the light. His gaze slid to my face, and my heart tripled its pace. His eyes revealed a world of questions and a big dollop of distrust.

"If you two will stop staring at one another for a moment, I can show you our latest variety," Waith said.

Staring? That wasn't exactly it, but I would play the music I'd been given… "Can you blame me?" I threw a grin in Lys's direction to fit our ruse.

His features fell into a blank look, then he shook his head as if to clear it. "Please, Master Waith, do go on."

As Waith plucked a dark grape from the nearest vine and blathered on about the skin and the juice and the soil, I kept an eye on Lys.

From his mannerisms, I could tell Lys hadn't wholly believed the tale I'd told about a pretend brother. But what specifically was he pondering at the moment? I didn't like being lost on my target's line of thought. Hunters who didn't have a handle on their targets were the ones who didn't return from missions.

A prickling sensation spread across my back and I turned away from the males who were smashing and tasting grapes. Beyond the first cluster of the forest, deep in dappled shadow, a dragon eyed me.

I shut my eyes and sighed. Arkyn. I shook my head subtly at him and he went invisible. Just great. He was being protective and had no doubt come to check on me. If the Fae noticed his scent, they didn't respond to it. I hoped Arkyn would remain in the forest because explaining how I, a farm gal, managed to bond with a dragon would take some painfully creative lying. The only tales I'd heard of a rare bond like Arkyn's and mine resulted from a warrior on a long trek through wilderness, where he had a traumatic experience with an Unseelie. Farm folk didn't tend to take off on long ventures in the wilds.

"I do believe it's time to harvest this section," Waith

said with a happy smile. He looked at me like I had been listening to the grape talk all this time.

I gave him a grin.

Lys brushed a hand down my arm, and my chest rose in a quick breath. His gaze snagged me. "Are you willing to pluck?"

My ears turned that word into something else and I coughed to cover a laugh. Lys's lips pulled up at one side, gaze dancing with mirth.

Gathering myself, I looked at him. "Yes, I am your servant, lord king."

Soon enough, a score of workers joined us and we passed baskets about. The small hooked knives Waith provided cut the grape clusters free with one smooth motion. Lys finished ten clusters to my one. I was quick with a knife, but my dexterity couldn't measure up to a full-blooded royal Fae's coordination and speed.

The next section of vines had produced even thicker bunches of grapes. I reached into the leaves to lop off another cluster at the same moment as Lys, and his fingers slid across the back of my hand. A shiver of pleasure danced up my arm and his focus turned to me, eyes burning like emeralds set before candlelight.

"You feel that too, don't you?" His tongue showed beside a vicious fang and warmth spiraled down my body.

I cleared my throat. I had to get a hold of myself. I would. Mentally cramming that desire into the box, I took a slow breath. But if he believed he had that sort of power over me, it could only be helpful. Misinformation would sway his actions and a confused target was an easier target.

"You know how handsome you are. I imagine any female has a response to your touch."

"Maybe. I can't speak to that, but I can say that I too feel a stirring sensation when your skin brushes mine."

This performance was part of the arrangement. The stirring sensation likely meant something far less delightful in his head. This act was played out so that the workers would witness our budding relationship and spread the rumor of our powerful attraction to one another. It would get the council off his back. That was the only reason for this conversation. He hadn't felt what I had. And that was perfectly all right.

I threw a saucy look at him over my shoulder, like a lady in the business of tempting a lord to bed, and a quiet growl issued from his throat. He stepped closer, easing his body against my back. My blood sparked, ready for a fight, but Berserker blood could also be roused for love.

We went back to plucking the jewel-like grapes and he remained close. His arm smoothed across mine as he set his basket down and our gazes met, sending heat through me despite my best efforts to only feign attraction.

"Ready for a break, my lady?"

"I'm no lady." I raised an eyebrow, set my basket beside his, then started toward the vineyard house, my hips daring him to follow. If we were to pretend at being a courting couple, we had to show those watching that we were desperate for some private time. It wouldn't be believable if not.

Plus, I needed to finish this job before I lost my hold on that locked trunk of emotions hiding inside me.

Hopefully, Arkyn would remain where he was. I could still feel his presence out there, not too far off. I couldn't always sense him and I often wondered if he could control the feel of his presence through some dragon magic. I was fairly certain he had hidden his presence from me now and then in the past.

I swung the side door of the house open and it creaked as Lys trailed me inside. Light from the front windows washed over the rushes of the floor and cascaded down a tight corridor leading to the rooms where we had changed our clothing. I entered the one I'd used and spun to see Lys playing along. The grin pulling at his full lips and the half-lidded look of his eyes was more than convincing. If this wasn't just an act, then… Errant thoughts whipped through my head and my heart beat faster.

I stood by the window. "Come. Kiss me here. If a worker passes by, they'll see us and you'll be off the hook with the council for at least a few days, don't you think?"

Reaching for him, I opened my mouth slightly and ran the tip of my tongue across my upper lip. His gaze snapped from the window to my face and he took a quick breath before lacing his large hands around my waist. A smear of vineyard soil marred his otherwise epically gorgeous face; even the scars here and there were somehow placed only to improve the steely look of him, the power of who he was and what he was capable of.

He set his mouth against the top of my head, his breath hot on my scalp and his fingers flexing around my middle. My body melted against him without even consulting me. I rolled my eyes at myself as I slid a hand under his tunic and up his smooth chest. His fingers curled into my hair, tickling the base of my neck where the death rune hid. None but the Witch and those also marked with such a rune could see it, so there was no risk that he would notice it. He bent his head and set his lips on mine.

The first brush of his mouth was soft and sent annoyingly lovely chills down the backs of my legs. He teased my lower lip with one of his fangs and a purr echoed in his chest, vibrating through my rebellious body. His tongue parted my lips and darted over my tongue, the heat exquisite. I fought a sigh. He was just so lovely and smelled absolutely divine...

I broke away, panting. "I need a drink."

Turning, I took up my poisoned cup of wine and held it to my lips. Pretending to sip, I kept my lips firmly sealed and tipped the beverage upward. I held it out and looked toward the window like I didn't care if he decided to sip or not.

"Oh, someone is there," I said. "She just looked over here. Sip that, then laugh like you're enjoying yourself."

Glancing at me, he sniffed the cup. He touched my wine-stained lip with his thumb, then studied the remnants of my feigned sip. With a nod, he set the cup to his mouth and drank. I fought the wicked grin of a Huntress on the edge of victory.

It was my life or his and I had to choose one. I chose myself because only I could fulfill my mother's dying wish.

REVNA

I took the cup from him, set it on the table, then put myself to work kissing his collarbone while he wrapped me in his arms. "Is she gone yet?" I asked, my mouth on the soft velvet of his throat.

"I don't see her." He stepped away, dropping his arms. But the smolder of his eyes remained. "A fine actress, you are, Resaynia. I suppose farmers must do their own mumming for holiday entertainment."

"We must, yes. All of us know how to act out a story or play the shawm."

Lys ran a hand through his mussed raven-black hair, and the tie that had been holding it back fell to the floor. I bent to retrieve it, then handed it over. Lys blinked repeatedly and took the tie. He smoothed his hair back and knotted it.

"Let's return to our work," he said as he opened the door.

I nodded and followed him, watching for any stumbling or mention of hallucinations.

As we continued our work in the vineyard, sweat beaded on his forehead. None of the other Fae were sweating, so I assumed the belladonna was at work, raising his heart rate and disrupting his body's natural rhythms.

The workers arranged a long table between the vines and servants carried a feast from the kitchens attached to the northern end of the vineyard house. Lys gestured for me to sit beside him and we dined on rosemary chicken, fire-roasted potatoes, and a berry tart smothered in a cream sauce that was delectable. We drank, the Fae toasted our courtship, and all the while, I watched Lys. If he began to falter, I would have to get him into a private room. Then I could end his life quickly with my blade and be gone on Arkyn's back before the others knew anything. I could have escaped without my dragon, but with him here, it would be even easier.

The feasting turned into dancing and soon Lys held my hand and we twirled through a web of Fae who clapped and cheered us on. The color in Lys's cheeks faded to a dull ashen hue and I urged him away from the dancing.

"Are you unwell?" I took his arm.

"I...yes, I was ill recently and perhaps this is a return of that particular ague. You enjoy the day. I'll be fine." He broke away and started toward the vineyard house.

Following him, I threw a wink toward Waith so the Fae would think we were merely slipping away for a lovers' tryst.

Lys made it inside but slammed against the corridor wall. Pain pinched his features and bright circles of red appeared high on his cheeks. His eyes were glazed as he tried to focus on me. I put his arm over my shoulders and helped him to the room where he had dressed. He dropped onto the bed, sitting up and looking out the forest-facing windows.

"I am definitely unwell. I just saw a dragon appear and wave its wing at me," he said.

I swallowed. Sure enough, Arkyn was out there mid-disappearance and signaling me. I glared at him, then put myself between the window and Lys.

I forced a laugh. "I wish friendly forest dragons appeared to me when I had a fever. I usually just imagine a failed harvest."

Lys allowed me to help him lie down and I fluffed the pillow around his head. Once his eyes closed, I would be on him and this would all be over. His eyelids shuttered, then opened a crack as I sat beside him, waiting to strike. He reached up a hand and touched my cheek.

"Your eyes are so strange," he said. "Have you been cursed by the Druid?"

My heart stuttered over a beat. Could he see through the potion's effect to my human ice blue eyes below? And what would the Druid have to do with it? The

Druid was the Fae's version of our Witch—people who had no kin and were not human or Fae—but most of his skills remained a mystery. Old tales called him an immortal earth wizard, a mage who could call up power from the ground and from trees and plants. Master's brief had only said that the Druid possessed magical abilities like the Witch and that he'd been seen at the Fae court twice since the Veil became passable and information began to be traded between human and Fae courts. The Druid was ageless in a way that surpassed even the long-lived Fae he served.

Maybe Lys could indeed see through to my human face due to some effect of the belladonna. If so, perhaps I could pretend Lys was hallucinating. Before I could fashion a response, his eyes shut and his breathing grew ragged and slow.

He was down and now was my moment.

I hiked up my loose farmer trousers, slid my dagger free, and—

A knock sounded at the door. Sweat rolled down my back. I sheathed my dagger and quietly called out, "Yes?"

"Mirnae said the king was looking unwell?" It was Waith's voice.

"Oh, he's fine. Just resting."

"Please may I come in and check?"

Because it would have looked suspicious if I didn't, I went and opened the door to the Fae male's narrowed eyes. He glared at me, then looked at the bed. Could he possibly know I was responsible? At Lys's side, he gently turned the Fae king's head and pressed the tip of Lys's ear between finger and thumb. The flesh grayed alarmingly. What in the name of the Old Ones did that mean? That he was dying? Well, good. My stomach twisted. I imagined digging my guilt from my stomach and locking it away. Good, yes. Good.

Waith was holding Lys's wrist now and tapping his foot. He whirled on me, his bushy gray eyebrows bunching. "His heart is unsteady. Too slow, then much too fast."

"Could it be the same illness that he suffered right before the Branle? I heard about it at court."

Exhaling, Waith pursed his lips. "Most likely. I assume, as one of his potential mates, you'd like to tend to him?"

"Of course." I'd tend to him all right. "What should I do?"

"I'll get a bowl of cool water and you can bathe his face, neck, and chest. He is burning up with fever. And then I'll have Mirnae find some verbena to administer."

While Waith and a few servants buzzed in and out of the room to tend to Lys and arrange a message to the castle's healers, I took Lys's hand to appear caring. I lifted it higher to study his sigil ring and found the mace, hare, fern, and drumstone etched into the gold. Age had worn down the etchings. Things weren't tallying up correctly here.

"Is there something wrong?" a female said.

A dark-skinned, curly-haired Fae I assumed was Mirnae crushed verbena leaves with a pestle and mortar on the side table. Humming as she worked, she added honey, then mixed it with a steaming mug of hot water.

"Did he used to wear two of these rings?"

"Oh, don't you start in on him about what those terrible humans claim. King Lysanael has always worn this one ring and that amethyst one from his mother's hoard. That's it. The humans lie, remember? They do nothing but lie and lie about our good king."

"Can't be worse than the courtiers."

Mirnae chuckled. "Too true, Lady Resaynia. Too true."

There was a tapping at the window and we both turned to look. Nothing was visible, but I knew that tapping pattern. It was Arkyn, fully invisible, thank the Old Ones. I didn't need another stick in my wheel here. I shrugged as if I didn't know what the tapping had been and Mirnae followed my lead, letting it go as regular sounds from the vineyards carrying oddly.

Handing me the hot mug, Mirnae gave detailed instructions on when and how to administer the healing concoction. I suppose they trusted me because Lys appeared to. Their mistake.

"This is wonderful," I said as Mirnae gathered her mortar and pestle. "I'll keep you posted on how he does once he wakes enough to take a sip."

Once she was gone, the outside door down the corridor had banged shut, and the house was quiet, I slipped out of Lys's room and back to the one where we had kissed in front of the vineyard-facing window. I had to clean up the belladonna evidence. Closing the door quietly, I got to it.

First, I dumped most of the wine into the wood sitting dormant in the hearth. Then I found a small book of poetry on the hearth's mantelpiece, ripped out a blank page from the back, then wiped the berries and leaves from the wine cup. I crumpled the page tightly, then pocketed it so I could dispose of it in a burning fire or somewhere safer than my hearth. I didn't want to burn it for fear the Fae would scent the plant.

When I returned to Lys's room, he was sitting up on one elbow.

"You look like death," I said, going for the mug that Mirnae had left.

"So full of compliments. I wonder, if we were truly courting and I was ill, would you be kinder or is this your usual way to behave around a potential mate?"

The word mate on his lips set my blood ablaze. I took a breath and smothered the heat of desire before holding the cup to his lips. He sipped and grimaced.

"Tasty, hmm?" I chuckled and placed the cup on the table.

He lay back down on the pillows and shut his eyes.

"Do you have any idea what might be wrong with you?" I felt his head. He was hot with fever. Using the items the servants had brought earlier, I dipped a clean linen cloth into the bowl of cool water and proceeded to wipe Lysanael's face.

This was a new low for me—poisoning and then aiding the one I'd set on the road to death in order to pretend innocence.

Smoothing the cloth over his forehead, I recalled what Master's brief had stated about a Fae's ears. They were considered sensual spots, so if I decided to touch him there, that would be crossing a line of our agreement. I would be urging him to mate with me. Instead of doing that, I dipped the cloth again and wiped the sheen of sweat from his throat. His eyes opened briefly, then closed once more.

"Stop fighting it. Just sleep."

I brushed the cloth over his chest and along his abdomen. Water droplets ran between the hard muscles and along the waistline of his trousers. The servants had removed his belt and weapons, a kindness to me even if they didn't realize it.

My Berserker strength sluiced through my veins. I slipped my dagger free, poised its tip where it would pass between his ribs, and drove it directly into his heart.

Blood poured around my hand, then the room grew hazy and I blinked to clear my vision.

I was lying on the bed with Lysanael over me, his eyes locked on me and his hands pinning mine beside my head. His hair was loose and he looked pale, but there was no blood on his chest. No sign of my work.

"What happened?" I felt like I'd stumbled into a goblinbloom den.

Lys cocked his head and raked me with his gaze. "You have been under my thrall, Huntress."

I froze. He knew. He'd tricked me with a thrall. "What did I say?" Most likely, he'd keep the truth from me in a very Fae manner, but possibly he'd be arrogant and tell me how much I'd given away.

"Only that you poisoned me and planned to stick me with that dagger in exchange for your life. You called yourself a Huntress, said it like it was a title of sorts. What does being a Huntress mean? Who ordered you to assassinate me and why? Who holds your life in his hand besides me?"

I could bump his back with my bent knee, hurl him forward, then head butt his nose, but what then? If he had recovered from the belladonna enough to work this Fae magic on me, drawing out my desires with that dreamlike thrall, he might be well enough to beat me to the door.

Sealing my lips shut, I tried to will Arkyn to blast through the room like he'd done for me the first night at the castle. Lys shifted his hold so that he held both my wrists in one large hand. With his other, he gripped my face and forced me to look into his eyes. I shut them as quickly as I could, not knowing in detail how the thrall worked. Did he need eye contact?

"Huntress, the thrall allowed me to see those human eyes of yours." His voice was a growl, a warning, a promise of coming death. "Your frail flesh is visible to me now and your stunted ears. The potion or spell work that created this illusion falters. I can see straight through it to the weak, lying human beneath. What made you believe you could end the Fae king?"

A warmth like honey left in the sun poured over me and my tongue loosened. The thrall again... My heart ached with the desire to please him, to do anything he wished. My lips spoke without my permission.

I opened my eyes. "I have killed many magical creatures in my lifetime. I could have bested you."

A dark chuckle left him and the heat of his body over mine flushed my cheeks and caused my thoughts to tumble into visions of our last kiss, of his fingers on my waist, of his tongue sliding over mine.

I fought the thrall, wrestling with the sensations rolling over me, pushing back at his influence with my will. Finally, my head cleared for a moment.

"And did you see my dragon?" I spat out. "Because he is just outside, and if you harm me, he will destroy you in a very creative manner."

Lys's smirk fell away and he glanced at the window. "That wasn't a fever dream?"

"Arkyn is quite real, I assure you." It was stunning how quickly he could pull back on his thrall, how fast I went from completely enamored and helpless under him to clear-headed and ready to win this thing.

The Fae king's gaze returned to me. His eyes were a forest river speckled with sunlight, a place where I would wade in, misjudging the depth, and drown beneath the beautiful shadows of the trees.

"Then we are at an impasse," he said quietly, dangerously.

I recalled the way he'd cut the head from the Unseelie spy. He wouldn't hesitate to end me. "We are cut from the same cloth, Lys."

"Lys?"

"Yes, I gave you a nickname. Deal with it."

He raised an eyebrow, tightened his grip on my wrists, and, with his free hand, tucked a strand of my hair away from my face. "You're so quick to lash out, my viper. Perhaps I like my nickname. Do you like yours?" His smirk returned and he used his free hand to fold back the edge of my tunic, exposing my collarbone. Though he didn't use his thrall, his gaze smoothing over my chest and throat felt as hot as if his mouth had followed along.

I cleared my throat. Longing to spit out that I didn't give a rat's arse if he liked his nickname and I sure as hells didn't like mine and that he needed to get his cursed body off of me, I instead adjusted my strategy. Adding truth would give me more time to kill him. The Fae king might not know of Master, the Hunters, and Isernwyrd, but he would eventually. It was only a matter of time. I could reveal a small portion of the truth.

But his thrall poured over me again, soft and delicious. My body melted into the bed, my pulse pounded in my throat, and heat gathered low in my belly. The urge to throw myself at him was nearly overpowering. I squeezed my eyes shut again as if that might help. My thoughts remained clearer, but I still couldn't control my tongue.

"We are both forced to do things we don't want to do," I said, my words slurring slightly. "I am owned by a man who would see you dead for reasons I don't know." Wincing but unable to stop, I went on. "The human king, King Darrew, blames you for his daughter's murder. They found your sigil ring beside her body and took it as a direct threat. He hired my owner to arrange an assassination." I opened my eyes and attempted to focus.

Frustration twisted Lys's features and the muscles at his jaw worked, his nostrils flaring. "They're truly passing around that falsehood? It's ridiculous. I didn't kill the human princess, and I told your king that through a messenger when the murder first occurred. I have no desire for a war with humans. I don't even wish to be king, let alone one gallivanting about the world spilling blood for no reason."

He was telling the truth—he was a Fae, so he had to be telling the truth. But it didn't matter, I thought, the thrall spinning my mind in circles. He was the job. Focus…

More words spilled from my enthralled lips. "A death rune is tattooed on the back of my neck and if I don't kill you, the rune will end me the moment my owner wishes it so."

Well, that ended my ability to barter. He knew I had to kill him or die. I snarled in frustration and glared.

Lys grinned wickedly. He knew he had won this battle and it infuriated me to no end.

"Why would I care if you die?" he asked, his voice silky and full of power that tugged at my heart and my Berserker blood.

I had lost this game and the cost would be my life.

Maybe I could still save the situation. Perhaps he would think there was wiggle room with my death rune and that I could be swayed to his side. "Number one reason, the dragon outside ready to destroy you. Number two, you need me for this fake wedding scenario and I can bet you'd be hard-pressed to find a replacement who would agree to your terms."

His eyes sparked and he leaned close. "Because it's impossible to resist attempting to seduce me?"

Delectable shivers danced down my body and my hips lifted of their own accord. "No," I lied, ignoring the warmth gathering inside me and the heat of my Berserker blood rising for the chance to let loose with violent passion. "Because they would want a throne beside you. From what I know of your kind, they are always hungry for power."

He straightened and ran a hand down my side and along my thigh, his gaze heavy on my trembling body. "And humans are so humble."

"We are more varied in temperament." I had to keep stalling. What was the out here? The solution?

"That is prejudice talking, Huntress. And you are lying through your pretty white teeth." His gaze snapped to my face. "I can scent your desire for me. I would bet my best stallion that your desire for me is nearly undoing all the training you've had with this mysterious master of yours."

Gritting my teeth, I prepared for another hit of his thrall magic, but it never came. He released me and stood. His glare was a brand, burning me as surely as a red-hot iron.

"You will tell me who sent you or you will die right now," he whispered. "I'm not afraid of a forest dragon. Did you happen to miss how I dispatched those goblins? It would be easy enough to use you as a shield against the dragon's attack. I would be gone before Arkyn had a chance to check that his bonded warrior was whole and unscathed."

"You underestimate my training and my dragon's as well."

Lys shrugged, but anger still rolled off him in invisible waves. "Do you care to put my prediction to the test?"

He moved his arm so quickly that it blurred, then

my dagger was at my throat. The point bit at my skin and a drop of hot blood trickled over my collarbone. He'd retrieved the blade from the floor—where I must have dropped it while under his thrall—with such speed that I hadn't even seen him do it.

"Tell me everything," he said.

"Try to understand my position here, King Lysanael."

Smirking again, he moved slightly but kept me pinned. "I suppose I've lost my nickname now that I've put steel to your throat."

"Correct. Now, if I tell you about my mission, why would you let me live?" I was riding a very dangerous line here, but he was so different from my previous marks. He knocked my strategies off-kilter with his barely restrained anger and his teasing manner. It was almost as if he was enjoying himself.

"For the same reason I let you live the first two, maybe three times, you attempted to murder me," he said. So he did believe there was some way I could get around the death rune. If not, he wouldn't be bargaining. "Because I need someone not of our society to pose as my intended mate."

"But you didn't know I wasn't of your society before today," I said.

"I knew you weren't merely a farmer's daughter, my viper."

He shifted the knife so that the length of it sat across

my neck at an angle. The position of the blade showed me that he knew how to end my life very quickly. Assumably that was his intention, to further frighten me.

"What did you think I was?" I don't know why I cared. Maybe I was just curious about what mistakes I had made to blow my cover.

"I had ideas..." he said. "A cursed selkie, a spirit from the Unseelie realm... Farmers' daughters don't stalk into the Branle like the Forest Queen come back to life."

The Forest Queen was a children's story, a cautionary tale about a Fae royal who had influenced all the animals of the Gwerhune to fight for her. Her lust for power caused her to forget the first bond she had with the creatures and they had turned on her, devouring her under a full moon. I had always wondered if a male had doctored the story in an effort to frighten girls into being submissive. I had no idea if the tale was based on a true story.

The door flew open and Waith stood glaring. "Your Majesty, forgive the intrusion. I came to tell you a horrible truth, but it seems you have discovered the assassin on your own. I am at your service, lord king. Let me know if I can be of any help in disposing of this vile soul." His eyes were crossbows aimed in my direction.

A low growl rumbled from Lys's chest and his lip curled, showing a fang. "You will not touch Resaynia.

She is mine to deal with. If anyone so much as breathes a word against her, I will burn this place to the ground with those gossipmongers inside."

Waith bowed low. "Your Majesty, we've been friends for ages and I say this only because I care for you. I..." He shook his head as if he was organizing his thoughts. Standing and locking eyes with Lys, he said quietly, "I won't say a word and won't lay hands on your intended mate, but please consider your well-being. I smelled the remnants of belladonna in the hearth where the female changed. She is a poisoner."

Only Waith knew about me, so it *was* possible to keep the game going at court and beyond. I was certainly up for it. I had no other choice.

Lys's growl increased in volume and my Berserker blood burned hotly, rushing through me with a fierce blend of desire and energy.

Waith bowed again, lower this time, his nose nearly scraping the ground. "Forgive me, lord king. I will not move against your mate." The vintner took two steps back and shut the door.

The second Waith's footsteps faded, Lys spoke. "If I can remove the death rune, will you agree to stay your hand?"

I swallowed against my dry throat. "You can't remove it."

Raising both eyebrows, Lys cocked his head. "Our Druid is very powerful."

Was it possible? Cold fear speared me. I didn't dare

to hope again. The Druid would want me dead for trying to kill his king, wouldn't he? A thousand things could go wrong in a meeting with the powerful magician even if he did have the ability to remove the rune.

I recalled the Witch's owl eyes and shuddered. When Master brought me to her home to retrieve the illusion potion, she had stared at me with those eerie eyes. Master claimed the Witch could read my mind. Would she know if I met with the Druid and he attempted to remove the death rune? Would she then alert Master and have me killed at that very moment? At *this* very moment? Sweat beaded on my upper lip and I fisted my hands to keep from shaking.

The edge of Lys's mouth lifted and his eyes softened. "I will take you there immediately after we marry and perform the ritual. We leave for Caer Du at dusk. I promised Waith I'd stay for dinner. Your dragon can fly us through this northeastern edge of the Gwerhune at night, yes?"

I was too stunned to say anything as he tucked my dagger into his trousers, then held out a hand. Taking it, feeling sparks of heat at his touch, I rose from the bed and followed him out the door. Finally, I found my tongue. "Yes. Arkyn can easily carry four men on his back."

"Fae, you mean?" Lys grinned at me over his shoulder as we walked the dirt path that led to the first section of vineyards.

Stones, I had forgotten to use the proper language. Again. Swallowing, I corrected myself. "Fae, yes. Of course."

Near a cluster of filled baskets and a few crockery pitchers of fresh water, Lys dropped back and put his mouth to my ear. "How long will your illusion last?"

Numerous Fae were still plucking and cutting and filling baskets with grapes. The vineyard hummed with quiet conversation, the huff of the two horses pulling the cart of already stuffed baskets, and the buzz of the bees. A Fae female with small antlers and emerald skin offered us a basket and a picking knife. I took the basket and Lys accepted the knife. She curtseyed, and with a polite smile, she moved away, giving us space.

"I'm not sure," I whispered to Lys as I adjusted the basket on my arm and reached in toward a bunch of grapes that looked ready to fall off. "Maybe five more days."

A displeased sound came from Lys as he began cutting grapes and filling my basket, his arm brushing mine. "We'll need to work quickly, then."

If the Druid did remove the rune—which was more than likely completely impossible—what happened after that? How long until Master came looking for me? The king wouldn't allow an asset like me to disappear into the Realm of Lights. Unless they believed I died by some other cause, of course. That was it. If I could get the rune removed, I would make certain Master's contacts heard of my death. I could find a contact. I had ways of accomplishing that discreetly. But then what?

Pain bit at my palm and I gasped. Distracted by my swirling thoughts, I'd stupidly tried to grab the cluster of grapes he'd been cutting and the knife had caught me.

Lys hissed and grabbed my hand as blood leaked down my palm. "Apologies, Lady Resaynia. You must pay more attention to our work." He spoke into my hair, his breath hot. I struggled with my control and breathed deeply only to be greeted with his intoxicating scent. "We've had enough of threatening one another for one day, haven't we?" A chuckle rumbled in his broad chest. "Save your next blood-letting at least for tomorrow when we've had a night's rest." Turning his head, he spoke above the vineyard's noises. "Anyone have bandaging handy?"

His teasing and his show of concern about my injury was a farce. I knew that. But my heart wasn't so easily convinced of the truth. My heart wanted to believe someone other than Raulian and Arkyn cared for my well-being, that there was a soul in this world that might come to love me despite my past and the horrors I'd inflicted.

As the Fae with antlers provided a bandage, I imagined full darkness. I slammed the black void over my emotions and shut them down.

I sighed, hugely relieved that my feelings were out of the way. "I appreciate it," I said to the Fae female.

She joined the others, leaving me with Lysanael, who studied the bandage, his deft fingers cradling my injured hand.

This was a job. Or a game of survival. Either way, love was not in the cards.

REVNA

I joined Lysanael in the front room of the vineyard house, where we were to meet Waith for a farewell. Dinner had been a pleasant affair, full of jokes told by those who didn't know I had poisoned their king. Waith had been silent mostly, keeping himself busy with talk of next season and the current harvest's production.

Now, as we prepared to leave, Lys turned to pick up a small bottle of wine one of the workers had given to him. He had his hair tied back again and something about the view of the knot at the base of his head was oddly familiar.

"We are riding your dragon home to Caer Du," he said, reminding me of what he had demanded earlier.

"We have horses. Won't a dragon cause some uncomfortable gossip or do all of your love interests ride upon scaly beasts?"

He didn't chuckle as he would have in the vineyard. No, his face was devoid of emotion and it reminded me of how he had regarded his court during the first part of the Brezhoneg Branle.

"It's none of your concern what my former love interests did or did not do," he said. "We will take your dragon because it is faster and we must ride in haste to the fest-noz."

The night festival—the portion of the Branle that took place in the hedge maze in the courtyard of Caer Du. Master's brief only mentioned that the event involved a search of some kind, body paints, and masks. It sounded like the most Fae activity that could ever be created.

"Did we accomplish what you wished here at the vineyard?" I asked.

Lys's eyebrows lifted, but still that cold mask remained firmly in place. "We did. Except for Waith, they see us as an infallible couple. They believe you helped me through an illness…"

His eyes darkened and I shrugged. His gaze flicked to the corridor, and the sound of shoes on floorboards carried through the room.

"Kiss me," Lys said in the lowest whisper, the tone of command clipping his words.

I didn't want to do as he told me, but he was right. Leaning into Lys's broad chest, I lifted my chin and parted my lips. His mouth closed in on mine, his lips pressing firmly as he gripped my arms roughly. Why did he have to smell so enticing? Why did I like the way his fingers dug into my skin almost painfully? A part of me longed to lose myself in this kiss, to melt against him and drown in sensation.

Heat rushed through me and my cheeks flushed hotly as Waith walked into the room, his footsteps loud now and near. I lashed down my desire and pulled away from Lys's mouth a fraction. His eyes opened halfway. A question appeared in his gaze, a twitch feathering the edge of his jaw. Breaking away from me slowly, he spun me around and placed an arm across my stomach to hold me against him tightly.

Waith bowed, but before he ducked his head, distrust flickered in his eyes. "Your Majesty. Lady Resaynia."

I gave Waith a slow nod. "Thank you for the hospitality, Master Waith."

Lys's mask cracked slightly and a true smile slipped through. "I always enjoy my visits here."

Waith straightened and regarded Lys with a grin that also seemed genuine. These two did indeed consider themselves friends. It boggled my mind that a king had befriended a vintner. But then again, if the Fae considered a female of any societal status appropriate for their king, they definitely had different ideas than us humans.

"We treasure your presence, my king," Waith said.

He sent us out the door with another crock of wine and Lys asked him to send the horses on in a few days, adding that there was no rush and the horses would enjoy the reprieve here in the countryside. Lys didn't mention my dragon, but instead we waved once more and walked across the meadows toward the Gwerhune.

I sensed that Arkyn hadn't gone far; a prickling sensation in my chest said he was eager to be near me and to protect me.

"How do you call your dragon?" Lys's mask was firmly back in place.

I wasn't going to answer that. "I suppose you must be cold to survive at court." I studied his chilly look and the flat line of his full lips.

Surprise flickered in his eyes and he glanced my way. "Yes. I learned long ago that no one at court is to be trusted."

"I certainly wasn't worthy of trust."

His mouth twitched as if he wanted to laugh but refused himself the joy of it. "No, you weren't, and you remain the very definition of treachery. I can't say that smile makes me feel any better about our arrangement."

"If you can get the Druid to remove my death rune, we have no argument against one another. I only wish to live for…" I stopped, not wishing to reveal the truth in my heart.

"What do you wish to live for?"

"Arkyn," I called quietly toward the dim of the forest.

The sunset pierced the tree cover here and there, setting coins of golden light on dark trunks and the red petals of another type of Fae ivy, the type that had tangled Arkyn and me on our journey to Caer Du. The dull beat of wings sounded and we looked up to see the dragon descending through a cluster of pines, his tail thrashing the limbs and knocking cones from their perches. He landed before us, his eyes narrowed and focused on Lys.

I walked forward, stretching out my hand. "It's all right. He's with us now."

Arkyn bumped my palm with his snout, then shifted his large head to keep an eye on the Fae king. I climbed onto Arkyn's back.

"We'll have to do without the saddle, I'm afraid, but Arkyn is quite good at keeping riders on his back as long as we aren't attacked."

With the grace that only Fae possessed, Lys launched himself easily onto the dragon. He set his hands on my hips and warmth curled out of his fingers, through my clothing, and into my flesh. The air was cool and crisp as Arkyn galloped and launched into the sky. With the spiced hue of the setting sun all around us, we flew toward Caer Du.

"To the castle gates," I said to Arkyn over the wind that tore at my braid.

Lys's chest touched my back and his breath ghosted over my ear. "How does he know what you wish of him?" Though his voice was cold, there was honest curiosity in his tone as well.

"I tap his scales in the direction I wish to go, but he

seems to know my will even when I don't use that technique. It's part of our bond. I...can't explain it. Yes, he is intelligent and understands language well, but it's more than that. He somehow senses my wants and needs."

"He can track you beyond anything I would have guessed."

I nodded as Lys sat back again, the chill of the air replacing the heat of his chest on my back.

Arkyn soared over the black-green edge of the Gwerhune. Mountains ringed in a thick white fog stood in the far distance. The Shrouded Mountains. Supposedly there were dragons there too, far larger than Arkyn's breed, and that kind could breathe fire.

"Do you ever visit the Shrouded Mountains?" I asked, hoping he'd mention the brother that the old council Fae, Bornien, had brought up at the castle.

His fingers moved over the leather belt his servants had given me to wear for our visit to the vineyard. "No, they are quite difficult to reach and a darkness surrounds that area as well."

"What does the fest-noz involve?" I asked.

Arkyn veered east and my boot bumped Lys's. His thigh pressed against mine, his body shifting closer. I swallowed. Lys cleared his throat and tried to ease away from me, adjusting his seat on Arkyn's smooth, scaled back.

"It's a dangerous celebration of the night," he said, "and you will remain armed until you find me. Once you do, you must then remain close to me until its conclusion."

"So you can protect me or so I can defend your back?"

"Both, viper. Both."

I hated the glimmer of bright joy his words gave me. "Tell me about your childhood at court," I said. "Have you always worn that cold mask of yours while at your home?" I didn't know if he would answer and I waited with only the sound of the wind in my ears.

"My mother tried to kill me," he said quietly.

I froze at the absence of emotion in his voice. No words rose to my tongue. Would this Fae king ever stop surprising me?

REVNA

I listened, keeping still as he spilled his heart to me.

Lys cleared his throat and adjusted his grip on my hips. "My father, King Illanius, had grown sickly and the council was preparing to name a new ruler. The council wanted me on the throne instead of her and she knew it. She had made too many enemies during her reign. On the pretense of visiting the menhir where we hold our sacred rituals, she took me into the depths of the Gwerhune. There, she dismissed our guards and attempted to plunge a dagger into my throat."

Even my steel-coated assassin's heart ached at that tale. "How did you escape?"

"I...slipped past her, but I returned and ended her life with the very dagger she had tried to use on me."

I fought the urge to place my hand over his as I would have done with Raulian—the only other person in the world with whom I'd shared personal stories of pain like this.

"How old were you?" I asked.

"Almost an adult. Not quite there, but I already had my strength, magic, and speed."

"More than her strength and speed, I suppose?"

He made a noncommittal noise. There was more to this story that he wasn't willing to tell.

The stars appeared in the darkening sky and the indigo Fae lights floated from the Gwerhune. The lights reminded me of the lanterns my people used to release every spring. A memory of Fjordbok washed through me, reminding me of the salt in the air at home and the way our homes resembled honeycombs set into the cliffs overlooking the water.

"King Darrew's men killed my mother because she refused to pay his taxes." My voice sounded too loud despite the wind in my ears. I lowered my volume because no doubt Lys's Fae ears could pick up my words even if I whispered. "His general claimed she was too old to be taught to work for Master and with her Berserker blood she was too great a threat to be left alive. She took down twenty-nine knights before they overtook her and she only failed because she had to protect me. I was still a child."

Her face flashed through my memory, blood caking her loose blond hair and the spark of ferocious rebellion in her eyes—eyes that had been as ice blue as my own. It was oddly comforting to talk about my past with someone outside of my world. The fact that I couldn't see his reactions made it easier too. I felt lighter now, strangely relieved.

"That's the scent I get from you," Lys said. "If I concentrate and work my senses past your illusion, I scent the cold black oceans of ancient Fjordbok."

I couldn't fight a proud grin.

The two rings of Caer Du's stone walls appeared and Arkyn flew over the outer bailey's quiet evening roads, thatched roofs, and shuttered buildings. We soared over the gatehouse of the inner bailey.

"Have him land near the stables. Just there." Lys pointed to a long wooden building roofed with dark slate.

I squeezed Arkyn's sides with my legs and leaned forward to point to where Lys had indicated, my hand visible to my dragon even if he didn't really need the direction.

Settling back on Arkyn, my body against Lys's, I felt Lys exhale, his chest moving against my back. I held myself steady as Arkyn landed in the courtyard by the royal stables. Lys dismounted first and held up a hand, his eyes giving away nothing. The mask was back in full force.

"My lady," he said quietly as the stable lads looked on, their eyes wide and flicking from Arkyn's mouth of long teeth and my face. So many juicy bits of gossip we were creating here.

After giving Arkyn a reassuring pet and tapping his

scaled neck five times to let him know all was going according to plan, I accepted Lys's hand and hopped down. He set my hand on his forearm and led me toward a set of side doors between the stables and another building—perhaps a workshop or an armory. My eyes took a moment to adjust in the dark of the interior and I blinked at a sconce that snapped as we passed by.

"What now?" I whispered as we walked the dark corridor and started up a set of back stairs.

"We sleep. Tomorrow, I will present you to the council. Just you, me, and the vultures. If all goes well, which it will unless they somehow can see through your illusion, we will display our affection at the fest-noz. I will be dismissing the other females I invited to stay."

"What does *displaying our affection* involve?" I asked.

His eyebrow lifted. "It'll be no more difficult than fighting goblins."

"You'll have to show some emotion at court though and you seem rather hesitant to do that."

His nostrils flared and he glanced behind us. "You're right. It will be more challenging for me because of the way I've handled my life. When one cannot even trust their mother, one becomes rather shut down in order to survive."

"I understand that," I said.

He looked at me as we passed under an archway that opened into the corridor I recognized as the one where my room was located. His gaze peppered my face.

"Because of what you have been forced to do and the threat of death always literally at your back," he said.

I cleared my throat. "Yes." Wincing, I pressed my thumb against my temple. "I need some sleep. My head is killing me."

"Fae don't experience headaches," he whispered.

"Really?"

Shaking his head, he looked forward again and his other hand moved to cover mine, which still rested on his well-muscled forearm. I didn't think he even realized his comforting movement; he appeared incredibly distracted.

At my door, he went in first, his body coiled and ready for attack, but everything seemed in place. A fire crackled in the hearth and the bed had been turned down. I supposed this castle worked like a human royal's did with servants always preparing for the lord and lady's return.

"Your life is in even more danger now that word will have spread about our arrival on dragonback," Lys said. "The entirety of the Realm of Lights will know you are my intended mate in mere hours, if I had to make a wager. Jealous females will attempt to get you out of the way. Council members with their own pawns in place at court will join you in the poisoning game."

He glanced at me, raising an eyebrow like a disgruntled tutor. Not that any of my tutors had ever looked like him. Stones, he was so tall, so broad-shouldered... His size was even more apparent indoors. His back blocked most of the starlight filtering through the glazed windows. He was eyeing a tray that I guessed had been left for me at some point during our trip to the vineyard.

"Do not eat this."

I joined him at the table where the tray sat, then picked up a sprig of something green. It smelled like mountbud. "Impressive. Mountbud is nearly impossible to render without killing oneself." I threw the poisoned veg back down onto the tray and covered the meal with the silver lid provided. "You don't need to fret on my account, Lys. I'm always watching for ways death might steal me away."

"Lys." His mask had cracked to show a pleased grin and a cocky look in his eyes.

A blush rose into my cheeks. "Yes, your nickname has returned."

His smile fell and his face grew serious. "Before I leave, allow me to teach you how to resist a thrall."

My blood rushed through my veins as I recalled the complete lack of control I'd had when he had performed that particular Fae magic on me. "All right. I'm listening."

He nodded once curtly and motioned to the chair beside the hearth, the amethyst ring on his hand catching the light. "Sit, human, and prepare yourself for my power."

REVNA

I sat and looked up at him.

"Fae can enthrall other Fae." His voice was low, dangerous. "They don't need to know you're actually human before attempting to work the magic on you."

"I had wondered."

The firelight blinked from the gold loop in the tip of his pointed ear. "When you first feel the warmth of the spell, imagine snow, ice, and perhaps that home of yours on the cold ocean."

The corner of my mouth lifted. I had never enjoyed an assassination job. Fighting Unseelie, yes, but murder was soul-eating to the killer and I felt the truth of that with every mission. But this, right now? I was enjoying myself, and the threat to my steeled heart and to that box of locked-down emotions increased with every moment here. If Lys failed in helping me remove the rune, I'd have to try once again to kill him. We were not allies. Not truly.

I realized then that he had stopped talking and was studying me.

"You're afraid." His voice curled around my throat.

My chest clenched, a fist of truth squeezing my heart. "I'd be stupid not to fear your control over me. I *have* tried to kill you multiple times."

He cocked his head to one side. "I told you I would take you to the Druid and help you to be free of your owner and your hideous king. I can't lie to you. You know that."

"But Fae are so tricky." I gave him a flat look, showing him I was no fool. This was such a thin line to walk.

"Definitely," he agreed. "What other way could I show you that I'm on your side as long as you remain on mine?"

I shrugged. "I'm not sure honestly. Any ideas?"

"We will simply have to go from day to day."

"Well, let's get on with my little lesson then, my king."

A pleased gleam passed over his slitted eyes and the room warmed. Heat rushed through my body, igniting my blood.

"Take your hair down." Lys's voice was honey poured over my chest and into my heart. "I wish to see your tresses loose in the fire's dancing light."

Before I could manage a defense, I realized I had

already obeyed him in full. The tie and pins that had been holding my coiled braid in place sat in my lap and my hair hung at my shoulders. More time had gone by than I'd noticed as well. I shut my eyes against the glory of his cruel smile, his tall form looming above me, and his hands which were now braced on the arms of my chair.

Swallowing, I imagined the cold ocean of my homeland, the black waves and the foamy lines of the tides moving in. I could almost smell the salt of the sea, hear the call of the gannets. The warmth of Lys's thrall faded and his voice dropped to a whisper that I ignored.

"Very good," he said in a more normal voice, if one could deem his deep, delicious, royal Fae voice normal.

I opened my eyes, feeling more clear-headed now though my headache from earlier persisted. "Try it again."

His eyes widened a fraction. "You're certain?"

"Don't hold back." This was training. I knew how to do this sort of thing.

A wicked gleam shone in his gaze and he leaned close, so close that I could have easily lifted my hand to brush my knuckles over his finely crafted stomach and hook a finger in his belt. His chest moved in a slow breath and the heat of his thrall crashed over me.

"Pull your tunic down over your shoulder."

Of course, I would do as my Fae lover ordered… The cool of the room washed over my bare shoulder as I obeyed his direction. The fire's heat mixed with the undulating warmth of the thrall. He drew his lips across my shoulder, his fangs catching my skin lightly and making it incredibly difficult to breathe.

"What else do you wish of me, my lord?"

I was dreaming. Everything around me—his handsome face, the firelight silhouetting him, my own hand—shimmered as if gilded. My body melted into the heat of his magic, into what felt like a dress formed to my every curve and line. Leaning forward, I longed for him to touch me again.

"Tell me your true name."

A haze of red washed over my vision. I blinked. What was that? King Lysanael was the best of males and I was his entirely. I had no doubts. My thoughts drifted and slid around in my mind as I imagined dancing with him again and kissing him and suddenly we were doing just that. He broke away from the kiss and I realized we were standing by the windows and the stars were gold.

"I thought stars were silver… What did you ask, Lys the beautiful? Oh, my name. Yes, it is…" The red haze dotted my vision again, a vision that appeared sometimes when my Berserker blood was past controlling. *Your name is Resaynia,* Master said in my memory. *Resaynia.* "Resaynia is my name."

"No." Lys's long black hair fell from its knot as he shook his head gently, his eyes as gold as everything else. "That's the name they gave to you for this mission. What is your true name, human?"

Another billowing rush of delicious warmth rolled

over me and I pressed my body against his, savoring the feel of his hard lines and tensing muscles. "That's easy. My mother named me Revna, the Fjordbok word for Raven."

The warmth from Lys evaporated and left me cold. He stepped back, his face shuttered, closed off completely. My mind cleared and I tried to remember what had happened a moment before.

"What...what were we talking about? I failed, didn't I?"

"No, you did quite well, Resaynia." He brushed a hair away from my cheek and tucked it behind my ear.

I shivered and cleared my throat. "Thank you for the lesson. I'll make sure I'm ready for the fest-noz and anyone who might try that on me."

"Snow. Cold. Your home. Keep it in the front of your mind." He bowed curtly and left me. Beyond the closed door, his voice echoed as he spoke to some servants, asking for a guard to be set on my room and for a bath to be drawn for me.

Had I truly fought the thrall as he said? I rubbed at my temples and when someone knocked, I let two servants inside. Along with a few others who scurried in and out, they worked hard to fill my tub with steaming water that smelled of honey and fresh leaves.

I sent them on, not wanting any more noise or hassle, and undressed myself before climbing into the bath. It wasn't as if I'd had a choice on whether or not to work on resisting the thrall. He could perform the powerful spell on me regardless. It had been just one of the many risks of this job. And, I reminded myself for the hundredth time, he had said he would bring me to the Druid to remove my death rune as soon as we were wed. He couldn't lie. I could trust in that, at least.

Swirling the water with my hands, I inhaled the sweet scent and worked on unclenching my jaw and relaxing my muscles. Arkyn was safe enough in the Fae stables. The Fae were known for their cruelty to one another and to humans, but they were far better with animals than humans were. I leaned back and rested my head on the tub, watching the steam rise into the lavish candlelit room that was attached to the bedchamber.

I could get used to this.

What would life be like if the Druid truly could rid me of that stones-cursed rune? If—and that was a large and looming IF—Lys followed through on his promise to gift me lands and money, I would sell the land immediately, pocket the coin, and head to Fjordbok with Arkyn. There, I would…I would look for my cousins. I doubted any were still alive, but if they were, we would have the very best of reunions. We would plan out a strategy for our people. I'd bring over steel for axes and arrowheads so that we could hunt, repair shelters, and get everyone their own fire to sit by, to eat over, to sleep near and grow healthy. Together, we could rebuild the port, then craft two large ships for trade. If I had enough coin, I could have us working on new trade routes in less than a season. The fish, whale, and seal trade had always been busy in late autumn.

My eyes drifted shut and I allowed myself, for the first time in ages, to dream of a free life.

Then my mind threw a memory at me—Master's knuckles white against the leather of his whip. I sat up in the tub and put a hand on my death rune. It pulsed beneath my wet fingers. Or did it? Was I just imagining things?

I sat back and tried to relax, but the moment was ruined. Even if I got rid of this rune, I'd still have a battle headed my way. Master might even have the king behind him if he came for me. But if I had the friendship of the Fae king to back me up, maybe they'd rethink attacking Fjordbok.

I laughed without smiling. Foolish woman. I threw myself out of the tub, wrapped up in a linen, and tromped out to one of the chairs by the snapping fire. Water drizzled down the side of my face and I wiped my palm over my cheek before slicking the water to the floor where my feet were likewise making a mess. As if this would all actually happen. A Fae king helping out a lowly human? Why? Just because she helped him get the council off his back for a bit? It made no sense. So why else was he helping me? Even if he didn't follow through, what was his real reason for going along with this ruse right now? Surely he could get some Fae to do what I was doing. Granted, they wouldn't be subject to his thrall since all court Fae trained to resist that particular magic, but…

It was like a door banged open in my head.

I had been under his thrall.

That was why he agreed to do this. I stood, barely keeping my linen bath sheet in place, my wet hair plastered to my shoulders and back as I stared into the fire and let out a slew of curses so foul they probably blackened the soul of every creature within a mile.

"My, that is quite a mouth you have on you."

I wheeled around to see Lys hitched to the door frame, to the door I had not heard opening or closing due to my crashing, banging, stupidly slow thoughts. My heart climbed up my throat. He held something in his right hand. Pocketing whatever it was, he tilted his head and regarded me like I was an interesting puzzle.

LYSANAEL

The Old Ones had outdone themselves when they'd created this female. Lysanael couldn't tear his gaze away from the view of Resaynia —Revna—standing before the fire in that bathing sheet. The cloth clung to each curve of her strong body. Water droplets slid down the battle scars on her shoulder, a place his lips ached to kiss. His fingers twitched, wishing they could follow the water's route under that sheet to explore the lovely lines of her form. He adjusted his trousers and forced himself to breathe evenly. She was angry. He could almost taste her rage in the air like a coming storm.

He commented on her rough language; teasing her felt natural. Whirling, she faced him, looking like a vengeful goddess to whom he would happily sacrifice himself. He shook himself mentally. Revna was truly lethal and so beyond anything he'd experienced in a person. A thrill buzzed up his spine and a wicked grin slicked over his lips. So interesting. He hadn't wanted to put her under his thrall. That type of magic was incredibly foul. But he had to keep his mind in this game and not allow his lust for her to endanger him and those he lived to protect. Unless Gwyn's safety depended on it, he would not use Revna's name.

She marched over, one hand on her bath sheet and the other clasping air like it was desperate for a blade. "What did you make me do while under your thrall?" Her tone cut him as surely as any knife. "Answer me."

"Why should I? Going to attempt murder once more?" He tsked her and delighted in the rage that boiled in her gaze. She was magnificent. "We've established that you're not capable," he said.

Revna threw a knee at his groin. He shifted his hips to block and her elbow flew at his nose. The strike missed his nose but hit his cheek, and pain bracketed away from the point of contact. With a snarl, she grabbed for his stones. He lifted his forearm to block, then latched his fingers onto her hair. Grunting, she clutched his hand—the one holding her hair. In an amazingly quick movement worthy of a Fae knight, she pressed his hand tightly against her skull, dropped back, then faked another elbow hit before balling her left hand into a fist and throwing a lead hook into his jaw.

Heat branched over his face and a growl escaped him. What a vicious little thing. He shook her slightly, still gripping her hair. She lost her hold and he pushed her to her knees. Looking down at the beautiful assassin, he narrowed his eyes. Her gaze belonged on a battlefield, not a bedchamber.

"Behave, my viper. I didn't come here to fight."

"Tell me what you made me do under your thrall," she said. "Who did I kill and why?"

Kill? He would never have used her the way her master had. It was insulting that she would believe such a thing. "I owe you no explanations."

Her chest moved in a deep breath, breasts rising and nearly escaping the damp sheet. Wet strands of thick hair drew lines over her sharp collarbone. What would the hollow of her throat taste like right now? Like lavender from her bath and the salt of her skin? His blood roared for him to take her, but he stamped the feeling down. He couldn't let this relationship evolve in any way; if he let her in, she might learn his terrible secret.

Her lip twitched and she bared her teeth. "You couldn't have had me accomplish much. I was still wearing the same clothing when I broke the thrall and the sky looked the same. You didn't have me under that long."

Such a clever viper. "No, I didn't send you away from this room, and before you suggest it, I did not enthrall you to take advantage of you carnally. I don't need such tricks. I only had a bit of fun with you. You're quite different when you are under my spell."

His jaw ached and he ran a finger over the small lump

already forming. "Yes, your venom rose up and struck true."

He pulled her toward him so that her face was close to his waist. His blood simmered with want and he wished they were a couple living far from court with no machinations, no ruses, and no secrets to keep them apart.

"Watch out for my teeth," she said very quietly, flicking her gaze lower.

In a flash of movement, he bent low and set his fangs against her neck. "Be careful of mine, human," he whispered.

Her pulse was a siren's song. In another scenario, he could have made her heart race for an altogether different reason. A wave of her scent washed over him —salt and snow. His throat bobbed in a rough swallow. Desire pulsed through him. She was so, so close. One turn of his head and his mouth would find hers. His heart drummed in his ears.

"Now, are you finished with today's attempt at bloodying me?" he asked, his voice breathier than he wanted. "Because I brought you a Fae herb to help with the headache you mentioned earlier tonight."

The muscles of her arm, braced against his body, relaxed. "I'm too tired to fight you now."

He released her hair, straightened, and held out a hand. She took it and stood. Trying very hard not to wish that sheet would fall away, he cleared his throat.

"Before I instruct you on this Fae healing herb, would you please dress yourself?"

Her eyelids lowered halfway and her gaze smoothed over his torso and face. Each sweep of her focus was like the brush of fingertips. He fisted a hand and gritted his teeth.

"Causing you some discomfort, am I?" She turned away, untucked the sheet, and let it fall to her lower back as she walked toward the bathing room.

Damned female. His breath caught. "You've been a fiery thorn in my side since the moment you crept into my keep."

She disappeared into the bathing chamber, and shuffling sounds and quiet knocks said perhaps she was doing as he'd requested.

Shaking his head to clear it, he went to the table near the windows, removed the herb Celin had provided for Revna's headache from his pocket, and proceeded to grind the dried plant between his palms as he'd been instructed. A goblet of watered wine sat ready for her and he sniffed it to ensure it was safe. Not that he'd been able to scent the poisons with which she had dosed him. Inhaling and cursing himself as a fool, he dusted the herb into the drink.

Revna's soft footsteps padded across the floorboards and he looked up to see her plaiting her hair over one shoulder. Her linen sleeping shift was thin enough that when she passed between him and the hearth, the firelight outlined her shape and poured heat into him. In the shift, she looked like a female who didn't know a male called Master who had turned her into a weapon. His heart gave an astoundingly tender squeeze. But he appreciated the weapon she was, the female she was. Perhaps it was truly possible to be both vicious and vulnerable. His throat tightened. He longed to be such a person too.

"Much better," he said, more brusquely than he'd planned. "Drink this and your headache should fade."

She sniffed the drink, then sipped. "How do you know what herb cures a human's headache?"

"I don't, but we use this herb on animals who become listless after an injury. I once used it on my favorite goat after he fell into a ravine and had to be rescued."

"I'm sorry." A chuckle left her and he was surprised to hear it. "You have a favorite goat?" she asked.

He shrugged. Was that so odd?

A fit of hilarity took her, a sure sign she was beyond exhausted. She wiped her eyes and tried to stop laughing. "Such a very serious Fae king enthralling me and using me to some dark and mysterious purpose who also apparently has a favorite goat."

Frowning, he crossed his arms and turned his sigil ring around his finger. He didn't want to love that laugh, but it was the loveliest sound in the world.

"The most skilled assassin in the world makes you think of small farm animals," she said, still snorting with humor. "Humans are doomed."

He nudged the bottom of her cup, and she drank the rest of the herbed wine and water down. She crawled into bed while he stood there, studying her. A very insistent part of his body expressed a wish to follow her under the covers.

"Go on now." She pulled the blankets over her shoulder and watched him as she lay on her side. Her lips parted slightly, showing the pink tip of her tongue and a slice of her white teeth. "We can spar more once I've had some sleep."

"Sleep well, my viper. I hope you dream of spilling my blood and flying to freedom." A smile pulled at his mouth.

"That makes two of us." She shut her eyes.

He chuckled and started to leave. "Dream of the dark hedges of the fest-noz where you will find me," he whispered as he shut her door quietly.

His dreams, he knew, would feature a female in a bathing sheet shooting arrows from her vicious eyes directly into his heart. It would be the best of dreams.

29

REVNA

S ervants knocked to enter eons before I wanted to rise.

"Come in," I called out groggily as I swung my legs to the bedside. I had dreamed of the fest-noz, yes, but my mind had spun possibilities while I slept as well. None of them explained Lys's long-term plan. I had to find out what he would do once we were wed and how he saw the situation settled, as he had mentioned. Did it involve his brother? The younger Fae male was dead. How could he matter here? Even if he were alive, he was the younger brother and therefore not the heir to the throne. I was missing large pieces of this puzzle.

Ignorant of my attempts at solving a life-threatening mystery inside my very tired mind, a veritable horde of brush-wielding, dress dragging, jewel-bearing Fae rushed in. I fought a yawn as they all began talking at once, obviously quite excited to prepare the king's intended mate for presentation to the royal council.

I stretched as a young female with skin the color of Laqqara oranges and a tail that spiraled absently behind her steered me into the chair by the desk. The watery light of sunrise filtered in over a set of horse hair brushes and bone combs that she arranged quickly in a neat row.

Yawning again, I rubbed my head, enjoying the fact that my headache was long gone. I had slept well, albeit not nearly long enough. It was odd to sleep so soundly during a mission. Everything about this job was strange. Unsettling, yes, but I had to admit, also hopeful. I hated the hope lighting up inside me, the beam of potential joy that refused to be locked away. It was going to get me hurt.

The young Fae set her hands on the back of my chair and leaned around to peer at me. "Good morning, Lady Resaynia. I am Sonaellyn." She slicked cream over my cheeks and rubbed it under my tired eyes. The cream smelled amazing—sweet and fresh. "I've never seen the king so enamored with a female and I'm absolutely thrilled that I get to dress you for the council."

Another female, this one much taller and with fair skin like mine, approached and held up two dresses, cocking her head left and right. "No one in the history of the realm has seen a king so wound up over a mate."

"But we've only just danced together. How do you know how he feels about me?"

They traded a look, then both laughed. "You're jesting, right?" Sonaellyn said.

"No. Why do you believe he cares that much for me?"

"As you wish, my lady." She picked up a large brush and began running it through my tangles. "He has never brought anyone to the vineyard. It is his... How would you explain it, Malaynia?"

The fair female clicked her tongue and examined a length of silk in shimmering dark blue. "The vineyard is the only place where our king truly smiles. Or so we've heard. We've certainly never been."

"Yes, he invited you to a place where he doesn't lord around like usual and instead shows his vulnerable side," Sonaellyn said, "his humility, his...heart."

"And from what we've heard," Malaynia whispered, light brows lifted, "you pulled a dagger on him and you're still here, living and breathing. A clever way to rouse the competitive nature in the male, my lady."

They believed my assassination attempt was a type of seduction technique? The Fae were most assuredly more cutthroat than humans. "Ah. I had thought that was a secret."

"Oh, we would never breathe a word of it to anyone," Sonaellyn said quickly as one of the other servants cleaned the hearth, her tools banging lightly as she worked.

Once again, I had to wonder at my situation with the Fae king.

Who was playing whom?

I was working Lys by showing vulnerability here and there with my tired laughing and my obvious physical attraction to him. Not that I could truly lock that down. I rolled my eyes at myself. Failed in that so far. But the Fae king was certainly maneuvering wisely around me what with the thrall practice. What a perfect setup for him. He could simultaneously prepare his asset—me—against outside influence while also wiggling into my brain to turn me into whatever he needed at that moment.

I had lost the first phase of this dark game. No way around that. I already knew it. But I would never stop looking for angles, trying for dominance, working for any chance at a way out. And for now, it was actually moving in my favor. I'd go along with this whole Druid possibility and pray to all the Old Ones that I didn't end up doing something terrible while under Lys's thrall. The only thing that would be worse than the thrall's control would be if Lys pried my true name from my head. But Master had trained me long and hard to avoid that. He beat us and shouted and hounded until adopting our false names became like breathing. I would see a spray of my own blood before I could break and tell him the name given to me at birth. That red haze, that remembered pain, would keep me from revealing it. My stomach turned at a memory of Master's knuckles and the crack of his stick on flesh.

Even though that training had been some of the

toughest I'd had to endure, I was glad for it now because if Lys possessed my true name, I would be his slave for life. All he would have to do is utter my true name under his breath and I would come running. It would be worse than a thrall because I'd be fully aware of his power and what he might make me do. And that magic didn't wear off when the perpetrator stopped concentrating like a thrall did. It was as permanent as the death rune—more so if the Druid could actually accomplish what Lys claimed he could.

"Finished. Now to dress you, my lady." Sonaellyn stood back and I lifted a hand to feel the various loops she'd braided and pinned around the crown of my head.

"I hope I don't have to let my own hair down tonight."

The two Fae snickered and wiggled their eyebrows.

"Now, do you like the blue?" Malaynia pointed to a dress hanging from the bed canopy. Another servant was brushing it out. The dress hanging beside it was as bright as noon. "Or would you rather wear the yellow? Oh, I can tell from your face that you loathe the yellow."

"Correct."

Malaynia gestured to another servant, ordering her to remove the second dress. "Of course, the fierce intended mate of our king would prefer serious shades of darkness."

I lifted the hem of the blue dress and examined the gold stitching and the underlying pattern of leaves hiding in the weave. "I was serious the day I was born."

Sonaellyn nodded approvingly. "She might just survive this courtship," she murmured to Malaynia.

"Tell me about the fest-noz," I said as they helped me into the blue dress and adjusted the wide gold neckline.

Malaynia clipped earrings that looked like little bells onto my ears. "The highest ranked member of each pair will hide in the hedge maze. Their lips will be smeared with a sparkling color that is unique to them."

The elaborate earrings dusted across my shoulders, which were left bare by the cut of the dress.

Adjusting the torc I'd bought at market, Sonaellyn continued where Malaynia had left off. "You are to find the king and kiss him." Her voice betrayed a barely restrained giddiness. "Then you leave the maze, marked by him. Once the firestars are ignited, he will be able to leave the maze as well and you will be greeted by the Court of Mischief."

"The what?" I remembered hearing about firestars, the blazing fires painted across the sky, a magic the Fae used to celebrate very important events. The Druid crafted the firestars and there were stories galore about them in the human realm. But I had no knowledge of this Court of Mischief.

"Oh, you will love them." Malaynia set out a pair of emerald-crusted court slippers and I marveled at the ability of a king's household to fit his ladies in the blink of an eye. How did they do that anyway? "They will do some sort of mock bonding ceremony with you and the king if all goes well. Sometimes, they make you trade clothing."

"They might have you dance the steps of a reel backwards or give you ridiculous tasks to do to one another like have him kiss the back of your knee or you'll have to lick wine from his palm like you're his pet."

They snickered and I joined in. At the very least, this evening wouldn't be dull.

"Do I get any hints on where the king is hiding in the maze? Will I have any help?"

Sonaellyn smeared dark blue cosmetics over my eyelids, then lined the edges of my eyes with Laqqara kohl. "No, that is against the rules. Once your council presentation is over, the king won't be permitted to see you at all."

Malaynia removed a silver pot from her pocket and touched my lips, leaving behind a slick bit of something that I hoped wasn't poisoned. "Listen to what he says in the meeting. He may try to give you a hint hidden in his words."

"Interesting."

Sonaellyn frowned at my hair, slipped one lock free, and fiddled with it until it hung at the side of my face in a soft curl. "Be careful of the maze though, my lady. Others will hide in the shadows and attempt to trip you."

"It's nothing too rough," Malaynia added. "Just a shove here and there, all in good fun."

So the maze event was a perfect opportunity for my rivals to kill me. "I appreciate the warning."

"Take this," Sonaellyn said, holding out a tiny dagger. The end was needle-sharp. She sheathed the dagger in a small pocket of sun-bleached hide, then tucked it between my breasts. "Just in case."

She and Malaynia patted me on the arm and back, their smiles genuine, and my heart warmed despite my efforts not to care about any of these Fae.

Another servant held up a mirror and my false face stared back at me. My lips were a soft pink and my eyes were still slitted as a Fae's, which honestly made me feel better. I had no guarantees on how long this illusion would last.

The females leaned over my shoulder to look at me looking at myself. I fought the urge to move away from them. "This is just a council room style. Tonight, for the fest-noz, we will turn you into a forest nymph. Don't worry," Sonaellyn said.

"I'm not worried. I've just…never seen myself like this." Acting as the farm lass they thought me to be, I reached out, touched the cool, reflective surface, and pretended to be in awe of myself. They had done a lovely job considering how tired I was.

Now, it was time to see if our ruse would pass the council's judgment. I wondered what Lys would do if they rejected me?

30

REVNA

After another once-over from Sonaellyn and Malaynia, I was escorted out of my room, down the corridor, and into a chamber where Lysanael sat at a round table with five older-looking Fae males. Lys's eyes widened a fraction and his gaze smoothed down my body, a look I could almost feel like a teasing caress. I swallowed. He wore a tunic that had both the blue of my dress and the yellow of the dress I had chosen not to wear, the colors set in a crosshatch pattern that also featured his coat of arms—mace, hare, fern, and drumstone. A fist surrounded the drumstone —perhaps as a symbol of the Seelie's control over the Unseelie, the bane of their lives here in the Realm of Lights. Unseelie were a problem in the human world too, but far more of the demonic monsters were here.

The council eyed me, each one of them serious, grave, not giving anything away with their features.

They could have been the best stag and fox players in the history of the world.

A rotund fellow with goat horns and tan skin leaned on the table and steepled his clawed fingers. His right-side neighbor pursed green lips, then crossed his arms and glanced from me to Lys. Bornien sat beside Lys, and the other two council members appeared to be twins, both of them silver-haired and adorned in an array of gold jewelry.

The questions began. What was my family's surname? How did they make their living? What level of income, both coin and bartering considered, did they bring in each season? Had my family held their lands for over five hundred years or were they new farmers?

I answered everything with ease, using the information from Master's brief. It was fascinating how they insisted on knowing my history down to the number of loves I'd had in my life and how many siblings I had—by-blows included—but they never asked for my real name. I knew they wouldn't because of the power the Fae held, but it still felt odd to be questioned so thoroughly and yet to keep that secret to myself.

A littleling burst through the door and ran to Lys, laughing.

"You little pixie!" A heavily bosomed nurse with red cheeks followed her in. "Apologies, my king, council," she panted out as she reached for the small female.

It was the same littleling I'd seen the first day of the

Branle, the one with honey-colored curls who'd been snatching sweet rolls.

Lys's mask cracked as he took her into his arms and held her tightly, his eyes shining. "My darling, what required my immediate attention? Is Snip being difficult?"

She giggled and gave him a sloppy kiss on his cheek. "Yes! But I'm here to ask you to ride with me. It's been too many days."

He sat her on his knee and tilted his head as he looked at her. "It certainly has. I will take you in one hour." Looking up, he set his gaze on the nurse. "Will you have her dressed for riding and meet me at the front stables then?"

"Of course, Your Majesty." The nurse curtseyed and tried to pry the littleling away from him.

The small thing went begrudgingly, sticking out her bottom lip and crossing her arms even as she was almost dragged from the room. The council looked on with tolerant smiles.

"That was my niece, Gwyn," Lys said to me as the door shut behind the nurse and the littleling. "Gwyn's mother is away right now."

"She adores you." Her mother would be Lys's sister-in-law if my memory served. She had to be the one who was married to Lys's younger brother, the one who died. Or perhaps he hadn't died if that conversation between Lys and Bornien held any truth. I might have it all wrong though. I didn't have enough information to know for certain.

The corner of his full lips lifted, and he looked at the ground as if remembering something happy, then his chest rose and fell in a slow breath, his features cleared, and the mask formed, his eyes as cold as Isernwyrd's training pond at Yuletide. "Council, please continue."

I shifted my weight and waited for the next question.

Bornien opened a tome slowly, his gaze on the aged parchment pages. "To which guild does your family belong?"

He was going to search for them on the guild list. Master had provided the guild name so I knew what I was to say, but would it be in that book? Would my false family's surname appear? What if the name I was stealing had history with someone in this room? I shook off the fear and steeled myself, breathing slow to keep my voice steady and confident.

"Brightleaf."

Bornien ran a gnarled finger down the page, turned to the next, and then tapped the center of the parchment. "Ah. Yes, right here."

Lys glanced at the book, then at me. His gaze was thorough, as if he was examining a threat and concocting a strategy. The horned Fae male watched us with narrowed eyes.

Gracefully shoving away from the table, Bornien stood. "Let us vote."

The horned Fae held up a hand. "I smell trickery here."

A bead of sweat trickled down my back as the silver-haired twins nodded in agreement.

"We want to see them at the fest-noz," the smaller of the twins said sharply.

His brother grunted. "Yes. The fest-noz will tell us if there is a strong potential mating bond between them."

The green-skinned male shifted in his seat to look at Bornien. "If we wait to vote, we must ensure we still have time to prepare for the wedding ritual. The astrologers say the best time for the king to mate will be during the full moon."

I tried to recall what phase the moon was in and how much time that gave them, or at least, how much time they believed they had to push Lys into begetting an heir.

"There is time enough to make a proper decision on this," the first silver-haired twin said.

Bornien glanced at Lys and traded looks with each of the council members. He watched me as he asked them, "Do we agree, then?"

I kept my features blank because I wasn't sure what he wanted to see from me—annoyance at having to wait to be approved, hope because I hadn't been denied, or some other emotion I wasn't privy to?

If they rejected me now, what would Lys do?

The silence rang in my ears as the council studied me, their gazes sharp and challenging. Bornien took a deep breath and I prepared for a rejection.

"Do we agree to wait on our decision and base it on the fest-noz?" the elder said.

The horned Fae called out, "Aye," then the rest slowly followed suit.

Our feigned relationship had been approved. For now.

Lys stood, his face giving as little away as mine did. We were quite a pair when it came to masks. He came around the table, took my hand, and brushed his lips over my knuckles.

"I hope you find your way to me in the fest-noz maze. It is a dragonic tradition, but if you plan to wed a king, you must acquaint yourself with such frivolities."

He gave me a meaningful look, his slitted eyes narrowing and his lips pursing slightly. With one last kiss on my hand, he left the room.

I was escorted back to my chamber, and the entire time, thoughts swirled around inside my head.

Had Lys said *dragonic* or *draconic*? How was searching for one's intended mate excessively harsh? My pulse tapped the side of my throat. Sonaellyn and Malaynia had mentioned Fae waiting in the shadows of the maze to trip and trouble me, but perhaps they were rougher than what I imagined. I'd find out tonight.

Ah, and I just remembered the phase of the moon. Lys had said the fest-noz took place during the waxing gibbous, when stars still reigned, but the moon was nearly ready to show its full face. His wedding ritual had to take place soon then in order to follow the astrologers' advice to mate during the full moon.

In my chamber, only Sonaellyn waited. I told her I'd love to visit Arkyn and go on a short flight. She had a tray of food brought and provided clean trousers and a scarlet tunic. I donned my riding boots and a thick black cloak, and I answered all of her questions about dragons.

"Yes, there are five types of dragons. Forest, like Arkyn. The tiny rock dragons. Mountain dragons are the largest ones. They live in the Shrouded Mountains with the Mist Knights."

"I do know about those," Sonaellyn said, her eyes bright with interest.

"The palm-sized rock dragons are rare, but I have heard they live on the coast of Deigs, the human kingdom across the White Sea. Supposedly, they have the power of telepathy, but I don't know if that's just rumor."

"I wish I had one."

I nodded. "They have to be adorable, right?"

"Completely."

I smiled. "And then you have the cave dragons that I don't know much about."

"I have never heard of those. How did you find Arkyn?"

I couldn't explain the true story because farmers' daughters didn't visit fighting pits; even the more vicious Fae had their limits. "I ran into him in the forest. He was injured and I took care of him while he healed."

"What does it feel like to fly on his back? Do you go invisible with him? The gossip is that he faded from view when one of the stable lads tried to bind his wings. They wanted to make sure he didn't escape."

"That lad is lucky Arkyn didn't snack on his leg."

Sonaellyn laughed. "How does he know when to land?"

I didn't want to give away all of my communication techniques. "He can sense what I want, but I also use hand signals and I tap his scales in certain rhythms."

The female only stopped following me and asking questions when I left through the front doors of the keep.

Once I had Arkyn readied for riding, I waved
farewell to my guards—two stoic fellas whom Lys had
obviously assigned to trail me everywhere—and sailed
into the bright blue sky.

Arkyn soared over Caer Du and I took a moment to
catalogue the number of guards at each of the three
outer bailey gates. The northwestern gate was the least
visited and the least guarded. Fae streamed down the
streets, their hair shimmering in the sunlight and their
bodies in every color of the rainbow.

I urged Arkyn to fly north, appreciating the crisp
wind on my face and the comfort of his warmth beneath
me. He clicked his tongue and swooped low suddenly
in a move that had me grasping to stay on.

"Brat." I smacked him gently and he clicked his
tongue again then growled playfully, the sound
rumbling from his stomach and through my legs. "How
are they treating you in the stables?"

He snorted and huffed, circling over a silver pond
surrounded by bright red flowers.

"You aren't enjoying horse oats, eh?" I laughed.
"Well, let's hunt, then, and get you some real food."

With a quiet growl, the dragon flew lower, and our
shadow painted the meadow and the sweet gum trees
dotting the rocky ground. Then we were diving. I
couldn't see his quarry, but I didn't doubt his nose.
Soaring impossibly close to the ground, his underside
drove across the tops of the trees and snapped branches.
He pulled his wings in a fraction, there was a shriek of a

smaller animal, and then Arkyn lurched higher into the air again. I leaned right to see a dead deer in his talons. He had always killed them quickly, and it was another thing I liked about him—he showed mercy to the innocent.

Once we had landed and Arkyn had his fill, I mounted back up and we flew toward our former hideout on the edges of the Gwerhune. The place was undisturbed, thankfully, and I removed my hidden pack and sword from the brush. I doubted anyone would trouble me about bringing in a sword now, but I tied it to my back, concealing it beneath my cloak regardless.

When we returned to the keep, the waning sun cast purple shadows across the stone walls and the expectant faces of the Fae who were very curious about the king's potential queen.

I swallowed. *Queen.* Of course, it wouldn't get that far. I'd never be his actual wife or his queen, but just thinking the word had my mind twisting over the possibilities. If the Druid failed to remove my rune, none of it mattered. I shuttered my imaginings and strode into the keep's front entrance, heading for my chamber.

The fest-noz would begin soon from the look of things. Already, the castle keep had that hushed but busy noise threading through its halls as nobles dressed in private chambers and servants prepped jugs of wine and trays of food. As I climbed the stairs, I looked out a window onto the inner courtyard where the maze zigzagged through a pebbled expanse of a large garden. A group of servants dressed in Lys's livery toiled over a set of wooden crates filled with red-painted sticks or... Ah, the firestars. It would be fascinating to see the display.

"Hurry, my lady!" Sonaellyn had her dress bunched in her hands and was rushing down the steps. She snatched my arm and verily dragged me toward my chambers. "It's nearly time for the search to begin. Old Ones save me, you smell like a knight gone for a year at war!"

She wasn't wrong. I smelled less than fantastic. In the bath chamber, I submitted to her rough hands and the other servants' work as they scrubbed and oiled my flesh, top to bottom. The oil smelled of jasmine and it was rather lovely.

Malaynia bustled in with a slip of moon-white material that she claimed was a dress.

"I'm not the modest type," I said, studying the dangerously low scooped back and then two slits that ran up to the hips on the front, "but won't the king take issue with me scampering about the maze half-nude?"

The servants chuckled. Of course they saw no problem with it. The Fae were half-naked all the time. It was fine with me, really, but I didn't love the idea of trying to hide my larger dagger in my thigh sheath in this dress.

Malaynia worked the dress over my head. "You have to keep most of your skin accessible for the painting."

"Painting?" The dress, soft as spider's silk, clung to every curve and line.

Sonaellyn urged me into the chair and began brushing out my hair. "Didn't we mention that bit?" She sprinkled a concoction that smelled like lavender onto the crown of my head. "The king will gild you in the symbols of power and fertility."

A curl of heat warmed my stomach and lower. His fingers would be on me. All over me.

Malaynia nodded as she watched Sonaellyn braid the top of half of my hair. "Some say there is true power in the runes painted on intended mates during the fest-noz."

"Interesting." I suppressed a shudder while Sonaellyn tied branches into my braids with tiny lengths of thin copper wire. I wasn't ready to even consider children. It wasn't a joy afforded to assassins. My body did, however, let me know that it wanted Lys's hands on my skin, no matter what he was painting and why. The room suddenly felt too warm.

"Oh, that's a nice flush to your cheeks, my lady," Sonaellyn said.

Malaynia winked, and soon they had me prepared for the fest-noz. The mirror showed me in a dress made for a bedchamber, my feigned Fae eyes dressed in deep green cosmetics, and my hair braided around an array of branches that gave the impression of antlers.

It was time to prove to the council that Lys and I were perfect for one another so I could complete the marriage ritual then visit the Druid to have my rune removed.

I followed them out of the chamber and down the corridor as I recalled what Lys had said in the council room, playing his words over and over in my mind to look for some sort of clue as to where he would be hiding in the hedges. The only thing that my mind tripped on was his mispronunciation of the word *draconic*. So far, that was the only mistake in speech he'd made. He was quick-witted and well-spoken; he didn't make mistakes. And he'd said *dragonic* instead of *draconic*. Could he have been referring to Arkyn?

"I need to stop by the stables," I said to Sonaellyn, who was chatting with one of my guards.

She turned and frowned. "Now? But you'll dirty your dress."

"Now, please." I gave her a smile to soften the demand of my tone.

With just one guard at my side—I left everyone else inside the keep—I made it to Arkyn's side. My guard waited just outside the stables.

"I need your help tonight," I said to Arkyn. "Can you go invisible and follow me? I must remain in view, but I need your nose to sniff out the Fae king. You remember his scent, I'm sure."

This was a lot to expect from a dragon, but as I looked into Arkyn's bright eyes, I could see that he understood. A tingling of joy touched my heart—a sensation that meant our bond was in play—and he leaned into me, already fading from view.

"I'm a lucky gal to have you as a friend, Arkyn," I whispered, giving him one last pat.

Joining my guard, I gave him a vague smile and nod, then we headed back inside since the only access to the maze was through the keep itself. I was glad the doors were wide because of the invisible dragon currently following me. Hopefully, he'd make this search in the hedge maze a success. Tonight had to be perfect.

REVNA

The stars above the hedge maze were like the bonfires of a vast and distant army here to see if I won this battle or lost. The hem of my diaphanous dress fluttered in the evening's cool breeze and every once in a while I felt my dragon's warm breath on my head. Sometimes the warmth disappeared and I knew he had taken off and was circling, but most of the time he walked behind me.

Despite Sonaellyn's arguing, I had donned my black cloak with a promise to remove it if I found Lys. It was too chilly to be half-naked this time of year, and who knew how long it would take me to locate him. Musicians strummed lutes and played pipes in the area in front of the maze where many lingered with goblets of Fae wine.

Three openings stood on this end of the maze and at each of them a group of Fae waited in clothing as dreamy and insubstantial as my dress. I joined the group in the center but kept my distance so no one would bump into Arkyn. Would any of the Fae sense his presence? They would detect his smell, but hopefully with the bonfires crackling every hundred feet in the area and the incense smoking along the boughs that decorated the various clusters of wicker chairs, the dragon's scent would go unnoticed.

His golden hair sweeping across his shoulders, Gyrion stood atop a large flat stone and held up his hands. "As Master of the Branle, I invite the lovers to seek their intended mates within the maze. May the Old Ones guide your heart and your feet."

Everyone bowed or curtseyed and I joined in. The crowd turned, and then we were off, heading into the dark of the maze. I pulled up the hood of my cloak and shielded my face from view. The hedges were at least ten feet tall and from the aerial view I'd had of them, the thickness of the growth had been held to a consistent five feet. There would be no passing through as the hedges were incredibly thick and the branches as firm. I reached a split in the maze and let the rest of those who had entered the same way move onward.

"Which way?" I whispered to Arkyn, hoping he was near enough to hear me. His warmth was nowhere nearby, so I had to assume he was airborne. I waited patiently at the split and was at last rewarded by a bump I recognized as my dragon's snout. He urged me to the right and I walked quickly that way. The corner ahead held a potted yew with branches that went all the way to the ground. A perfect hiding place for mischief makers or assassins.

I pretended not to notice the spot and walked by, giving the area a wide berth. The sound of a foot shifting on the round pebbles of the maze had me spinning. A Fae male in a hooded cloak lunged for me, something silver flashing from his fingertips. Arkyn wasted no time slamming the male backward with what was most likely his tail. My attacker dropped backward against the hedges and exhaled roughly.

"What magic is this? Who are you?" the attacked asked.

Bleeding slightly from whatever weapon he'd wielded, I turned away and hurried onward. He must have cut me before Arkyn hit him. Would the attacker follow me? So what if he did? I had a dragon at my back. The scratches weren't serious, just three lines of red marring my moon-white dress. Arkyn nudged my elbow at the next split and I went left. We kept on like this, avoiding more potted trees and the occasional tangle of ivy spilling over the hedges like dark waterfalls. We had made nine turns and I memorized every direction Arkyn had suggested in case I needed to escape quickly. The maze was now a map in my mind, its paths white and the paths I'd taken black lines in the white.

Two figures in dark masquerade masks walked out of a dark corner of the maze and aimed for me, their fingers silver as the first male's had been. Ah. They had donned metal claws. Hmm. I kicked one of them in the chest and drove him back while Arkyn threw the second to the ground. Their shouts of surprise and confusion were loud but no louder than the music churning the cool night air as I continued on with Arkyn behind me.

Three paths opened up, and my cloak was tugged toward the center. I wiped dragon drool off my shoulder.

"Take it easy," I whispered, heading along the center path. "I need to remain tempting for this whole thing to work out, you know."

A snort of hot air blew my hair away from my cheek and he bumped me again, sending me into a diagonal offshoot from the path. He made a clicking noise and then the wind of his wings pumping told me he was lifting into the air.

On a high-backed stone bench tucked into a narrow angle of hedges, Lys sat with his legs wide and his arms crossed. Glittery golden paint sparkled across his sharp jaw line and on his sensuous mouth, and his eyes—lined in kohl—were as cold as the stars above him. His black hair was loose and swept back from his forehead, where a diadem of woven black metal rested. Wearing just a pair of tight-fitting trousers and a decorative sword in a sheath of tooled leather and gold work, he looked like a god, like he truly did hold the blood of an Old One.

"Well done, my viper." His low voice sent shivers down my spine. He glanced upward and tilted his head, eyes narrowing. "You noticed my *mistake* in phrasing, then?" he whispered.

Dragonic. Draconic. "Yes, thank you, my king." I glided forward, and he stood, his fingers already working the clasp of my cloak. He set his mouth near my ear. "We have an audience," he whispered, his breath making my skin pebble.

His hands grazed my collarbone as he removed my cloak. The garment fell to the ground and cool air swept over me as his palms cupped my face. He drew my chin upward. Old Ones save me but he was beautiful. Those big dark green and gold eyes of his simmered with such believable desire and care… It was difficult to remember this was an act, a show for the council's spies. Boots shuffled behind the hedge and a shadow moved inside the greenery—someone had worked their way into the very branches of the maze by way of clever garden shears or magic.

He lowered his head, closing his eyes, and his lips hovered over mine.

How long could I play this game and not slip up?

33

REVNA

His breath smelled like honeyed Fae wine and flowers and I wondered how much he had imbibed. With his hands on my jawline and his mouth so close, my body rebelled against my control. My skin went hot, my Berserker blood rose to a simmer, and heat pooled low in my belly. I pressed myself against him and he kissed me, drawing his tongue over mine and making my heart crash into my ribs. He deepened the kiss and a low purr echoed from his throat, a decidedly Fae sound. My muscles tensed. The heat inside me slid lower until I was gripping his hips and pulling him to me. His bare stomach warmed my flesh through the thin dress, then he urged me to straddle him on the stone bench. His body reacted to the position, the purr in his throat increasing to a quiet, almost feral growl as my arms curled around his neck and his hands slid to my thighs.

This didn't feel like an act.

I broke away from the kiss, shaking my head to clear it and easing away from him though I remained on his lap. "I..." My voice was ridiculously breathy. "Aren't you supposed to paint runes on me now?"

His half-lidded gaze made my heart turn over. "Yes." He reached to the side and produced a small cup of what appeared to be paint, starlight reflecting off its gilded surface. "Be very still."

I set my mouth to his ear and he paused, one finger in the paint. "Will you paint true runes on me?"

Turning his head, he whispered back, "It matters not. We won't be married in truth. Or did you forget this is a ruse?" A dare colored his words.

A sound told me our spy was still there. Worried he'd hear my response, I decided to dive back into the act and I nipped the tip of Lys's pointed ear, his earring cold on my lip. He sucked in a breath of surprise and buried his face in my neck. His teeth dragged across my throat and I let my head fall back, savoring the touch of his warm breath and the feel of his hand just below my breast. He pulled away and, with a wicked gleam in his eye, began painting runes on my body. Every stroke of his finger sent pleasant shivers over me. He drew a long line down my back, his lips brushing my shoulder as he worked. I could hardly sit still on his lap. I had been through missions of partial seduction before now but this, this was worlds different. My breath caught as he swept his palm across my lower back, then dotted another bit of paint under the edge of the back of my dress, above my hipbone.

He placed the paint cup beside us, then gave me a heavy look. "Finished with that, but I'm not quite done with you yet."

It's a show. An act. Just a ruse. I forced a flirtatious smirk onto my lips to replace what had to be a painfully open look of desire. "And what do you wish to do now, King Lysanael?" I doubted our spy needed the reminder of who sat in these shadows, but if I was going to stumble my way through this, I was going to make certain it counted toward our end goal.

He stood, holding me tightly, fingers flexing on my sides, then set me on the bench. Kneeling, he slipped off one of my slippers and kissed the inside of my ankle. "I want to taste your skin, to claim you…" His mouth smoothed up my calf and then he was kissing the inside of my knee. "…to mark every inch of you with my scent."

My blood roared in my ears as I ran a hand up Lys's bare arm and let my fingers drift over his muscles and the broad expanse of his shoulder. I slammed my eyes shut, willing my blood to cool. The Berserker in me had decided it was long past time to mate with this proud, powerful, full-blooded Fae male. Trying to shove my feelings into the locked trunk in the back of my mind was proving impossible at the moment because Lys had made it to my inner thigh. His gaze flicked upward to meet my eyes and a promise of absolutely torturous pleasure gleamed in that look.

I ran a hand through his hair, mussing it until he looked like he'd just risen from his bed. Black as the night, his hair felt like silk through my fingers. "How long do we have until the—"

A boom cut off my question and orange, purple, and pale blue fire erupted across the sky as if the very stars had burst.

He stood and held out a hand to help me up. "You must go. You're late in leaving and I can't leave with you."

"Time for the Court of Mischief to make an appearance?"

"Yes." He retrieved my cloak from the ground and fastened it at my neck. "Now hurry so they can see my markings on you."

I watched his face as he smoothed a flipped edge of my cloak and a warmth stirred in my chest. Surely, he didn't actually care for me, but the action felt, well, I wasn't sure, but it felt like more than nothing.

"See you around, my king." I winked, then headed back the way I'd come.

I didn't feel or hear any signs of Arkyn, so I assumed he was gone for the moment or flying above to keep watch. I'd been trained to remember difficult routes, so leaving the maze was no hardship, especially since all of my attackers seemed to have left while I was…busy with Lys.

The taste of his wine lingered on my tongue. I tugged my cloak away from my throat, then unclasped and folded it over my arm.

At the opening of the maze, a group of wildly dressed Fae females and males cheered and threw handfuls of curled parchment that had been painted gold.

"Is she marked?" A female with goat horns and light pink skin scurried forward, grinning. Like the others in what I assumed was the Court of Mischief, she wore red-, green-, and blue-striped trousers that ballooned out at the thigh and a sleeveless shirt that showed Lys's coat of arms.

The female studied my body, lifting my arms and walking a circle around me. She ended up facing me and wearing a wicked grin.

She slicked a finger across my lips, spun, and held up her hand. "She bears the mark of King Lysanael!"

The mock court hurrahed and the rest of the attending Fae—as well as the servants—let out a cheer as another volley of firestars blasted into the sky.

The back of my neck tingled and I put a hand to my death rune. A warning? Was my time drawing to a close? I turned just in time to see Lys leaving the maze, his gaze pinning me where I stood between two other members of the Court of Mischief.

34

LYSANAEL

In the maze, Lysanael sat on the cold bench, willing his heart to stop pounding and his body to cool. Red and indigo firestars thundered overhead and he couldn't help but draw a comparison between them and his desire for Revna. When her body was near, every bit of his good sense exploded in a riot of pleasure. The feel of her skin under his hands, the way her head fell back as he kissed her sweet thighs…

This bench wasn't nearly cold enough to do the job. He needed to leave the maze, but at the moment, that was nigh on impossible. Leaning forward on his knees, he stared at the ground where her footprints showed in the pebbles. If they had been truly alone, he would have stretched her out on this bench and not stopped until she was shouting his name at the volume of the firestars. His blood longed to claim her as his in truth; marking her had nearly been his undoing. Magic had sparked against his fingertips as he'd painted the runes over her soft skin. Her quiet gasps had almost driven him over the edge, beyond the moment when he could continue to act as though his desire for her was false.

And when he left here and joined her in the festivities, he would have to restrain himself again, holding his heart away from the growing care he had for her. Because it wasn't just lust that drove his gaze to hers and turned him into an animal. It was everything about her. Her intellect, her flirtatious nature, the courage she showed in the terrifying life she'd been forced into, and the way she had respected the vineyard and its inhabitants. She was kind and determined, brave, bold, and utterly unique.

With another deep breath, he began to walk out of the maze. He was already tarrying here far too long. He couldn't allow the council to think he didn't care about leaving Revna alone during the Court of Mischief's appearance.

As his mind cleared, he recalled the cuts on Revna— no doubt from the nature of the fest-noz. He wasn't supposed to grow angry with the tradition. It was a long-standing Fae tradition and the injuries only further proved the lengths to which lovers would go to find their mate. But the thought of someone putting their hands on her...

A sword of cold anger pierced his chest. If he found out who had gone so far as to draw blood, that Fae would suffer.

The maze opened up and there stood his false mate.

The crowd cheered him and she turned, giving him that serpentine smirk. His heart jolted and he touched his chest as if the injury could somehow be witnessed.

If she only knew how much he cared…

🦋 35 🦋

REVNA

There was another shout of joy at Lys's appearance and suddenly I was being pulled toward him. Our bodies met and the mischief-makers began lashing us together with ivy. A male came up behind me and laughed, the sound low and sultry. Lys's eyes flashed with warning.

"Don't fret, my dear king. I come not to steal your intended mate but to ensure she stays by your side. Or perhaps not your side but by your sword, and by your sword she will be happily pierced this night and onward!"

His words made little sense, but of course, I understood the leaning of the jest and could indeed tell how close I was to every part of him.

Heat rushed up my neck and into my cheeks. Lys's eyebrow flicked upward as he looked down at me; the corner of his lips twitched before his features went flat, then he looked at a spot over my shoulder.

Lys was so challenging to read. Yes, he hid his emotions at court. That much was obvious. But when his joy or interest sneaked through, was that true feeling or an orchestrated move on his part? The way he reacted to his niece, Gwyn, wasn't played up. I would have bet my dagger on that. But the rest? I just wasn't certain. Some of his kisses hummed with desire, with genuine heat. Or perhaps he was as skilled at pretending attraction and care as I was. I snorted at myself. I wasn't playacting the entire time and I knew it. My body betrayed me every time Lys was near.

"I must know what you are thinking," Lys said, his body pressed to mine as the Court of Mischief bumped us around the area in front of the musicians. I fell against him and his body tightened and kept us upright. Anger flashed in his eyes as he glared at one of the mischief-makers. "Careful."

"I never know when you're acting and when you're being true," I whispered, shocking myself with the admission. But perhaps this would gain me insight and give me a leg up.

He studied my face. "I hardly know myself."

I began to ask him to explain, but the wildly dressed Fae snipped our ivy bindings with a golden set of shears as they started a bawdy song about a pixie and Mist Knight from the Shrouded Mountains, part of a tale Raulian had told me when we were children.

The mischief-makers spun us away from one another, and a silver goblet of Fae wine was held to my lips. I sealed my mouth shut as Lys was spun toward me again.

"My taster says it is clean," he whispered, motioning to the goblet.

I opened my lips and let the spiced wine flow into my mouth. It set my head spinning almost immediately. Fae wine must be stronger than human wine.

The music increased in volume and the tune turned dark and twisting, the notes bringing to mind the massive trees of the Gwerhune, the indigo lights that floated above us now, and the rumble of thunder.

"It's beautiful." I meant it. The music was absolutely divine.

The Court of Mischief drew our hands together and forced us to dance, turning us around and around until the world and Lys's handsome face blurred. More cups of wine were forced down our gullets and we linked arms with other Fae who laughed and pulled us into group reels and circle dances. I stomped my feet alongside the Fae, my head wonderfully light. Lys's wicked grin warmed my insides and had me longing for another visit to the shadows of the maze. He must have sensed the drop in my guard because he broke from the others and stole my hand from a blue-skinned Fae male who had been slinging me and two others left and right in a raucous jig. Lys pulled me away from the music and we slipped out of the garden courtyard and toward a wall of thick ivy at the back of the keep. A hill rose beyond the wall, and past the ivy, the inner curtain wall loomed.

"Where are we going?" I asked, my voice sliding in spots due to the wine.

"We should take a ride on Arkyn." A gleam lit his eyes in the dark corridor. "Catch his attention and have him follow us to the north of the keep. Can you do that?"

I looked up and waved a hand, hoping he had been keeping a watch. My heart tingled with anticipation and I knew that the dragon was indeed just above us.

Lys pushed past the ivy to a wooden door. He set his palm against it and the wood glowed as gold as his painted body. We entered a place of complete darkness that smelled of turned earth.

"Where are you taking me?" Panic threaded through the fun I'd been having.

Was he going to slit my throat here and end this bizarre game of ours? *He can try*, I thought as I narrowed my eyes and trailed him farther into the dark.

"Hold on," Lys said, his voice telling me he had stepped forward even though he still gripped my hand with his long, calloused fingers.

How had he opened that door? Was it magicked to open for his hand alone? The Fae certainly had magic we humans weren't aware of, that or their Druid was more active in their everyday lives than we had previously believed. Of course, Lys was the king, so maybe the Druid was more involved in the lives of the royal family than we had thought.

I blinked, trying to clear my head, but the Fae wine had me in its grip. I couldn't stop grinning like a fool and my body was soft as warmed honey.

"I'm going to let go for a moment. Don't worry." Lys released me.

The sound of shuffling and the drag and snap of a

flint sounded as a spark lit the dark and blinded me. A torch blazed to life. I lifted a hand against the sudden brightness, eyes aching. He snatched my hand again and pulled me farther down the earthen corridor.

"Not far now and we'll be free of the walls completely."

This was a secret path under the inner and outer walls? No way he'd let me live after showing me this. Oddly, the fact made me giddy because this show of trust might just mean he truly meant to bring me to the Druid to remove my death rune. Either that or he was going to try to kill me, but I wasn't going to allow that.

We hurried on and on while his thumb ran up and down the outside of my hand and shivers rode along my flesh. He glanced back at me now and then, a grin pulling at his glimmering lips and the torchlight cutting a deep shadow under his jawline.

The scent of the Fae night reached my nose and then he was setting his hand against another door that flashed brighter than the torch before swinging open. I turned back to look and indeed we were beyond the walls and in the wilds north of the Caer Du. Near a bank of wide and twisted trees, Arkyn shimmered into view. Starlight painted his slightly expanded wings silver and he jerked his snout my way in greeting.

Lys held up the torch and the light flickered over his dark diadem. "Greetings, Arkyn. May we ride on your back on this lovely evening?"

I led Lys to the dragon, then rubbed Arkyn's side,

enjoying the feel of his warm scales. "We'll have to ride bareback…"

Nodding, Lys set the torch on the ground and dug up dirt to smother the flame. He stood and dusted off his hands. The wine made his eyes hazy and he swayed on his feet. I laughed, not sure why, then hopped on Arkyn. Lys climbed on behind me and Arkyn wasted no time in launching into the starry sky. Amid a flurry of the indigo Fae lights, we soared through the heavens, Caer Du growing smaller and smaller.

Lys put his hands on my hips and thrust his legs against mine. I could feel his muscles tensing to hang on to the dragon's sides. His fingers slid up to my waist and my breath caught, my blood rising. My thoughts swam through the murk of the Fae wine's effects and I closed my eyes. Leaning back into Lys's hard chest, I savored the cold air on my cheeks and the heat of the Fae king's body. He ran a hand along my thigh where the dress's slit showed my pebbled skin. My breathing became erratic despite my half-hearted attempts at ignoring the wine's lure to relax and enjoy myself. Some of the glimmering gold paint from Lys's lips shone on my knee and the image of him kneeling before me flashed through my head. Suddenly he was kissing the side of my neck. Heat flew into my chest, then ran down my body.

Working his way to my ear, he whispered, "You are unlike anyone I've ever met. It's wrong, but I trust you."

"As in you trust me to gut you when I get the opportunity?"

His laugh rumbled against my back. He licked the spot below my earlobe and I shivered with pleasure. "Your goal to kill me doesn't make sense anymore now that I have promised to take you to the Druid." Pressing another feather-light kiss to the back of my neck, he pulled me closer. "It is in your best interest to keep me alive. For now, at least."

"Lucky you," I said, more breathily than I wished.

He set his mouth against my cheek and I felt him grin. "I don't have to pretend with you. I don't have to hide my true feelings."

"You're drunk, my king. Best to watch your words." The stars blurred across the sky and the scent of wine permeated the air.

Lys was uncorking a flask with one hand. "If I'm deep in my cups, it makes sense that you join me."

"It really doesn't."

He handed the flask over and leaned forward to look at me, a dare in those forest and gold eyes.

"Fine." I took a swallow and the wine's flavors burst across my tongue—cinnamon, roses, and sugared plums. "If we're allies for the moment, one night of revelry can't hurt."

With another swig, I handed it back. The locked-down emotions at the back of my mind shook like they wanted to be free. Only a portion of the desire I felt for Lys leaked out...

"Ask Arkyn to land here," Lys said.

I looked down beyond Arkyn's flapping wings to see a small wooden structure and the ruins of what might have once been a keep. Ivy crawled over time-nibbled stone.

"It's my hunting lodge," Lys said. "A private place for me. No guards here. No courtiers."

I tapped once and pointed to the small clearing in the trees near the lodge. "Will you take us there, Arkyn?" I said into the wind.

He clicked and growled in acknowledgment, the sound reverberating through me. Sweeping from the sky toward the ground, Arkyn flew us to the clearing. But once he landed, he lifted his head and let out a low growl in warning.

We climbed off, both of us eyeing the forest surrounding the lodge.

Glancing from Arkyn to me, Lys whispered, "What does he smell? I can't quite scent anything out of the ordinary."

I raised an eyebrow. "The wine robs you of your keen sense of smell, hmm?"

Lys nodded. Interesting.

I walked to Arkyn's head and set a palm against his scaled cheek. "What is it?"

He snorted and glared at the trees and the indigo lights floating thickly in the area. Arkyn growled as a rumbling vibrated through my feet and the edge of the forest flashed green with drumstone light. The emerald illumination was everywhere, brightening the entire landscape. My stomach plummeted to my knees and my hand searched in vain for my sword and dagger. How were there so many drumstones here? And all of them active at once?

A host of Unseelie burst from the darkness.

37

REVNA

The demons were varied. Gargoyles, goblins, and a handful of grotesque pale orange beasts I'd never encountered before raced at us. My body shuddered as my Berserker blood rose hot and sure. There was no holding back the wave of rage my ancient bloodline sent gushing through my limbs.

"Take this!" Lys tossed one of his two swords to me —the longer one, which was a kindness.

I grabbed it and immediately swung at one of the orange-colored beasts. The thing had a hairy thick hide and my sword seemed to do next to nothing as I swiped the sharp edge across the monster's middle. The monster did fall back a step and in his place a gargoyle launched itself at me, clawed hands outstretched and eyes bulging.

Roaring above me, Arkyn whipped his tail into the

face of a gargoyle, busting its nose and sending it reeling.

Lys cut down two goblins with sword strikes and mace hits too fast for me to see clearly.

My head pounded as I whirled, faster due to my Berserker blood, my borrowed blade slicing through the gargoyle's abdomen. I leaped high and cut the orange beast's throat. Both fell dead as I turned to face more monsters. Bloodshot eyes. Limbs that dragged the ground. Teeth that dripped with drool in some cases, venom in others.

My world became a blur of jumping, striking, cutting, breaking, and loosing monster blood. My Berserker power thrummed through my veins and no pain, fear, or worry for what to do next tripped me up. I knew what move to make and the exact moment to make it. I launched myself nearly as high as Arkyn flew above us, aiding him with a strange white monster with massive pinchers and the body of a snake. Once that beast was slain, I leaped onto Arkyn's back and he shot over Lys.

The last monster standing, another orange one, balled a fist the size of a vegetable cart and aimed for Lys. I held onto Arkyn with one hand on a wing joint and used my other to slice the monster's arm open. The beast crowed in pain and that gave Lys the opportunity he needed. He lunged, jumped, and cracked the monster's skull with his mace. The creature fell back, dying on the bloody ground.

Arkyn landed and Lys joined me on the dragon's back.

"Fly," Lys said, his voice filled with the unrepentant, dominant tone of a king.

I tapped Arkyn's scales and lifted myself slightly off his back, and he shot into the starry night sky.

"Why were there so many?" I called out to Lys over the wind. Thankfully, I didn't see any more anywhere around the hunting lodge.

"I don't know," Lys said, "but as I mentioned at the vineyard, sightings have increased markedly."

Beyond a stretch of trees, Caer Du glimmered darkly in the starlight. Figures moved all around the castle, through the inner and outer baileys.

My blood went cold. "They're being attacked."

"Go!" Lys pointed, and Arkyn, guessing what we wanted, flew straight for the castle.

At least thirty Unseelie beasts rampaged Caer Du as we sought a place to join the fighting. Gargoyles ripped roofs away. Goblins smashed massive clubs into stone walls and scattered knights armed with maces and swords. A group of Fae townsfolk spun the sleeping spell from their palms, the rose-colored cloud of magic sending one gargoyle to the ground, where his body smashed a gate house. Two Fae jumped from the debris, bleeding profusely. Shouts, calls for aid, and the bang of metal on metal tore the night apart.

Arkyn soared low and we dropped off his back into

the courtyard in front of the keep, where screaming and the clang of swords greeted us.

A crowd fought in front of the keep's main doors, some fisting their free hands at their throats to ward off the Unseelie as they wielded blades and sticks. A host of knights only half-dressed in their armor fought with maces while a cluster of castle workers in aprons wielded everything from ladles to kitchen knives. A bevy of noble Fae in their flimsy fest-noz attire battled the monsters with sword, daggers, and a few ceremonial maces that broke far too easily under a goblin's strike.

I fought alongside Lys, my borrowed blade singing death to every beast that came within reach. Each sound was clear and easy to place as I ducked, struck, spun, and dove to defeat the Unseelie demons who had passed through the drumstones to this realm.

"Gwyn!" Lys's strangled cry had me turning to see his niece backed up to the wall of the stables, a small knife in her hand. A goblin the size of the guard tower loomed over her.

Lys tried to run to her but blood poured from his leg and he stumbled.

I wasn't too far away. I could get there. Stabbing the gargoyle in front of me, I spun to go to her, but a sound drowned out every other noise.

"Revna."

My true name, spoken by Lys, hummed inside my ears like a song even though it was obvious that somehow no one else in the courtyard could hear him.

"Revna," Lys said again, the ground vibrating with the syllables of the name my mother gave me. "Revna, please. Please protect Gwyn."

My body obeyed because he was using my true name. Muscles quaking and blood gone cold, I was a marionette on strings, and his voice, repeating my true name again, was the puppeteer. There was no time to ponder and my mind was intent on following Lys's orders anyway. I launched myself between the goblin and Gwyn, thrust my blade into the monster's gut, then snatched Gwyn's knife from her shaking hand. I spun, leaped onto the stumbling goblin, then stuck the knife into its eye. I jumped free as the beast fell backward into the stables. Horses fled as the structure collapsed under the goblin's weight.

The sensation of being led by a puppeteer's strings dropped away and I exhaled in a rush.

Turning, I glared at Lys, who was hobbling toward Gwyn and me as he held his bleeding cut closed.

"What did you do?" I hissed, enraged that he had not only stolen my true name but also used it.

He ignored me and went to Gwyn. The littleling fell into him, her legs collapsing and her eyes shuttering. Bruising already showed on her neck and down her side where her clothing had been partially ripped away. The goblin must have struck the poor little one hard and injured her internally.

Anger at Lys pulled at me and sparked in my blood.

"King Lysanael," I growled. "How did you get it? Why did you use it?"

"Get your dragon over here now or I'll do it again," Lys snapped, his eyes wide with panic as he looked down at Gwyn.

"Arkyn!" I shouted over the din of the last of the fight with the monsters.

The knights had rounded up the only living Unseelie and would soon have the battle won.

Arkyn bounded over to us and lowered his neck and wings so we could all three climb onto his back. I sat behind Lys, who was holding Gwyn. She looked like a broken doll in his arms. As we soared away from the castle, I longed to demand answers from Lys, but I held my tongue. For now, the littleling's life mattered more. She was an innocent in all of this.

"Where to?" I said to Lys.

"Toward the hunting lodge again. The Druid lives just northwest of there." Lys's voice was tight with concern as he spoke over the wind in our ears.

I tapped Arkyn's side to direct him and he lifted a wing to steer us in a northerly direction.

I held onto Lys's stomach because I was tired from fighting and didn't care to plummet off of Arkyn's back. I hated how strong his flat stomach felt under my fingers and how velvet smooth his skin was. I hoped he was bleeding to death from his leg wound. Leaning forward, I checked it out. Sadly, his Fae body had reacted in a far better way than my human one would have and the cut had stopped bleeding and had partially mended itself. He'd still need stitches if he were to fight on that leg again though.

"I would have fought for her," I snarled. So much for holding my tongue. "There was no need to use my true name. How did you discover it anyway?" Then it came to me—that night at the fire in my chamber when he'd trained me to repel his thrall. I gritted my teeth. "Never mind. I know how and when."

"Upset that I didn't trust an assassin?"

"We had an agreement," I said. "I haven't tried a thing on you since our agreement."

"Your agreement mentioned nothing about avoiding the topic of your true name or about thralls."

Infuriating Fae. I shouted in rage and frustration.

We flew through the night, now silent and me fuming like a bull ready to charge. Gwyn occasionally muttered incoherent phrases and her small body shuddered in Lys's powerful arms.

"Forgive me, Revna." Lys's voice was low and sincere. "I know you would have fought for her. I… I panicked. My sister-in-law put her in my care and…and I love her so very much. She looks just like my brother did when he was young. He was as obsessed with horses as she is."

My heart shook with the truth of his words. I would have done the same for Raulian or Arkyn. But that didn't cool my anger enough to bend. "I understand that," I spat out, "but now that you have my name, you can do whatever you wish to me. I can't allow that…"

I stopped myself from saying that I couldn't let him live with that information. Fighting so many Unseelie at once had left me unsteady in mind and body. Shutting my mouth was probably my best move right now despite my desire to tear him limb from limb and demand justice.

"Please ask Arkyn to fly us above those three hills to that hollow just there beyond the waterfall," Lys said.

A stream of water glittered under the stars as the indigo lights bobbed in the distance. I tapped Arkyn to give him a direction, and he eventually had us safely landing between the hills near a cottage made of stone and thatch.

We had arrived at the Druid's house.

38

REVNA

The dark wood door of the stone house swung open as we approached. Anger at Lys and fear for the innocent littleling had me striding quickly over the mossy ground.

We were here for Gwyn, but would Lysanael ask about my rune? Should I?

Lys didn't have to duck to enter; the whole place had a larger scale to it than most thatch-roofed homes. I could tell why too. Clad in snow-white robes, the Druid stood before a huge sparkling tree in the center of the main room. He was just shy of Lys's height and nearly as broad.

The tree stole my attention with its ghostly green light, shimmering and falling leaves, and the way its roots slithered over the house's floor through invisible soil. Its leaves shuffled in a magical breeze and I could hear the stretch and rub of its roots over the sound of the Druid's mumblings. He still hadn't turned around.

A cooing sounded from the corner. A great horned owl perched on a branch that appeared to be growing into the house from the outside. Then I realized there were owls everywhere. Small gray ones lodging in holes in the walls. Slender brown owls with long yellow beaks on the hearth's mantel. Snowy owls sitting here and there on rocking chairs, a tall stool, and above a hook that held a white cloak.

Finally, the Druid faced us. He held a tall staff that glowed green at the tip, and his beard stretched to the floor. He wore a short sword at his braided belt. "Greetings, King Lysanael." Dipping his head in respect, he whispered a few words I couldn't make out.

"Greetings, Druid." Lys bowed his head over Gwyn's inert form.

I curtseyed. This meeting was eerily similar to the one I'd had with the Witch alongside Master. My mind whirled and buzzed around the amount of Unseelie we'd fought, seeing the infamous Druid, Gwyn's condition, and the fact that a Fae king knew my true name. I squeezed my eyes shut. I wished I could wake up from this disaster and realize it was all some sick dream.

"Druid," Lys said, bringing Gwyn to the wizard, "she suffered a strike to the head and has other wounds as well." Lys leaned hard on his good leg as he held her out to him. "Can you heal her?"

The Druid took the littleling and set her on the flagstone floor at the base of the magical tree. Its emerald light flickered over her pointed ears and apple cheeks. She was a lovely little Fae and the family resemblance to Lys was unmistakable. Her chest rose and fell erratically and her brow furrowed as she slept. Setting a hand to the side of her throat, the Druid muttered something and grass-green sparks leaped from his fingers, then danced down Gwyn's body before circling her head.

"I am not certain I can repair what has been rent." The Druid's voice was calm and low-pitched. "Her soul hangs to her body in rags." He looked at the air around Gwyn as if he could see the very tatters of her essence blowing in the unnatural breeze that flowed through his home.

Lys's hands fisted at his sides but no emotion showed on his features. "I only ask that you try, Druid."

Arkyn's roar from outside echoed through the window. A bang and a crash sounded and the corner of the ceiling caved in. Owls flew in a panicked rush around the room, some escaping out of the hole in the roof.

Limping but obviously still strong, Lys kicked the door open and I ran after him. Outside, a giant the color of a stormy sky drew its huge fist back, its eyes focused on the Druid's house. Arkyn lay knocked out on the ground. Lys glanced at me, pressed his eyes closed for a breath, then his hair and flesh turned black, into long feathers…

I fell back, gasping. "Lys!"

He had shifted form into… Into what? I had no time to process. My Berserker blood flowed hot through me and I leaped onto the giant's arm as it smashed into the house and widened the hole in the roof. I could see the Druid still working over Gwyn. I drove my blade into the meat of the giant's palm. It shrieked and shook me off. I landed hard on the ground, the breath knocked out of me.

Where Lys had once stood, a massive peak raven hovered. He had shifted into the form of a peak raven. Shock threatened to stem the heat and power of my blood. I tried to shake my focus from him back to the giant.

With wings as wide as Arkyn's and a viciously sharp black beak, the raven shot for the giant's eyes. Flapping its wings and jabbing with its beak and talons, the raven blinded the giant.

The giant fell onto its knees, just barely missing the house, and I launched myself at the blinded beast. As the peak raven—Lys in animal form—jabbed at the back of the giant's neck, I rammed my sword into the giant's throat. Spinning, I jumped free of the dying monster and landed under the peak raven that hovered, its wings spread wide enough to block the sky from my view.

Shaking, I tried to understand. "You…" I looked the bird up and down. He was beautiful, with wings so black they seemed almost blue and amethyst feathers at his neck. Peak ravens were the largest birds in all the realms. "You are a shapeshifter." I swallowed around a lump in my throat and held my blade up. "You… You must have Unseelie blood."

I should have been horrified, but I was simply shocked and awed by his otherworldly beauty. I couldn't stop staring as the raven's obsidian feathers shimmered and became Fae flesh, dark hair, and Fae bone again. Lys's eyes—back to his normal forest and gold hue—were as cold as a winter night. He looked the same as before he'd shifted. Same clothing. Same wound. But he was depleted in a new way. Hollowed out. Why?

I started toward the door to the Druid's house to check on the wizard and Gwyn, but Lys gripped my arm and dragged me toward Arkyn, who was up now and shaking his head. Relief at his activity warred with confusion at why Lys was dragging me to the dragon.

"What are you doing?" I asked.

"There are no more monsters here. I don't smell a single one, so Gwyn will be safe with the Druid for now." His voice was short and strained and rage colored every syllable. He hurled me onto Arkyn's back, then climbed on after me. "Order him to fly to the hunting lodge or I will use your name and do it myself."

Seething, I did as ordered. "What are doing? How do you have Unseelie magic?"

Silence was my only answer.

Arkyn landed near the lodge and Lys frog-marched me inside. The interior was too dark for me to see clearly as no fire was lit nor any torches nor candles. We were entirely alone here.

Lys threw open a side door and pulled me up a winding set of stone steps. We were inside the partially ruined tower. Arkyn roared outside, asking if I needed aid.

Stopping me halfway up the steps, Lys yanked me against him and glared down at me, his eyes like arrows aimed at my stuttering heart. He looked so cold, every softer emotion I'd seen from him stripped clean away. I had no doubt he saw me as the worst of enemies now.

"Tell your dragon to stand down," he hissed.

Why was I suddenly his enemy? Because I'd seen that he had demon blood, that he was part Unseelie? Yes, his folk and mine would completely lose their minds over the fact that Unseelie blood held a throne in this world, but I knew more about the real Lys than most. He wasn't evil. Dangerous, yes. And he would probably kill me if the need arose, but he wouldn't enjoy it. I sensed that truth just as I sensed that Arkyn was currently flying in circles around the tower.

"Arkyn, I'm fine," I called out, my voice going raspy from fatigue, fear, and thirst.

Would Arkyn know I was lying? I hoped he would. Of course, Lys could set that sleeping spell on him if he tried to attack, but if Arkyn moved fast and caught Lys by surprise, he might succeed in injuring Lys further and giving me an opportunity to strike. Together, we might take Lys down. But only if I could keep Lys from using my true name. My teeth ground together.

Dragging me the rest of the way up the stairs, Lys tugged me into an empty room where a set of shackles hung from chains on the wall. Windows cut the darkness in three places and the swath of black beyond the nearest one showed Arkyn for a split second as he flew by. His presence was the only comfort in my heart. The room smelled like old blood and rotting wood.

"Well, this is a lovely spot," I said snappishly. "Is this where you were going to take me when we first landed outside? Perfect place for a tipsy and ill-advised kissing session, hmm?" I practically snarled as he latched my wrist in a shackle. "Do you even have keys to these things? What's your plan? Now that I know your terrible secret—"

Lys went preternaturally still. I froze, fear icing my Berserker blood.

Never once had my rare blood reacted like this…

The Fae king raised his hand and acted as though he might grip my chin, my cheeks, but his long fingers paused, hovering and curling in on themselves.

"Do not speak of my fouled blood," he whispered, "or it will be your last moment." He stepped back.

My blood blazed through me, all fear torn away in a flash of heat. "Then why keep me alive and chained here? Why not kill me now?"

It wasn't reckless to ask. He had some sort of plan

here or he wouldn't have been chaining me up. I needed information to work out an escape plan and a murder scenario.

"You are the king. Would they dethrone you for your blood?"

I knew the answer. Yes. The council would toss him out and quite possibly hunt him as they did all Unseelie.

"Talk to me, Lys. Why must you hold the throne and deal with politics and a court that you despise? Why not just leave if you don't care about your people losing their magic?"

His hair, torn loose from its knot during the fighting and shifting, covered half his face as he stared. His eyes glittered with menace and another emotion I couldn't place.

"Because of Gwyn," he said, his words the sound of a knife on a whetstone. "If they find out I'm a bastard born to my Seelie mother but seeded by an Unseelie male, they'll have me killed and put Gwyn on the throne. She has no magic. She is a littleling. The courtiers and council will eat her alive. I will not put her in that position."

Gwyn was the temporary heir to the Fae crown. Interesting. His brother's child... That second emotion in his face was his need to protect his niece. "Is she the offspring of the brother you think might still be alive? Who is seeking him out? Your sister-in-law?"

"If they all lose magic, Gwyn will be safer."

"Not against the..." I stopped. I had started to say

Unseelie, but he was also Unseelie. I didn't want to lump them all in together.

His eyes darkened, hurt flashing through his gaze before he turned away. "I know. I am a demon just as the rest of them. But this demon must keep his secrets and hold his vows. Goodbye, assassin."

He strode quickly down the stairs, leaving me linked to the wall by way of that one wrist shackle. And I knew then what he had planned for me now that I held his dangerous secret.

"You coward," I hissed.

Halting just before he disappeared in the stairwell, his hand on the blackened stone of the wall, he turned to glare.

"You're going to let my death rune do your dirty work." As if it heard me, my rune pulsed at the back of my neck. I winced.

His labored exhale echoed through the stairwell and into the room. "I swore an oath to protect her and this is what I must do. I take no joy in it." His footsteps knocked down the steps and he was gone.

L ysanael stormed down the stairs as his pulse hammered his throat. His weak and easily swayed heart demanded that he go right back upstairs, free Revna, and to the nine hills with the consequences.

But he knew better.

His desire had to be denied. He'd thought she was different, that she wouldn't see him as a demon because of their strange connection, because of the way he felt around her. He had been wrong. Revna was just like the Fae at court. She held the same beliefs—he had seen the disgust in her eyes when he'd shifted. His eyes shuttered, and his heart gave another violent lurch at her betrayal and his own terrifying response.

And Revna wasn't wrong. He was indeed half demon, a child of the Unseelie, a monster to be disposed of as quickly as possible. But he was also Gwyn's shield and he would hold on to this life as long as that was true. If he freed Revna, she would kill him or force him to kill her. She had been trained to fight those of his blood. It was her entire life. And if she failed to kill him herself, surely she would use the prejudices of his people to bring him down.

Gwyn would be left defenseless with her mother beside her.

Neeria didn't have the standing to push back at the council or hold a position of influence with regard to Gwyn. Someone would have her murdered the day she attempted it. Her ancestor had killed a queen and been caught outright, so her house and thereby her blood was considered not much better than his Unseelie half.

Swallowing bile and ignoring Revna's shouts, he strode past Arkyn, who slept under his spell, and ran toward Neeria's home on the outskirts of the village of Budocdour. A messenger had sent word that Neeria had returned from her search and awaited his arrival.

This was the only hope he would allow himself. Perhaps if he told Neeria everything, she would think of a way to allow Revna to live without endangering the rest of them.

Revna's words echoed in his mind and the truth in them rang through his bones like a death knell. *You coward.*

He was exactly that. Anger at her betrayal burned his soul, but she was still the one who lit him up inside, the one he had never known he would crave. By leaving her, he was simply allowing the course of her life to continue. Her Master and the Witch of the human realm would end her life and then he would continue on. Or Neeria would help him devise a plan and they could return and free Revna.

But could he give Neeria his secret after working so hard for so long to keep it? His throat tightened and he blew out a frustrated breath. His stomach rolled and burned and he was unsure of every decision he had made since the last Fae king died. Had hiding the truth been the wrong thing to do? He had driven away every close friend, every potential mate—save Revna—just to keep his people from finding out he had demon blood. During the years of hiding his Unseelie side, he had refused to fully rule his kingdom. Fear that the council would discover the truth had kept him from battles he should have been fighting for his realm. He'd worried he would shift into his raven form during the bloodshed and that they would turn their weapons toward him, endangering Gwyn's chance at a childhood.

Was it all a waste? Had he been wrong this entire time?

Shaking his head, he tried to let the past go. He had to make the right choice going forward. Pushing away the fear and regret, he focused on his intuition. What should he do? He imagined his brother's wife, Neeria, with her earnest dark eyes and her honest way of life. Yes, he had to tell Neeria. He needed advice. He'd been arrogant and secretive for what felt like ages, so long, in fact, that he had become the sort of evil he fought each time the drumstones activated.

He allowed himself to grieve and to hate himself as he ran, the world blurring around him like he had been poisoned once more.

I truly am a demon now, he thought as he pushed open Neeria's door and prepared to tell his brother's wife what she had to know. Neeria would never understand his stance if he didn't reveal it all and she would keep Gwyn's well-being as the top priority. Neeria was a true mother, unlike Lysanael's mother had been. It was honestly difficult to believe that she wasn't the Unseelie half of his parents. He shuddered, recalling the way she'd lifted that knife to slay him when he was still a gangly youth.

Neeria walked out of the back room, her face still wet from washing and a linen towel in her scarred hands. "Lysanael."

Tears shone in her eyes as she threw the towel onto a chair and ran to hug him. They wept together for a while, then Lysanael began to tell his story.

"A human?" Neeria asked after almost all had been told.

"You're not...abhorred by my Unseelie blood?"

"Of course I am, but I know you, Lysanael. Granted, we have never been close. You kept Aragael at a distance, as well as me once they forced you to take your father's place."

"You mean my stepfather."

She nodded and blew out a breath. "I never would have guessed it. You had me fooled. But no one has to know, and besides, who is to say your offspring would be anything different from you? They would have even less Unseelie blood." She started to make a fist, her hand going to her throat in the same habit as every other Fae, but she stopped herself, eyes widening.

Lysanael waved off her concern. The fact that she seemed to be accepting him as he was even after knowing the truth had him stunned to silence.

"So this human that you're in love with, does she love you back?"

"I'm not… It's not like that. She is disgusted by me. She'll never keep my secret."

"Hmm." Neeria crossed her arms and studied him. "You thought I would be horrified, and I'm stunned but not in any way that would make me think less of you. It's not your fault who your seed father was. I bet she is as wild for you as you are for her."

"How do you know how I feel?"

She snorted. "The great and stony-faced king blushing? Stammering? It's as obvious as the day is long, dear brother."

"She hates me now. Of that I can assure you."

"Why?"

An imaginary claw gripped his heart and squeezed. He shut his eyes as pain pinched his chest and his blood chilled. He set his gaze on Neeria.

"I chained her up at my lodge and her death rune will take her life soon if it hasn't already."

Neeria's eyes went wide as plates and she grabbed Lysanael's tunic. "What in the nine hills made you treat her like that? Your fear for Gwyn?" She was already running out of the door.

He trailed her to where three horses stood tied to posts. She lived with two other warriors and it seemed they had all been prepared to ride.

"We were about to head back to your keep." Taking a slip of parchment and a slender stick of charcoal from a small bag at her belt, she ordered him about. "Get on the black one. He's almost as fast as my girl here." She scrawled a quick note, assumably to her fellow warriors and the owners of the horses, and pierced it on a nail hammered into the hitching post. Once she'd mounted her gray mare, they took off.

Heart seizing up against his ribs, Lysanael climbed atop the gelding and worked to catch up. "But—"

"I am Gwyn's mother," Neeria shouted over her shoulder as they rode through the mid-morning light. "Do you think I would risk my littleling? I'll answer that. No, I wouldn't. You are being an impossible male, my king, and from now on, you need to let that human and me guide your clueless self."

Panic lanced Lysanael's chest as his love for Revna burst through his fears for his niece. His pulse galloped in time with the horses' hooves and he didn't blink the entire desperate ride to the lodge and tower. How had he gone so off track? How could he have hurt Revna? He would never, ever forgive himself if she was gone from this world. He would never forgive himself anyway for the chains and the rage that had resulted from the way he'd misjudged her.

"She'll never forgive me. I'll never forgive me."

Neeria glared. "That's her choice and yours, but if we don't make it in time, she won't have the freedom to decide."

He kept quiet as they drove the horses as hard as was possible, his heart plunging into darkness all the while because of the terrible crime he had committed against the one person who had gone against all to trust him and care for him.

Please don't die, Revna. If you do, you won't have the chance to throttle me, which would surely give you the greatest pleasure.

❧ 40 ❧

REVNA

The worst part of the next hours wasn't the dangerous pulse of my death rune. It was the absence of my sense of Arkyn. He was either deeply asleep by way of Fae magic or... I didn't want to think about the other possibilities.

I swallowed against my dry throat and tried to call for him for the thousandth time. "Arkyn."

Tethered to the wall, I leaned as far as I could, peering out of the window. I could only see a sliver of the ground as it swept upward, away from the ruined tower that had once been a fine keep. I couldn't see Arkyn in the sun's morning light.

I'm sorry, Arkyn. Go, if you can. Just...go.

Lys was most assuredly gone. There hadn't been a sound for hours. I kept trying to work my hand free of the shackle, my skin growing swollen and hot as the morning turned to noon and the pound of horses' hooves sounded beyond my prison.

Leaning, I tried to see who it was. It was three—no, five males in fine robes.

The Fae council had arrived without Lys.

Heart hammering, I tried to figure out why they would have come here. They must know that Lys visited this place from time to time. Or perhaps the Druid told them of me? Or were they here on Lys's orders? If so, what did that mean for me and my promise to my mother?

"My king?" Bornien's aged voice called out several times before the lot of them began slipping up the stairs.

"What is that scent?" another voice said.

A deep cold wrapped me from head to toe. If they could scent my true self, my illusion spell was fading. I felt exposed, without proper armor behind enemy lines. My rune pulsed painfully and I hissed, grinding my teeth together.

Had Master asked the Witch to set a timed effect on my rune before I'd left or did he know I had been compromised? I hadn't seen any of his contacts at the Fae court, no sign of two fingers held by the right hip or any whispered versions of the Hunters' phrase *We are the rising night*. I didn't think Master knew. I didn't see how he would. But time told tales certainly and I had never been gone this long on a mission and succeeded. He wouldn't let me be captured by enemy hands. I was too dangerous.

"Human," another whispered as their footsteps sounded on the stairs.

Bornien and the council members walked into my makeshift prison. Their faces told me they did indeed see me as a human and they were not best pleased about the change. I shivered.

Raising my chin, I prepared to meet my end with my head held high. "Afternoon, fellas," I said. "Bring me a mead, did you? I'm frightfully thirsty."

Bornien swept forward, his eyes wide. "What is this magic?" He looked at my ear and then studied my face.

Another council member, one of the silver-haired twins, rushed forward and grabbed my throat. Pain burst down my body and my Berserker blood rose up. The room tilted as fatigue pulled at me, weakening the effects of my rare blood.

"This is the human Witch's doing, isn't it?" His black eyes raged over my features and his lip curled to show a fang. I could smell minted wine on his breath. "Tell us all."

He smiled wickedly and heat poured over my body.

"You have no approval to use a thrall on a human, Yonnis," Bornien said.

I barely heard him. The thrall felt nothing like Lys's…

A fire burned in my stomach and I fell into it, too tired to fight. I felt my mouth open, ready to tell him anything. Everything.

Then my blood reared high and I shook myself.

Cold, black ocean. Salt. Crashing waves and calling gannets. My head cleared and I glared at the silver-haired Fae male.

"You'll have to try harder, my lord."

He snarled, drew back, and smacked me across the face. I balled my free hand and punched his jaw, sending him spinning across the floor, where he landed beside his twin's feet.

Bornien looked shocked but not altogether displeased. "Now, enough violence. We must find out what has happened here. Our king chose this female as his mate and we must discover why she is chained here and why, well, why she is human."

The horned Fae with the clawed fingers strode across the floorboards to stand in front of me. "It is obvious, Lord Bornien. This human and her Witch have tricked the king."

He tilted his head and licked his lips as he ran a claw down my cheek. Hot blood ran down my face and dropped from my chin as he glanced at my free hand and my legs, practically daring me to attack him. He wouldn't pout like the silver-haired Fae was. This male was ready to kill me and ask permission later. Death looked at me, dark and sure, from the pupils of his slitted eyes.

"The only answer we need is whether or not there are any more of you in our kingdom," he said quietly.

"I am the only one."

He laughed and set his claws against my cheek. The

tips pierced the skin and sent pain rushing over my face. Were they laced with poison? He dragged those claws down the side of my neck and fire erupted in my veins.

I bucked my hips, bumping him backward, then I shoved one foot into his stomach. I launched myself at him, but my chain held me fast. Shouting, raging, I pulled, but I was stuck and my bones were near to cracking with my efforts to break free. Blood ran freely down my face and neck, and my clothing stuck to my chest and stomach.

The horned Fae shot to his feet.

The bolt holding my chain to the wall snapped away from the stone.

I was free.

A grin that could have belonged to an Unseelie crossed my lips. "I think it's past time for this meeting to end."

Unleashing the fury of my Berserker blood, I swung my chain and caught the horned Fae male. He slammed into the floorboards with a grunt and a crack of bone. Jerking the chain free of him, I whipped it at the green-skinned Fae who had started toward me with a mace. Quick as a bolt of lightning, he ducked the chain and slid across the floor toward my left leg. I slammed my boot onto his knee, then lifted my foot to kick him in the jaw. He hadn't even had time to do more than scratch me. Bornien held back, face grave, as I stormed toward the silver-haired twins. We fought like rabid mountain lions, my own human nails not doing half bad a job at scratching eyes. I slammed a palm into one's nose and he dropped back. I kneed the second in the chin as he tried to tackle me. With that one down for the time being, I jumped onto the one with the nose bleed and finished him with a kick to the groin.

I whirled on Bornien. "Are you with me or against me?"

"With you." Something akin to mischief lit his old, slitted eyes.

Something terribly hard and unforgiving hit the back of my head and the room went dark.

A light broke through the dark and I looked at the blurry room. That green-skinned Fae must have rallied and knocked me out. Where was I? Still in the tower at the lodge or had they moved me? I had no idea how long I'd been out. I was not in the tower, but instead, in the council room. New shackles on my wrists and ankles chilled my bruised body.

The council members chatted around their table, enjoying a nice little meeting as if there weren't a human beaten and chained in the corner.

"As much as I love receiving new jewelry from exciting males, I wish you would've consulted me on this purchase." I held up my shackles and shook them lightly.

Bornien regarded me with a wary expression. "It's in your best interest to be quiet."

"Being knocked out kept me pretty quiet and look

where that's got me." I shook my chains again. Where
was Lys? Had he ordered this?

"You're to die once we finish questioning you. The
king has your true name and we simply await his
return."

Someone must have noticed him using my true
name during the fight with the Unseelie in the
courtyard. The magic was odd; it had a feel to it when
used, and from what I'd been told, no one but the owner
of the true name, the one given the name by the person
with that name, would be able to hear it. It was a
sensible magic; at least enemies couldn't trade names
like coins.

I sat back against the wall and tried to feel for Arkyn.
The bonding sensation in my chest was quiet. I didn't
dare ask about Arkyn just in case the council hadn't yet
gone after him. Most likely they had him chained
somewhere, sleeping under their spell. I rescued him
once; I would try to do it again if I lived long enough to
make a plan. Hopefully, Arkyn was long gone, off in the
Gwerhune. It wasn't likely. He'd probably stayed
around to see if he could help me in some way. He
wouldn't give up on me just as I wouldn't give up on
him. The thought both touched and grieved me.

The council was discussing what possible spells the
Witch could have used on me to affect Lys. I'd never
heard of half the magic they brought up.

"We must use the thrall on her and find out who sent
her," one of the silver-haired Fae said. He was

completely healed from our fight. Disappointing. "The king had her chained up. He won't care what we do with her now."

Bornien cocked his head and looked down at the table. "I don't know about that."

The green Fae waved a hand dismissively. "Ach, the enchantment had to be broken if he had her in such a condition at his lodge."

"We should wait until he returns," Bornien said.

Leaning on the table, eyes narrowed, the green Fae glared my way. "It's not as if the king truly fell for her. The enchantment is broken. He will want her dead as much as we do."

"He may want to kill her himself," the second silver-haired Fae said as he toyed with one of three torcs hanging around his neck.

The horned Fae that I had cracked on the head with my chain while we were at the lodge's tower pushed away from the table and sauntered over to me. He had a bruise the size of an apple on his temple and I was happy to know that even with the Fae's excellent ability to heal, this one was still suffering.

He set his clawed hand on my cheek and grinned as pain leeched into my face. "Tell us what you know, human, and I'll make your death quick."

The door burst open.

Lys strode in, his long black hair unbound and wild. His feral gaze locked me down better than any chains could manage. His nostrils flared, and he lifted his head like a wolf on the hunt. The chill of fear rattled me. A blaze of hot desire shot through my blood. The air in the room crackled like lightning was about to strike.

Lys's stare latched onto the horned Fae. "Take your hands off my mate."

His mate? What had changed?

The male stepped back quickly. "My king." He bowed and the rest of the council stood and did likewise.

Bornien glanced from Lys to me and back again. "My king, she is human. We assumed you had discovered her trickery, as you had her chained in your lodge."

Lys turned his head slowly. "Lord Bornien, unlock her immediately."

His lips tightened into a line but the elderly Fae removed a key from his robes and unlocked the shackles quickly. I rubbed my wrists but remained where I was as Lys regarded me with a searching gaze. What was he wondering?

He came close and inspected my face and body, going so far as to lift an arm and glance at the back of me, taking stock of my wounds.

"I'm fine," I whispered as he leaned toward me to look at the cuts on my cheek. "But why do you suddenly care?"

His eyes burned, his gaze piercing me like an arrow, like he could see every side of my soul and he claimed me in whole. My cheeks flushed hotly.

He whirled and threw a dagger at the horned Fae.

The blade struck true and the male fell dead to the floor. "He drew blood from the intended mate of the king."

The council murmured agreement, their faces wary.

"Do you…" Lys started, then glanced at me again before looking at Bornien. "Do you have any questions for me?"

What was he getting at?

"Did you know she was human?" Bornien asked.

"I found out very recently. She was sent here by the human king," Lys said. I had to be grateful that he left out the whole ordered to kill him part of the story. "The Witch set an illusion on her, but I found no other spells cast on her body or mind."

Bornien's mouth fell open. He raised a finger and frowned. "So, King Lysanael, you are saying you truly have feelings for this human female and you still wish to mate with her? I know your magic is powerful enough to continue through a mating with one such as her, but it isn't wise to mate with a short-lived human."

Regaining my position here was the first step toward escaping this council. I'd figure the rest out once Lys and I were free of them. "I have Berserker blood. My folk live nearly as long as Fae if the magic is strong in us. And I am very strong."

Lys's gaze shimmered as he studied me. Was it pride in his look? "You see?" he said to the council. "I claim her as my mate. I know it is unconventional, but one cannot always sway the heart's desires."

I was more confused than I'd ever been.

First, I remained infuriated about how he'd tricked me and stolen my name. Granted, I had attempted to kill him time and time again. How could I blame him for taking such a grand opportunity? It was what I would've done if I'd been Fae and capable of name magic. But blame him, I did. And then there was the fact that Lys hated me for knowing his secret—he'd made his view of me very clear with the treatment he'd given me at the lodge. So why was he so incensed at the council's violence against me? Why was he reforming our ruse of his desire to marry me and mate with me?

The green Fae steepled his fingers on the table. "What did she come to learn for her human king and what will you do to keep the human king from attacking when he learns you have stolen his spy for a wife?"

"That is none of your concern. I will handle it. Do you doubt my ability to defend our realm?"

I couldn't breathe. What had happened to change Lys's mind? I forced my feelings to go silent under my imaginary lock and key. I didn't dare to hope for what part of my heart wished were true, and besides that, I was incensed at the way Lys had treated me.

The green Fae male stared at Lys, defiance pouring off him. Lys's gaze was unbreakable steel.

"Maybe we should discuss this—" Bornien was cut off by the shift of muscles in Lys's jaw. "We do not doubt you, my king." Bornien bowed his head.

The green Fae bared his teeth, then at last, he too

bowed his head and kept it there. "Of course not, my king."

"Good." Lys held out his elbow and I took it, though I remained coiled and ready for a fight. "We will marry at the sacred menhir. Make the necessary preparations."

The council erupted into questions, but Lys turned and led me out of the council room. He set a brisk pace down the corridor toward my chamber, slowly but surely dropping his elbow so that we were no longer touching.

"You didn't tell them," he whispered, his eyes glittering in the firelight of the sconces on the stone walls.

"Tell them what?" I snapped.

He huffed and scowled down at me. "You aren't a fool. Why didn't you use what you knew of my Unseelie blood to ruin me after I handled you roughly, chained you, and left you to die?"

"I should have," I bit out, anger leaking through my words.

His eyes shuttered briefly. "I know. But it was a security measure. A mistake. A horrible mistake. I didn't want to leave you to die by your rune, but I—"

I held up a hand to stop his excuses. "Save it. You decided you liked me better as a corpse back at your precious lodge and now you're my hero? I'm confused, Lysanael."

"You could have ended me with a word to the council and you didn't," he said. Then he looked down the corridor, his focus miles away. "I was sired by an Unseelie, a demon. I am a monster."

I exhaled roughly and gritted my teeth. "No, you aren't," I said reluctantly. "Unseelie are beasts driven purely by instinct; even the high Fae are more beast than reasoning creature, right? No Unseelie would have gone to all this trouble to keep a littleling from suffering at the hands of his court. Also, I didn't want to destroy Gwyn's life before it started either. Ruining you would be destroying the plan you have for her. Now, where is Arkyn?"

The corner of his lips lifted. "Your dragon is in the stables. He is asleep by way of magic because he would not stop trying to tear me apart."

Relief uncoiled my tense muscles. Arkyn was alive and healthy. Thank the Old Ones "You should have let him rip you to pieces. Perhaps I would have forgiven what was left of your sorry arse. Looks to me like someone got a strike in here and there." I eyed his bloodied arm and the bruise on his sharp cheekbone.

"The Druid healed Gwyn and my leg too. But yes, Arkyn is responsible for some of these bruises and cuts, but most are from another drumstone waking near the southern gate."

"You still haven't answered me."

"About what?" he appeared genuinely confused.

"Why did you decide you wanted to continue our ruse instead of letting me die?" I asked.

An exhale that spoke of some internal struggle left

him in a rush. He ran his free hand through his mussed hair, waved the guards at my door away, then escorted me inside. While I checked the cider and watered wine left on a tray by the window, he examined the shadows and the bath chamber for intruders. He joined me at the hearth to continue our conversation while I drank every drop of liquid in sight.

"When I shifted into my raven form, you were shocked," Lys said quietly, "disgusted."

I shook my head. "I wasn't disgusted. You were magnificent." The memory of his wide obsidian wings and his powerful talons flooded my mind. "You're still an arsehead though."

He closed his eyes briefly and let his head fall back. "I saw what I feared to see. But my sister-in-law, Neeria, set me straight. We were on our way to you when the council beat me to it." His lip curled to show a fang that caught the firelight.

My rune pulsed and sent a crackling pain down my entire body, shaking my very bones. I dropped, my legs going out, then Lys caught me in his arms.

"Revna?" Lys said, his voice jagged with fear.

My true name echoed as the room spun and the heat of his arms warmed my back and behind my knees. Pain lashed through me, beginning at my neck and coursing down my flesh like a thousand fire-hot brands being pressed into me inch by inch.

Time grew meaningless.

My ears rang.

I was cold, then burning.

I thought I heard Lys whispering as he carried me in his arms. "...and I don't understand it myself, this draw to you. I am probably the greatest fool of all. But there's something about the way you see me. I never thought I'd fight beside someone like you, someone not of my world. Watching you move, it's like watching an artist with paint or stone. You're mesmerizing, Revna. The stark divide between what you have been raised to do and how you show kindness to the innocent is so much more than admirable; it's a miracle. Truly. I will never stop groveling, begging you to forgive me for what I did to you."

My mind buzzed and I fell back into the pain pounding from my rune.

The next time I was aware of myself, wind rushed along my fevered cheeks, and my hand dropped from my stomach to touch warm scales. We were flying on Arkyn. The pain hummed in the background of my foggy mind...

Taking my hand, Lys turned it over. "Please don't die. We could have a life I never imagined. Maybe..." His lips brushed across the soft skin of my wrist and a shiver danced up my arm. "I never should have doubted you, my viper." Though he held me close as we flew, his words sounded distant behind the ringing in my ears. "You are vicious enough to brave the dark that hides in me and find it beautiful."

Searing agony ripped me limb from limb as I felt Arkyn land.

Had Lys urged Arkyn to take me to the Druid? I couldn't open my eyes to look. It didn't matter anyway.

It was too late.

"Lord King," the Druid said over me. "I don't know if this can be done."

On my side, I lay at his feet among the glittering roots of the magical tree. The Druid's hands were as cold as his words and I fought a shiver as he traced the death rune again and whispered words of power. The roots crawled over my legs and tangled in my hair but somehow their touch was a comfort. The pain from the rune remained, but the Druid and his tree had pushed it away somewhat, enough so that I could think and feel more than the agony.

The magical tree cast webs of emerald stars across Lys's stern face and proud nose. His hand held mine, his warm and calloused fingers a second unexpected comfort.

"Please try again," Lys said.

The Druid lifted his head and raised an eyebrow at

Lys. "You love her, this assassin, this human woman with the blood of hundreds in her lifelight."

My heart skipped and dropped into my stomach.

He did? The Druid sounded as if he knew Lys loved me. Loved me? But how? We hardly knew one another and the time we'd spent together had been filled with poison and blades, deceit and false kisses.

But maybe they weren't all false?

Memories washed through me. Lys smiling at Waith and talking to the vineyard workers over his ale. The feel of his mouth on mine in the maze. The glint of joy in his eyes when Gwyn ran into the council room unannounced. His gentle hands cradling my body on the way here. The fierce, protective fire in his gaze when he found me in the council chamber today.

Lys's throat moved in a swallow and he locked eyes with me. My very soul trembled. I wished I didn't feel the jolt of pure emotion that I did. I locked the feeling down and shut my eyes.

The Druid set his hands on the sides of my head. "She blocks her feelings for you. You shouldn't lock your emotions away, assassin."

I opened my eyes to see Lys studying me like he often did. "Emotions are a liability in my line of work," I said, my words rough with pain and truth.

The Druid huffed. "You are a living being. You must release your feelings. Even if I could unwork this rune and give you a longer life, you'll die…" He stopped, his hands leaving the back of my neck.

"What is it, Druid?" Lys stared at the earth wizard as the Druid hurried away to the far side of the room.

The Druid rummaged around in a set of drawers under the snowy owl's perch. "We will unravel the rune as she unravels the myriad of emotions she has been locking away in her mind." Glass bottles clinked as he shuffled scrolls and long strips of parchment covered in drawings.

I didn't like where this was going. It was disconcerting that he knew the exact wording I often used to think on my process for remaining stoic during jobs—locked.

The rune pulsed, and pain launched itself down my chest and into my heart.

I gasped and rolled forward, and Lys caught me gently, keeping me on my side. The magical tree's roots slithered around my boots and I focused on them and the feel of Lys's grip as the pain receded. Once it faded, I took a breath and imagined my emotions locked so incredibly securely in that box in the back of my mind.

The rune whipped my senses again and blinding pain lashed me. "We're running short on time." I looked to Lys, who had gone gray around the lips.

"What do you wish for Arkyn?" he asked, his voice strained.

I smiled, glad that he knew what mattered most to me even though we'd met only a short while ago. I felt as though I'd known Lys forever, but of course, that was impossible, ridiculous.

"Let Arkyn mourn over me to accept that I am gone," I said, "then encourage him to find happiness in the Gwerhune. Unless you're headed to the Shrouded Mountains at any point?" I didn't want to bring up his lost brother. "He'd love to see the fire dragons that live there."

The edge of his mouth lifted. "I will treat him as one of my family."

A flash of golden light washed through the house and we turned toward the tree and the Druid, who was staring at the magical tree's branches.

"Did that light come from your tree?" I asked.

The Druid nodded and glanced from the tree to Lys. "You just made an oath, King Lysanael, and the earth respects it. You…" He frowned at the tree as he hurried back to us. "…you have a new littleling?" The Druid stared at my belly. "Are you with child?"

"No," I choked out, the pain gripping me tightly. "Definitely not."

"Then you have one who depends on you? One to whom you are bonded, assassin?"

"Arkyn. My dragon." I squeezed my eyes shut as my body howled under the relentless sting and lash of the rune.

I opened my eyes to see the Druid wave his hand and a wall of shimmering blue light cocoon the old wizard and me.

"Tell me your true name, assassin."

I blinked my aching eyes. "Why? You aren't Fae. You can't use the command magic, can you?"

"No."

"You could be lying." Of course, I was nearly dead. What did it matter? "Just heal me or let me die," I said, fully exhausted. A memory of my people in Fjordbok shimmered through my mind and tears leaked from my eyes. I was failing them all. "I'm sorry, Mother," I whispered.

The Druid took hold of my cheeks gently and turned my face toward him. "If I lie, the tree shows the deceit. Watch." He looked at the tree. "I am not the Druid." The tree trembled, shaking the floor as it turned a sickly yellow. Then the light returned to its usual shade of emerald green. "You see?" The Druid asked me. "Tell me your name. I have a guess and if I am right, it means everything."

"Revna. My name is Revna."

Light shone in the Druid's triumphant gaze. "Yes! I knew it." He lifted his hand and the blue cocoon around us fell away. "My king, I think we can save her. Please listen to me in full before responding."

Lys bared his teeth in frustration but nodded his head. "As you will it, Druid."

The Druid took Lys's hand and set it on my rune. The inking pulsed and I winced as the Druid began speaking again. "In the Fjordbok language, Revna means raven."

I glanced at Lys, who was wide-eyed like a frightened deer.

"Raven," Lys said, his voice dangerous. "Why does that matter?"

The Druid tilted his head. "Don't fret, my king. A prophecy came to me when you were but a littleling. A tale of two ravens, and though I'm not sure how that term applies to you, my intuition says it names you. If my guess is right, this raven of Fjordbok, this assassin with the blood of the ancient Berserkers, is your fated mate."

My name meant raven and when Lys used his Unseelie magic to shift form, he became a peak raven. We were both ravens in our other lives. Maybe the Druid was right. A flood of warmth cascaded through me, easing my pain. But it couldn't be true. Could it?

"And," the Druid continued, "when you, King Lysanael, took an oath to treat your fated mate's chosen dependent as your own kin, you took on an heir."

Lys's eyes went even wider and though I was still twisted in pain, I found myself laughing, more tears leaking from my eyes.

"Arkyn is now heir to the Fae throne?" I couldn't stop laughing then and Lys shook his head.

The Druid leaned close. "You must unlock your emotions and reveal your love for your fated mate. If you do so, I believe the rune will unravel under my additional unlocking spell. I cannot promise you your life, but it is a possibility you will survive if you open yourself to your feelings."

I swallowed against my dry throat and let Lys help me to a seated position on the floor. The tree aided me with roots that curled around me like the back of a chair. The Druid sat behind me, his fingers touching my rune. He whispered a spell and his power, cool and calm, laced the pain that rumbled down my spine.

I met Lys's gaze and tried to lose myself in the forest and gold of his beautiful eyes. "Could it be true? Do you feel it?"

His lids lowered a fraction and he set a hand on my cheek. His thumb rubbed my lower lip and his gaze smoothed across my cheeks before landing on my eyes. "I have seen only you since the moment you walked into my keep. Try as I might to deny it, to fight it, to reason the sensation away, you are the center of my world. Using your true name to defend Gwyn nearly undid me. I hate myself and yet I would do it again to save my niece."

I couldn't breathe properly. My lungs burned and my chest ached. I tried to reach for his hand, for the fingers tracing my jawline, but I was too weak and everything was a humming haze of pain. "I…" What could I say? My body wanted him from the second I saw him in his bed that very first night, but my mind and heart? What did I want? Was he my fated mate? Could I love him? "I don't know what to do. I have trained myself to remain removed all my life."

The Druid set his flat palm on the rune and a rush of magic sparked over my skin. "Where are your emotions stored, Revna?"

"In a box. I mean, in my mind, there is a locked trunk." I felt foolish saying it aloud.

"Close your eyes," the Druid said, "and imagine the trunk in the best detail you are able."

I did so, seeing the dark wood of the container, the black iron of the bars that held it fast, the heavy lock that kept my secrets safe.

"Now, find the key and place it in the lock."

Only emptiness greeted my mind. "I have no key."

Lys growled. "What can we do to help her, Druid? Her face…"

I must have been going pale or ashen. The pain remained and now it felt as though the death rune was eating at my very bones. I was a glass goblet near to shattering under the hail of winter.

The Druid moved away and I opened my eyes to see Lys staring at me, his slitted eyes stormy with frustration and banked rage at what neither he nor I could control. I looked to the Druid as the earth wizard flung his door open wide. Arkyn peered inside and a smile pulled at my chapped lips.

"My friend."

Wings knocking loose thatch from the top of the entryway, Arkyn sidled inside, and the owls perched about the room fluttered and hooted in protest.

"What are you doing?" Lys demanded even as he set an easy hand on Arkyn's side.

Arkyn lay beside me, eyes flicking to the slithering roots as he rested his head in my lap.

"This is our key," the Druid said. "Tell Arkyn about Lys, Revna."

I smoothed my hand over Arkyn's scales, savoring the gentle warmth there. I felt ridiculous. "Arkyn, do you believe Lys could be my fated mate?"

Arkyn huffed, shutting his eyes, then his tongue flicked out to touch Lys's fingers, the ones curled around my other hand.

Lys smiled. "I hope that means *yes*."

"You do?" I asked, pulling his attention from Arkyn. My heart drummed against my chest and I pushed back at the rune's pain.

Lifting my hand like he had earlier, Lys flipped it over and kissed my wrist. His breath was so warm and lovely. He looked up at me through his thick black eyelashes. "I do, Revna of Fjordbok. You are the only song I hear, the only color I see, the only light that guides my heart. I tried to hate you. It did not take."

Arkyn bumped my leg and I glanced down to see him eyeing me with a questioning look. He wanted to know what I thought.

"Help me feel, Arkyn." My stomach rolled and I forced myself to breathe. "Can you do that?" I had never understood the bond between us. There weren't many folk who had familiars or anything like that. The tingling sensation that his presence often sent through my heart shivered through me now, the intensity increasing as I pressed my hand to his scaled head.

"Can you feel what I feel?" I asked Arkyn.

The dragon leaned into my touch and the tingling sensation increased again. I felt his answer somehow —*yes*.

"See him as the key," the Druid said. He whispered his spell louder, the ancient magic words like the scratch of branches on the wall during a gale. His cool hand kept contact with my death rune.

I shut my eyes and imagined Arkyn lashing at the locked trunk with his tail. A wave of fear chilled me and Lys's hold on my other hand tightened. In my mind, Arkyn swiped at the trunk with a talon.

My breath caught in my chest and then I was falling, spinning, gasping...

REVNA

A whirlwind of bright colors—spring green, scarlet, rich honey brown, brilliant indigo—spun through my mind. They bounced off one another, sparkling like stars, until they formed memories.

My mother's eyes, just like mine, stared at me. Her smile widened and her hand brushed my cheek. My heart shivered…

Raulian's laugh echoed, creating streams of blue across my mind's eye. His face materialized and he winked as he wiped blood off the corner of his mouth. Then Master's stick struck him and he fell. Stomach rolling, I felt hot tears run down my face. But was that in the memory or now?

The glare of a brash red blinded me and I winced as pain exploded across my body. Every inch of me hurt from training first, and now from the strikes of Master's fists and feet. He glared at me, then grinned. I was going to be sick. Why did he hate me? Why had he taken me from my home? I looked at my bloodied knuckles and saw a child's hand. I was only a child...

I reached for the darkness at the edge of my vision. All I wanted was the blessed, cold, unfeeling dark. Arkyn's scaled snout appeared and one of his bright eyes blinked at me knowingly. *Brave*, he was thinking. He thought I was brave. He was wrong. His wings wrapped around me and a hand held my fingers tightly —a hand that I knew somehow... Lysanael. I gripped his hand back and curled into Arkyn's body as sobs shook me and the darkness refused to come.

Over and over the memories came and went, brought new ones I'd forgotten into view.

So much grief. So many feelings.

Not all of them bad, but each and every one of them enough to overwhelm me. I was falling again. I'd lost hold of Lys and Arkyn. The feelings besieged me, hit me from every side and angle. I had no defense. Curling into a ball as I dropped into the bright, colored madness, I screamed and screamed and screamed. There was no fighting this onslaught and so I let the rage, sadness, lust, love, desire, fear, hope, frustration, and longing wash over me like a great wave. It took me under and I couldn't breathe. My right hand felt warm scales. My left held Lys's hand once more. I opened my mouth, my heart, my soul and let the storm in.

❧ 44 ❧

LYSANAEL

Her body twitched and thrashed in her delirium and he held her hand like she was the one who could save him. Because she was. Hells, what had this amazing woman been through and survived? He'd thought the Fae court was the worst of the world, but the words she uttered, snippets of what had to be memories, stole his breath and chilled him to the bone.

Master would die. He would see to that. The king was also living on borrowed time. They would feel her wrath and he would not rest until she was satisfied with her revenge.

His blood boiled as her life spilled from her lips in phrases that spoke of a child's broken bones, Master's lies and mind-twisting acts, lost loved ones, and the horrors Revna had been forced to be a part of when she was no more than Gwyn's age. He squeezed his eyes shut, his muscles coiling with the desire to tear from the Druid's home and ride the wind to Saxonion and destroy those who had done these terrible things to his mate.

But for now, he had to keep hold of her; he had to help the Druid continue whispering his magic into her death curse or he would lose her before their lives had even had the chance to begin.

I opened my eyes and licked my lips, tasting the salt of tears and sweat. Arkyn rested on my thigh and Lys sat beside me, still holding my hand as he had been during my hallucinations or whatever that had been. Lys smiled, but his eyes were on fire with rage.

My Berserker blood sizzled through my veins and I gripped his fingers, feeling his bones shift under my too-rough hold. Every inch of me wanted to touch every inch of him. I wanted to listen to every story he had to tell and I longed to spill my every thought.

"I…" My words stuck in my throat and he helped me to sit up.

"I know." His voice was honey and woodsmoke.

Arkyn lifted his head and shifted back as Lys took my face in his hands. Lys kissed each of my eyelids, his lips soft and at such odds with the anger that had flashed through his gaze.

"We have time now," he said. "You are free."

I pulled away and looked toward the Druid, who stood at the far side of his one-room house, tending to a small smoking cauldron set onto a candle of sorts. "Did you succeed?"

The Druid glanced at me over his shoulder. His eyes nearly glowed in the dim light, the magical tree flickering over his wrinkled features. "What do you think, Berserker? How do you feel?"

I touched the back of my neck and felt... "It's gone." I swallowed air, gasping, unshed tears searing my eyes.

Arkyn shuffled forward, his wings cramped between a black stool and a tower of wooden crates. He sniffed the back of my neck and his hot dragon breath made my hair stick to my skin. With a grunt of approval, he licked my cheek.

"I can't believe it." Was I truly free from Master and King Darrew? I felt everything at once—a dizzying relief, fierce joy at what might happen next, and a gut-wrenching fear that this might be a mistake and I wasn't free after all. "It's so much." I balled my fist and pushed it against my stomach in an attempt to ease the nausea. My blood was sparking up and down my body, not like I was about to go wild with violence, but as if I was more alive now and my blood wanted to sing and shout and scream about it all.

"Take this," the Druid said, pushing a cup at me.

Lys helped me to drink. My hands shook like a madman's. The drink was bitter but had the aftertaste of vanilla and something smoky.

The Druid watched me take a second sip of the warm liquid. "It will help you calm yourself and sort through the emotions. I've never seen someone so blocked in heart and soul."

He kept talking, explaining how the death rune had been woven into the way I'd been trained and the manner in which Master had twisted my mind as a child. The Druid went on to talk about the complexity of the Witch's work on the rune and how I would most likely need to visit him now and again to be sure the rune didn't reappear and take my life when I least suspected it.

I barely listened. It was too much. It was all too much.

I don't know when but the Druid and Lys had started discussing the drumstones. I drank down the rest of the brew the earth wizard had given me and we all sat on stools around the magical tree. Arkyn gave me a nod, then went outside, probably to stretch his wings.

"The drumstones are far more active than I've seen in ages. They need a blood rune to seal them once more," the Druid said. "The last seal worked fairly well for three hundred years. For years after the seal was set, we saw no Unseelie at all. Of course, the blood breaks down in the weather and fighting the dark Unseelie magic."

I wondered if the Druid knew that Lys had Unseelie blood. It didn't seem like he did, but maybe he was protecting his king by keeping it from me. He wouldn't know that I was aware of Lys's secret.

Lys glanced at me then at the Druid. "How does the sealing work?"

Taking a shimmering leaf from the magical tree, the Druid blinked. "Well, it begins by capturing a powerful Unseelie." He smoothed the veins of the leaf he'd plucked, then blew on it. The leaf transformed into a bat and flew out the window. "I've sent a message to my apprentice. Perhaps he's seen signs of an Unseelie high Fae at some point in the northeastern lands."

Lys looked at me, a question in his eyes. I thought maybe he wanted my opinion on whether or not to expose himself. Could he trust the Druid?

"What are the signs of an Unseelie high Fae?" Lys asked.

"You've never seen one?" I asked Lys. Aside from looking in a mirror, perhaps he hadn't.

He shook his head. His wary gaze went to the window where the bat had slipped away.

The Druid spread his hands, and a flickering emerald scene appeared between them. A drumstone sat in a glen and shimmering indigo footsteps led from the stone into the scene's misty hills.

"Though the Unseelie high Fae look much like you, my king, and all of our people here in the Realm of Lights, they do not dress as we do," the Druid explained. "They wear very little and certainly not any shoes. Where they step, they leave an impression of their magic. It is a temporary thing and difficult to track certainly, but I've seen the prints once before in the Shrouded Mountains and again near your hunting lodge, my king, though that was when you were just a toddling littleling."

Near his lodge? Could that have been his father?

The Druid dropped his hands and the image dissipated, the magic scattering like stars. He raised an eyebrow. "We must use the Unseelie high Fae blood to rebuild the seal and more firmly divide the realms."

"How much do you need?" Lys asked. "Is it a matter of painting runes on the drumstones with the blood? How many stones must be sealed?"

"They are connected in their power, so to seal one is to seal them all. Yes, we paint runes in blood on the stone," the Druid said, "but we must also pour a measure around the drumstone while reciting the sealing spell."

Lys's gaze dropped to the floor. "I must tell you something about myself, Druid. If it can help our people survive and rid us of the destructive Unseelie, I can't hold back my secret any longer."

"I am your servant, my king." The Druid clasped his hands and set them in his lap, adopting the pose of a patient listener.

"My mother, the former queen, set out to gain more power through dark magic. She went so far as to break her marriage vows with the king. My mother welcomed a high Unseelie Fae into her bed and I am the product of that foul union."

A small gasp issued from the Druid's lips, and his hands gripped his knees through his long robes. He looked toward the window as if in thought then said, "I had no idea that a union between a Seelie and an Unseelie could produce offspring, let alone a person such as yourself, King Lysanael. When did you find out?"

"You've heard the talk, I'm sure. The tale of me murdering my own mother."

"I have."

"It's true. She brought me deep into the Gwerhune when I was still a youth and attempted to end my life there. My fear and grief sparked my Unseelie power and I shifted into the form of a peak raven. I shifted here, just outside, when the giant attacked while you were healing Gwyn."

Crossing his arms and tugging at his beard with one hand, the Druid hummed. "Fascinating. Will you do it now? I'd love to see it. Oh, no, of course not. You must return to the keep and deal with your council."

"They will be in full rebellion if I don't return soon." Lys faced me. "We have a great deal of work in front of us if we are to wed."

My stomach fluttered at the burning look in his eyes. He wanted me. "I need time to think about all of this. Will you make me queen? I have no idea how to be a queen." My mouth was dry as dust. "And I'm still angry with you, Lys, even though you did save my life today."

Lys dropped to his knees and tilted his head to gaze up at me. "Forgive me. I was a madman. I have a list of excuses, but I won't spill them onto your heart now. I was a fool."

The Druid's lips lifted into a grin as he left us and went to work at his potion table.

I stared at Lys, at this Fae king kneeling before me. "I can't deny the love I feel for you or the incredibly powerful connection." My blood simmered and I flushed. I longed to run my fingers through his long black hair and I wanted to drop into his arms. "But my anger remains. I want to let it go, but I feel like it has me in its grip."

"You only just now found the ability to feel properly, assassin," the Druid said over the clinking of glass vials. "Do not smother your rage or you will grow tangled again. The rune could return. I doubt it, but it is possible."

Lys reached for me and I set my cheek against his large palm. "I can grovel daily until you feel amenable to me once more. I am more than happy to do it. I will bloody these knees for you, my viper."

I couldn't fight the smile that tugged at my mouth. "I love a good groveling."

Light sparked in his eyes and he grinned. "I will beg for forgiveness in one thousand ways."

Reaching up, he drew his thumb over my chin, then

ran a finger down my throat, between my breasts, and down to my stomach. My skin pebbled and my desire burned hotter than my anger.

I did my best to loom over him though his head was level with my chest even while on his knees. "Let's return to the keep and you can grovel there. We will take this hour by hour."

Standing, he took my hand, turned it over, and brushed his lips over my palm. "I will do exactly as you order, Queen Viper."

I raised an eyebrow, pleasure rising in my chest. "Oh, I quite like that title."

"And will you agree to marry me?"

His eyes softened, and I touched his lip with my thumb. His lids shuttered briefly and then he looked at me again, worry showing in the tightness at the edges of his gaze.

"If the groveling is sufficient, I'll consider it." I couldn't hold back my smile as my heart nearly burst just looking at him. These new feelings were like the sun at high noon, too bright. Too much. But I wasn't about to let Master take this from me too. I had been locked up, unable to make my own choices. "I would love to marry you, King Lysanael Oakthorn." I reached up and kissed him. He tasted like Fae wine. I pulled away, then grabbed his tunic. "No more secrets."

"No more secrets." He drew me close, his chest on mine, then he pressed another gentle kiss to my lips. He whispered my name, his left fang lightly touching my bottom lip as he spoke. "I will work my entire life—every heartbeat, every step, every word—to be worthy of you."

Happiness galloped through me and I let it run wild, stretching my mouth into a wide smile. His features echoed mine and he took my hands as we faced the Druid.

With a few more words to the wizard, we were off for the keep, where the council would be waiting, fuming, ready to destroy at least me but possibly the both of us.

LYSANAEL

After they'd bathed and dressed in court finery, Lysanael took Revna's arm and escorted her into the throne room.

Earlier, the Druid had arrived at the castle to discuss sealing the drumstones, insisting that Lysanael learn the words to say and how to draw the runes in his half-Unseelie blood. Lysanael had listened carefully, but the Druid had been forced to teach the ancient spell work to him at least ten times before Lysanael had been able to mimic the process. He hoped the Druid would be there when the time came to do the sealing. Magic like that didn't come naturally to Fae like it did to the rare Druid. Regardless, the earth wizard had done right by coming. If push came to shove, Lysanael would be as ready as possible.

As Revna walked with Lysanael, he marveled at her posture of power and the cool gaze she set on the openly gaping courtiers who never once suspected Lysanael would choose a human for a mate. Revna appeared as comfortable in this imposing chamber as she did dragging a blade through a gargoyle. Such an amazing female, so multifaceted. The meaning of her name, raven, linked them in a way neither of them truly understood. Revna was also his viper, a vicious creature that struck with venom. And she was a female, one of frightening beauty and complicated mind.

He would have already been blissful with the idea of their nuptials if the threat of the council's response to his choice of mate and the mystery of how the human king and Revna's Master would retaliate weren't pressing on his mind and soul.

She glanced up, her eyes like the purest ice. He permitted himself a quick look down her lovely body, relishing the idea of worshipping her flesh at a point in the very near future.

"Every council member agreed to meet here?" Her lips twitched like she was fighting a laugh. "They have to be absolutely incensed."

"Yes, and I'm sure they are. But it's long past time for me to reassert my dominance over them. Let them see me as the terrible King of the Fae who flouts all tradition and refuses to be tamed."

Her eyes sparkled with mischief, and what he hoped was desire lowered her lids a fraction. "I dare them to test you. I hope they do. I'd love to watch the show."

Chuckling, he leaned down and brushed his lips

over her smooth temple. "I will be sure to provide you fine entertainment." He would do anything to keep that naughty smile on her face.

An upstairs maid with two horns that curled about her pointed ears walked toward them. She dropped into a low bow and though her movements were quick, Lysanael didn't miss the fact that she had slipped a tiny piece of parchment to Revna.

Revna opened the note while they walked on.

"What is it?" he asked.

"She made the sign of the Hunters." Revna showed Lysanael by holding two fingers against her hip, then went back to reading the note. "The maid…she will report to Master that I am successfully in your trust." She looked up, worry etched into her features. "She doesn't know my rune is gone. I don't know if Master or the Witch will be able to tell. I suppose I shouldn't stop the contact from going back to Isernwyrd with news of my success in fooling you." She raised an eyebrow and pursed her lips. "It may buy us time."

They both knew at some point Master or the human king would come for her. *Let them try.* Lysanael and Revna had been over this a dozen times already and hashed out the possibilities.

Two guards opened the back door to the throne room and the layered carpets on the floor muffled his and Revna's slow and measured steps. The court was in attendance, a multitude of familiar faces glancing their way before bows and curtseys were performed.

Lysanael and Revna climbed the dais, but as planned, he did not sit on his throne. She had no seat and he didn't want her to feel out of place. This would be a short meeting regardless.

The doors beyond the gathered court burst open. The council strode in, faces grim. Old Bornien, his eyes swollen as if he'd had little sleep, led the way. Yonnis smoothed his silver hair away from his face as he followed a step behind, his twin, Corae, like a shadow behind him. The council formed a crescent at the base of the dais.

Lysanael's heart beat a staccato rhythm between his ribs. Would they rebel? "Welcome, Lord Bornien," he said, keeping his voice smooth and even. "I hope you and your fellows come to offer congratulations on my announcement."

Bornien's frown answered that—not that Lysanael had truly expected a change of heart. "My lord king." He bowed and the rest of the council did as well. Lysanael's old friend looked up then, his gaze imploring. "While the council is pleased you have at last come around to the idea of a wedding and taking a mate, we must respectfully withhold our approval of your chosen bride."

Bornien had the decency to put a hand to his chest and bow his head in apology to Revna. That was more than any other council member would do. The rest of them eyed her like the viper she was. Good. They needed to be afraid.

Yonnis edged past Bornien, and Corae took up the spot at Yonnis's elbow. "King Lysanael, never in the history of the Realm of Lights has the Fae king taken a human as his wife. It is not done and will not be done. We have no idea if such a pairing would even fulfill the magic's requirement that you produce an heir to retain our powers."

The green-fleshed Gorgel glared, nostrils flaring. "This is insupportable. We cannot permit such a union. You have gone too far, King Lysanael."

The other council members stared at Lysanael as if they were in full agreement.

Heat built in Lysanael's blood and he wondered if that's how Revna's Berserker power felt when roused. He gave her a small smile, then left her side to walk slowly down one step so that he stood over Yonnis's head. They never would have spoken to the former king, Lysanael's stepfather, in this way. He had nothing good to say about the former king—a Fae thoroughly distant and just as cruel as Lysanael's mother had been —but he had kept the council firmly under his thumb. Lysanael had been lackadaisical about his reign for too long. The time had come to rise up and be the true king.

"I'm certain I misheard your words, Lord Yonnis, Lord Gorgel." Lysanael's anger sharpened his words as they left his lips. "Do repeat yourself."

Yonnis's hands fisted at his sides and Gorgel's throat moved in a swallow.

"What if this…choice of yours means that all Fae

lose their magic?" Yonnis toyed with one of his many rings, a sign of nervousness.

"That response was markedly shorter. I do think I missed something. And Lord Gorgel, what was it you said? I have *gone too far*? Interesting. I thought I was your crowned king and that my every word was law."

The lord's eyes widened and he flinched, his gaze flicking to the mace and sword at Lysanael's belt.

Lysanael descended one more step and let his hand hang on his mace, the black adamant of the barbed weapon cooling his fingers. "I'm fairly certain you told your king what will and will not be done."

Yonnis paled and dropped to one knee. He tucked his chin. "I didn't intend to offend Your Majesty."

Bornien held up his hands. "My lord king, surely you can understand our concern. To be stripped of our magic might end us all."

"Do you not suppose I have thought of that, Lord Bornien?" He didn't loom over Bornien because he respected the fellow, but he didn't blink as he met the lord's wise eyes. "Do you not think that my people are always at the forefront of my thoughts and actions?"

Lysanael turned and looked to the side door of the throne room. Exactly as they'd planned it, the Druid opened the door and entered to a rush of gasps and murmured exclamations. Many had never laid eyes on the Druid except from afar during the long-ago wars. He was more legend than person to most.

"Druid, welcome to my court," Lysanael said as the earth wizard made his way through the crowd like a ship's prow through the sea. "Will you explain to my council what you told Lady Resaynia and me at your abode?"

The Druid positioned himself beside the council, then he bowed to Lysanael and dipped his head to Revna as well. His long robes gathered on the ground around his feet and he had drawn blue runes over his cheeks, making him appear even more otherworldly than usual. The light of his magic glowed about his fingers and wrists.

"When these two came to me, I saw that they were fated mates."

A shocked hush fell over the room.

Bornien's mouth fell open while Yonnis and the other council members traded looks of astonishment. "In the sense that they are already bound in spirit by prophecy?" Bornien asked.

The Druid nodded. "It is so. I have seen it. Furthermore, when our king accepted the bond in his heart, a choice one makes without truly knowing it, he thereby adopted an heir."

All eyes turned toward Revna.

She grinned. "As I'm sure you know, I have a dragon familiar. It seems familiars are as bonded to a soul as offspring. Although I doubt Arkyn has any desire to reign over the Fae realm, it is within his power to do just that."

The room erupted into arguing and shouts of confusion.

Lysanael held up his hands and silence poured over the crowd. "We are not fools. Dragons have far finer things to do than deal in politics." A few chuckles peppered the court. "But with this bonding and his life, he fulfills the magic's demand for an heir and so our powers are secured."

A cheer rose up and Lysanael felt his mouth spread into a smile. He faced Revna, and her dancing eyes warmed him from head to foot.

"But of course," Bornien said once the crowd had quieted, "you still plan to marry and produce a high Fae heir, my lord king?"

"We do." Lysanael didn't bother to mask his pride.

The Druid raised a palm that glittered with emerald power. "Rest assured, the offspring of these two would retain Fae capabilities. You see, Lady Resaynia is no ordinary human."

Curious gazes fell on Revna and she raised her chin. "I have the blood of the ancient Berserkers of Fjordbok. Magic simmers in me as well."

Excited conversation bounced off the high ceiling.

"And," the Druid said, "such power will only make King Lysanael's magic stronger when they bear littlelings."

At the Druid's house, Revna had been quick to state that she would not be forced to bear littlelings no matter what the outcome. Lys had agreed, of course. After all,

Gwyn could inherit the throne if they never did have offspring of their own. But the court and council didn't need to fret about that. It was his and Revna's private business.

A thrill ricocheted through him at the thought of having a life with her, of experiencing their own private world of adventure, pleasure, and joy. He glanced her way and found her staring. The heat in her eyes made breathing evenly difficult and turned his attention to activities that had nothing at all to do with courts or councils. He could hardly stand the wait to have her in his arms in the darkness of their wedding night.

Lysanael held a hand out for Revna, and she descended the steps to join him and take his arm. "Now," he said, facing the council, "bow to your king and the one who will be your queen or you may choose to lose your head this day. It matters little to me." A truer word had never been spoken. He loathed this room of deceivers and grasping nobles.

The courtiers and council dropped in obeisance, Gorgel and Yonnis the last to bend the knee.

Finally, it was time for a wedding. Lysanael had to laugh at himself. Never had he thought to be excited for such an event.

❧ 47 ❧

REVNA

My head whirled with everything that had happened during the last seven days. I hadn't seen Lysanael at all, a period of separation being required by the Fae for the marriage ritual. Honestly, I was glad for the space because my emotions remained chaotic and I swung from gleefully excited about my future with Lysanael to boiling with rage about all the damage Master had done and how to exact revenge. Because I would have it.

Unlocking my feelings had been necessary and good, I knew that, but I felt raw. At first, even the light of a lovely morning was too bright, Arkyn's playful growls too loud, and every touch from my well-meaning handmaids too harsh. But oddly enough, when I began to feel the need to curl into a very prickly ball, armed and ready to hiss and spit, my Berserker blood simmered and burned the overload away. I never could have predicted that. I'd always guessed letting all of my emotions out to play would have me on a murderous rampage in seconds.

"Stop fidgeting, Lady Resaynia," Sonaellyn said quietly as she pulled my hair into yet another elaborate looped braid.

"Apologies." I set my hands on my thighs and watched her reflection work in the polished metal surface set on my table. "Do you have a smaller reflective piece? I'd like to see my neck again."

A sad smile crossed Sonaellyn's face and she bent to rummage in the bag she brought into my rooms daily. She retrieved a circle of finely polished silver, handed it to me, and lifted my half-up styled hair. I held the silver piece at an angle with the one in front of me so I could once again view the bare skin at the base of my skull. Seeing the absence of my death rune never stopped unraveling the tightness in my chest, a vice that had gripped me ever since the Witch set the mark on me with Master looking on. I still didn't know quite how the Druid had accomplished it. The earth wizard had only said that good magic of the soul and the earth can always wash the evil from the past.

What did Master think now? That I was dead? Truly, if Master had wanted me dead from the death rune, I would already be cold in the ground. One thing I knew for certain, that rune could drop someone in a heartbeat. Perhaps Master had merely started the process of enacting the rune to give me pain and remind me of my mission. A bit of *Get to work, Hunter* type of thing.

Or did Master believe the rune had finished its job and killed me? I wished I would have asked more questions about the rune and the details of how it functioned, what sign it gave Master and the Witch when it worked its dark magic.

Had the maid—the one who had passed me the note on the day Lys confronted the council—delivered the message that I had ingratiated myself with the Fae king? She'd surely heard more news since and had to be doubting my drive to kill Lys. If not, she wasn't a very good spy.

I handed the silver circle to Sonaellyn and she returned it to her bag. She removed a wooden box and opened it to show me a golden arm cuff. An array of silver and gold links hung from one side of the cuff to the other. She slid it onto my upper arm and the links brushed my skin softly.

"You have such strong arms, my lady," she said kindly.

"They were hard earned."

"I'm sure." She bowed her head in a show of respect that surprised me. "As were those scars." Her finger glanced across one Raulian accidentally gave me during our first bladed sparring match when we were both around eleven years old. "You are the perfect queen for our vicious king."

I grinned and she studied the arm cuff.

"What's that twinkle in your eye mean, Sonaellyn?"

A full grin pulled her lips wide, and her orange cheeks dimpled. "King Lysanael designed this piece of jewelry for you. Do you see the lovely doves on the end of this metal loop?"

This craftsmanship… I ran a finger over the detailed shapes of the cool metal. The Fae from the market—the one who'd made my torc and Lys's—had created this too. I would have bet on it. I smiled as Sonaellyn continued.

"I don't know what the doves signify," she said, "but I am guessing they mean fated love somehow. Usually an animal denotes that rare and special bond for the Fae. These hares tell of his respect for you since they are the animal on his sigil ring and his coat of arms. And these stars," she said, the twinkle rising in her eyes again, "these stars are telling of how much he desires you. Stars are the symbol of physical longing, my lady."

Heat rose in my cheeks and sped down my torso, gathering in my belly. I turned and lifted the links to squint at the various charms hanging from the cuff. The birds were peak ravens, not doves, but I wasn't about to correct her, of course. No one except Neeria and the Druid knew of Lys's Unseelie power or his demon blood. Lys and I planned to meet the Druid out of view after our ceremony and seal the drumstones with Lys's blood.

Malaynia hurried over with my dress. "Quickly now."

They worked it over my head, which wasn't difficult seeing as the neckline boasted a dramatically deep drop in the front and just barely hung from my shoulders. The fabric was the softest material—some textile we didn't possess in Saxonion—and it was the exact shade of Lys's eyes.

Someone knocked at the door. "Can't keep me away, I'm afraid." Neeria's musical voice sounded through the carved wood.

I nodded and Malaynia opened the door to allow my soon-to-be sister inside. She rushed forward and took my hands. Her eyes were positively luminous.

"You are beauty incarnate, Lady Resaynia. Our king is going to rush the ritual to get his hands on you."

A laugh bubbled from my throat, and my heart warmed as Neeria hugged me then released me to more of Malaynia and Sonaellyn's ministrations.

"I hope so. I was never a fan of ceremony," I said.

Malaynia tsked me. "It is a very important one to our people."

Nodding, I patted her hand. "I'll behave. I promise."

An image of Lysanael washed through my mind, his hand grasping mine, his fingers sliding down my throat. A shiver ran down my body. Thankfully, the others didn't seem to notice my distraction.

Neeria took a cup of Fae wine from another servant who had entered when I wasn't paying attention. She held it out and I sniffed it. Sonaellyn insisted on sipping it and making me wait to see if she suffered any ill effects. Once we were fairly sure it was safe, Neeria made me drink the goblet in full. I didn't mind the lightheadedness. It took the edge off my whirling mind and winding emotions.

"It's time, Sister." Neeria hugged me again, then she placed a coronet on my brow.

I wasn't yet queen—that would have to wait until our marriage and mating were confirmed—but Lys had wanted me looking like his queen today.

Bronze peaks reached from the coronet outward and some had been fashioned into the shape of wheat and grapevines. A few were styled into roses, their edges gilded with bright gold.

"This is madness. Me being a queen," I said more to myself than any of them, but they all responded at once, interrupting one another.

"You have the blood of ancient warriors. You will lead us well if that human king tries anything," Malaynia said. "The marriage bond will protect you both too."

"How?" I asked.

"None can use your true names against you after you are bonded at the menhir. That magic will never work against either of you after you are bonded."

I blinked at that. "That is great news." It had to be another reason the Fae insisted on their rulers marrying.

Sonaellyn moved a hair that must have been out of place. "King Lysanael wouldn't have been fated to you if you weren't meant for this role."

"He loves you. You love him." Neeria had tears in her eyes. "That's truly the only thing that matters. Now, let's get going."

It was time for me to wed the king I had been ordered to kill.

✣ 48 ✣

LYSANAEL

Flanked by his foul, pretty-faced cousins, Lysanael stood awaiting his bride. Gyrion, his steward, hadn't stopped rearranging his golden hair or barking orders to servants since they'd dismounted here, deep in the Gwerhune. A circle of chrysanthemums had been laid out, mimicking the mushrooms that ringed the menhir stone. The menhir stood a foot lower than Lysanael's head, and in the center, about stomach-high, a circular opening passed all the way through the middle of the ancient magical stone. The circle played an important part of this ritual.

When the bustling servants halted in strewing petals and other nonsense and the courtiers turned to face the path leading to the menhir, he knew Revna had arrived.

His heart flew into his throat. Dressed in the deepest shades of the forest and wearing a coronet that made her look like the Berserker goddess she was, his love walked toward him slowly, gracefully. The way her dress clung to her curves shot fire through his veins as if he held Fjordbok magic.

He would tear down a world to bring a smile to her lips. All she need do was ask.

The cuff he had designed for her—crafted by the always amazing Alaina—pleased him to no end. He would never say it aloud, but he loved how the cuff marked Revna as his. She was too strong to truly belong to anyone, but at least for this morning she wore his sigil symbols, the stars that showed his desire for her in body and soul, and the marks of his respect for her.

She came close, her golden slippers peeking from the drape of her gown, then she met his gaze. "Can we have a moment to ourselves before we continue?"

Gyrion's eyes widened and he opened his mouth, surely to argue against this break of tradition, so Lysanael held up a hand to silence him.

"As you wish, my viper."

He took her arm and escorted her past the gawking crowd and tittering courtiers. The fall-hued boughs of the Gwerhune stretched high overhead and soon the only sounds were those of a herd of moss deer nibbling down the animal path a ways from them and the snick of leaves trailing from the canopy to cluster underfoot. Revna's gaze flew over the emerald and gold coats of moss on the deer's backs and flanks and the white fur that graced their necks and heads. She smiled and shook her head as if still in disbelief at the Gwerhune. Then she faced Lysanael and he fought the urge to pull her to him and feel the warmth of her against his body.

She swallowed, and he enjoyed the way her gaze flitted from his partially bare chest to his jaw then to his eyes. "What will our lives be like? How is this going to work?"

"It will work as you see fit," he answered. Her throat begged to be kissed, the smooth skin beckoning.

"I must help my people."

"We will go to Fjordbok whenever you wish. I can either facilitate rebuilding and fortifying defenses there or we can aid them in relocating to our kingdom."

The light that danced across her ice blue eyes sent his pulse racing. "Thank you. We should ask them."

"Of course. You will be a wise queen."

She shook her head, once again showing disbelief. He took both her hands and held them between their chests. He wanted her to feel the true beat of his heart.

"I mean it, Revna," he whispered.

Her eyes shuttered closed and she pressed her forehead against his. "I know you do. The human king may come for me."

Heat sparked along his forehead and anger built like a blaze in his chest. "Let him come. We will defeat him and I will set his head at your feet."

"I don't want to start a war, but of course, he is the one who framed you."

"Yes. He began this fight long before you had it in your head to leave his…service," Lysanael spat out.

An amiable growl—more like a large cat's purr—sounded behind them. They turned to see Arkyn landing on the fire-colored leaves. He lifted his snout and let out a grunt.

"Nice of you to show up," Revna said, going to him and rubbing his chin. "Any questions we should ask the king before we are forever bound?"

Arkyn eyed Lysanael, which made Lysanael pause, feeling nervous. Lysanael bowed his head. "I will answer whatever you ask, Sir Dragon."

The dragon stalked toward him, then stopped his snout barely an inch from Lysanael's nose. Arkyn turned one bright, unblinking eye on Lysanael. Was he going to attack? Show dominance somehow? Perhaps Lysanael needed to do so? He certainly could if that was what the creature required.

A quiet growl issued from Arkyn, and Lysanael held his ground. The creature made a series of clicking sounds with his tongue and the upper part of his throat. Arkyn glanced at Revna, then at Lysanael again, and the way his brow moved and the eye roved Lysanael's face, the dragon seemed to be saying *Hurt her and I will kill you.*

"Arkyn." Revna's voice held a request and a warning.

Lysanael held out his palm and Arkyn set his snout against his hand. "Don't worry. I live for her now."

He glanced up to see Revna's eyes shining with

happiness. Arkyn trotted back to Revna, brushed his wing over her back, then took off into the canopy.

Revna joined Lysanael where he stood watching the dragon fly away. Leaves floated down from the point of his exit far above.

"Tell me about being a Berserker," he said quietly. "I know that your blood rises and the magic in it gives you great strength and speed. I've seen that in action and I've heard the tales of old. But how does it feel when your power is banked? What helps your power rise up?"

"Anger." Her finger ran along the embroidered phoenixes, hares, and ravens on the edge of his floor-length open tunic. "My magic sits deep inside me, like a coiled snake."

"Fitting metaphor."

A smile pulled at one side of her delicious lips. He loved how her top lip stuck out farther than her lower one. The desire to nibble at it was nearly unbearable.

"But yes, anger wakes it and then it is very difficult to control." Her eyes widened a fraction and her finger stopped its exploration of his tunic. "It can be very dangerous. I have injured friends and I once killed someone by mistake."

"Who did you injure?"

"I hurt Raulian, my one friend at Isernwyrd."

Lysanael studied her face. Regret showed in the line between her eyebrows. "How badly?"

"I broke his arm," she said.

"Was he upset with you?"

She laughed at some memory she didn't share. "No. He...Raulian isn't like that."

"I would love to meet him."

Her gaze snapped to his face. "Oh, you will. Once we are through here... Well, I have plans."

"What else should I know about your power?" He took hold of her hips and brought her body to him. Relishing the feel of her warmth against him, he brushed his lips over her bare shoulder. Her skin pebbled and he delighted in the powers that he possessed.

"The other thing that wakes my Berserker blood is lust."

"Oooh." He purred against the outer shell of her round human ear and felt her shift against his stomach and chest. His tongue touched the lobe of her ear and his fingers dug into her hips.

She made a soft gasping sound that had his body growing far too hot to worry about any sort of ritual. He pulled away to see her open her eyes very slowly.

"We should return. Unless..." He raised an eyebrow in question. If she wanted to take him here in the middle of the Gwerhune, he would do as she pleased. In his mind, he was already her husband. They were mates, now and forever.

She squeezed his bicep and gazed up at him through her eyelashes. "Let's head back. I want every last one of those fools out there to know I'm yours and you're mine."

Heat lashed through him, hot and delightful, and he lunged for her neck, setting his lips across her collarbone. "I like the possessive side of you," he purred.

Grinning, she broke away, took his hand, and led him back to the menhir and the waiting court. He didn't bother suppressing a chuckle at how put out they all appeared to be.

Sonaellyn and Malaynia fussed with Revna's coronet while he waved off Celin. He refused to be fancied up in front of the court. Revna must have felt the same because she thanked her maids graciously but firmly sent them on their way.

Gyrion announced them and started to speak the words of the ceremony as Revna took a spot on the far side of the menhir and Lysanael stood on the near side. They reached through the hole in the sacred stone and clasped fingers.

The wedding ritual had begun.

49

REVNA

I couldn't get enough of looking at him. My Fae king. My mate. I nearly laughed, which probably would have all these Fae eyeing me like I'd lost my mind. It was absolutely wild to stand here, in the process of marrying one of the most powerful beings in the world, a male who, despite being my target for assassination, had awoken my sleeping heart and driven me to break the chains locking down my soul.

He had freed me from Isernwyrd, from Master, from King Darrew. I would see to it that every Hunter visited the Druid and had their death rune removed. We would all be free.

One corner of Lys's lips lifted and his gaze smoldered, making my body hum with anticipation of the night to come. He wore a deep green cloak that pooled on the autumn leaves piled around the sacred site, and a ground-sweeping tunic graced his body, open, of course, to show off his fine physique as was the custom. Black as night, his trousers hugged his strong thighs, and dark boots reached to his knees. His brow held the same crown from the first day of the Branle—a dark adamant creation with skystones decorating its peaked sides.

We both wore our torcs and I took a moment to nod to the craftsfae female, Alaina, who had fashioned them, the kind one I'd met at the market. She grinned at me, her wrinkles bunching. Lys had said Alaina was an old friend of his, a tutor of sorts who had taught him to work gold during lessons as a child.

Lys's thumb dragged slowly across my knuckles as Gyrion droned on with a load of archaic words about promises and vows. The golden-haired Fae steward threaded a braided length of emerald-hued wool through the menhir's hole and wrapped it around our joined hands.

"Once separate," Gyrion said over my head, "your two lives are now joined forevermore."

Lys's gaze never wavered. The intensity warmed my belly and sent a flush into my cheeks.

"King Lysanael, please voice your desire to mate with this female." Gyrion stepped back, giving us space.

"I, King Lysanael Oakthorn of the Realm of Lights, do wish to mate with this female. I find her to be my heart's desire, my body's demand, and my soul's song."

The vows were told to us beforehand, but hearing him say them gave the words so much more meaning. I took a shuddering breath, a small part of me wishing I could use that lock to hold back my emotions once more. I didn't want to show weakness before the court.

"Lady Resaynia, please voice your desire to mate with this male," Gyrion said.

Arkyn's clicking sounded across the leaf-covered ground and through the quiet crowd. I smiled his way before gazing at Lys.

"I, Resaynia Fjordbok of Saxonion, do wish to mate with this male. I find him to be my heart's desire, my body's demand, and my soul's song."

The scent of the forest—dying leaves, damp soil, and late-blooming autumn flowers—strengthened and Lys's nostrils flared. Sparks of indigo magic danced over our joined hands and a deep satisfaction filled me, relaxed me, rejuvenated me.

We were bound.

Joy shone in Lys's eyes, and Old Ones save me, I just could not stop a tear from trailing down my cheek. How was this my life?

Mother, I said silently, *I will see your last wish fulfilled. This king will fight for us. Bless him, Mother.*

A breeze brushed across my cheek, cool and soothing. I pretended it was her saying *Yes.*

Gyrion removed the braided wool from our hands very carefully, keeping the knot in place. Lys walked to my side of the menhir and I recalled what we were supposed to say in unison as we turned to face each cardinal direction. Gyrion rewrapped our hands.

"To the east, we give our breath," we said, his voice low and rumbling under mine. We shifted, facing Saxonion. "To the south, we give our passion." Rotating toward the western side of the Realm of Lights, we said, "To the west, we give our tears." At last, we faced the direction of the northern regions where the Shrouded Mountains loomed. "To the north, we give our bodies."

Gyrion led us to a stone basin of water that reflected the orange, red, and yellow colors of the canopy. He drew a palmful of water and poured it over our bound hands. "These two are fasted and none shall break their bond. Rise up and greet your king and the lady who will be our queen."

Lys slipped the knotted fasting braid off our hands, slid it into his cloak, then took me in his arms and threw me backward into a dramatic kiss. His mouth was soft but insistent. Fire blazed through my veins as his breath mingled with mine. One of his hands cupped the back of my head and the other splayed across my hip. We straightened as the crowd cheered. Tossing acorns and bits of bread that symbolized fertility, the courtiers shouted bawdy phrases. Even Bornien waved a hand and gave me a smile. The rest of the council…well, that would take a while.

Lys followed me to Arkyn and we climbed onto his back to the continued shouts of congratulations.

Then the sacred site burst into chaos.

50

REVNA

Unseelie exploded into the crowd, throwing Fae and clawing at the knights who had been on guard at the edges of the ceremony. Scorpions the size of Arkyn, trolls as wide as houses and with drooling mouths and meaty fists, giants wielding clubs, and gargoyles with clawed paws and burning eyes filled the formerly peaceful place.

Lys and I ran to Neeria and Gwyn, then dragged them toward Arkyn and pushed them onto his back before we mounted.

"Up, Arkyn." I slapped his side and he launched into the air above the madness. I unsheathed my sword. "Take us to that oak."

I eyed a thick fork in one of the many massive trees, a perfect place for Neeria and Gwyn to remain out of reach. Arkyn flew us so high our heads brushed the canopy.

"Stay here," I said.

Neeria and Gwyn seemed to understand because they hopped from the dragon to the tree limb quickly.

Lys's breath dusted over my ear and his thighs pressed against mine. "Get me to the nearest drumstone. It's just south of the menhir." He slid his mace free of his belt loop and unsheathed his sword.

Arkyn swooped low and I swung at a giant's blocky skull. Lopping off an ear, I dodged his defensive strike. Arkyn tilted his wings and flew higher. Lys held to Arkyn with his legs and leaned farther than I could have managed. He whipped his mace at a gargoyle who had taken flight beside us. The mace cracked the gargoyle's outstretched paw. The beast howled in fury, only dropping back momentarily before coming at us with rage in its beady eyes.

"Faster, Arkyn!"

My dagger slipped easily from my new thigh sheath and I threw it at the gargoyle, my blood rising and lashing like the wind of a coming storm. The dagger struck the monster's throat. Blood surged from the wound. The beast gurgled and dropped into the fighting below, scattering Fae knights in dark leathers and a group of shining Unseelie with tentacles and pinchers.

The drumstone flashed with bright emerald magic just a stone's throw away. I twisted to see Lys, who was seated backward on Arkyn. Lys raised his mace and sword as two more gargoyles flew toward us.

"They'll see you seal the stone," I said. "They'll know about your blood."

He glanced over his shoulder, blood spatter on his forehead and his fangs bared. "So be it. With us wed, everything is different. I am their king and they will be forced to accept me as I am."

I grinned. "That's my kingly mate."

As Arkyn landed, I leapt off with Lys doing likewise beside me. We engaged the gargoyles. Arkyn struck out with his tail at the taller of the two beasts. I ran behind the first monster and lashed my blade across its spine, dropping it. Lys sheathed his mace and knelt at the drumstone. The light painted his face and threw shadows behind his broad shoulders onto the forest floor.

Arkyn jumped onto the chest of the gargoyle and ripped out its throat while a giant lumbered toward us.

Two Fae knights took down a scorpion by surrounding it and lopping off its vicious tail.

I scrambled onto Arkyn's back and we flew at the giant's head. I tapped Arkyn to get him to veer sharply and I rose up as best I could, my blood giving me strength and speed. My blade slashed across the giant's eyes, making the beast growl and shriek. Arkyn roared even louder and the Unseelie stumbled backward, blind and afraid.

I turned to watch Lys drag his bloodied forearm across the drumstone. Arkyn flew toward him as he drew runes in the scarlet liquid. Crouching, he moved back and let drops of his blood fall. The stone flashed a bright moon-blue and the forest went silent.

The Unseelie turned toward the drumstone they had used to portal here, then they watched Lys with eerie gazes.

"Finish them," he said as he charged a scorpion.

The battle rose once more and Arkyn hovered over the dirtied, bloody assemblage. I urged him to fly toward the last of the Unseelie, a hairy thing that I had no name for. Arkyn bashed the creature in the face as he zipped by and I stood on Arkyn's back, my blood roaring, and launched my sword into the back of its neck.

Arkyn and I landed hard. The dragon grunted and I hissed in pain. A gash showed on my upper arm.

Slicked with Unseelie blood, from both his arm and from the monsters, Lys stood and faced his audience.

51

LYSANAEL

L ysanael let his blood run down his forearm. His hair stuck to his damp forehead and neck as he lifted his head to speak. "I am the son of a Seelie queen and an Unseelie high Fae."

A chorus of shocked gasps echoed through the courtiers and Lys hardened his heart against the pain of their disgust. He had Revna, Neeria, Gwyn, and Arkyn. The rest could go hang.

He lifted his arm and his mixed blood glistened in the dappled sunlight. "Yes, I am half nightmare, but this monster," he said, placing a fist over his heart, "is loyal to you, to our Seelie court. The Druid recently informed me that the blood of an Unseelie high Fae could seal the drumstones for a time. I didn't know that fact until he told me or I would have sealed them sooner. The Druid didn't know of my bloodline until the day he told me about the sealing."

Murmurs of disbelief echoed through the crowd and every gaze either sharpened or widened in horror.

He had to push them. To be the ruler here. "Now," he said, raising his chin and voice, "bow to your king."

Would they?

None moved. Silence reigned. Sweat beaded along Lysanael's upper lip and his heart drummed unevenly against his ribcage. If they did bend the knee, he would still have to keep the council under his thumb to avoid a coup, and there would be moments when he'd have to lean on their fear of his Unseelie blood to encourage obedience. But all of that could be accomplished. Possibly. But if they rebelled now and took him, his life was forfeit.

With a heavy flap of wings, Arkyn landed, and Revna nodded at Lysanael approvingly. Her crown shimmered and her icy eyes promised she would annihilate anyone who stepped in his way. She eyed the council members, who shot glares at Lysanael. They were plotting already.

Revna called them out by name. "Listen, you lot. He saved your ungrateful arses today. You can beg his forgiveness for your poor attitude and bow or he can unleash his fellow Unseelie so you don't have to make any more difficult decisions. Ever."

The court dropped into deep bows and curtseys, their eyes lowered respectfully. Yonnis practically snarled, but Corae yanked his arm, forcing him into a bow.

Lysanael's heart surged with gratitude for Revna and with a relief that untied the tension of his entire adult life.

Winking at him, Revna leapt from Arkyn's back to stand with him.

Yes, his reign would be possible because of the Berserker goddess at his side.

52

REVNA

Ribbons of black and indigo fluttered from the trees of the courtyard beside the keep. Lys's coat of arms showed on at least a dozen banners hanging from posts that lined an area set with long feasting tables. Musicians plucked lutes and played wood pipes at the far side of the gathering. Though many wore bandages or walked with new limps, the Fae seemed more than ready to celebrate our marriage. Sonaellyn, Malaynia, and Gwyn were trying to talk Arkyn into wearing a ribbon-festooned blanket made of ivy and indigo flowers.

Good luck with that, I thought, grinning as I took Lys's arm and walked out to meet our court.

"Everything to your liking?"

I smoothed my flimsy indigo gown and tugged my ebony cloak higher on my shoulders. "It's all lovely until a dragon bites your head off for trying to drape him in flowers."

Lys followed my line of sight and chuckled. "I know how he feels."

I eyed his feasting attire. Everyone in attendance had been forced to bathe, bandage, and redress for the feasting after the Unseelie battle and sealing of the drumstones. Now, Lys wore all black and I had to say it suited him. The gold loop in his pointed ear and the torc at his neck stood out against the simplicity of the clothing. He'd let his hair fall loose over his broad shoulders, making him appear less formal. Catching me staring, he grinned wickedly and his hand ran farther down my back. I shivered with delight and he leaned close.

"I say we make our toasts, enjoy the first course, then leave. Unless you're set on staying for the dancing?" The kiss he set on my temple was warm and gentle.

He wanted to begin our wedding night early. I swallowed, face flushing. My neck and cheeks were probably as rosy as the sunset glowing around us. "I never cared much for dancing."

His chuckle rumbled through his body into mine. His sandalwood and cedar scent made my heart do a dance of its own.

We ignored the fact that most of the council wasn't present for the feasting. Bornien was there and the majority of the court. Lys had said he'd most likely force the others off the council and out of Caer Du for good. I agreed and would be happy to see the back of them when the time came. There would be work to do, certainly. But we would handle it. I had no doubts about that. The real trouble on my mind was putting my past to rights. Vengeance was coming.

But for now, I would enjoy Lys and a freedom I had never known. I welcomed Arkyn to rest beside my end of the feasting table. Lys and I sang and ate and relished the joy of being alive.

ॐ

The moment I shut the bedchamber door behind us, Lys and I were in motion. Tearing off cloaks, boots, slippers, and weapon belts. Kissing. Holding. My hands in his long hair and his fingers digging into my hips. My raw emotions, so recently unleashed, only made every touch of his hands on me and each sweep of his mouth on mine more intense. I pushed him back onto the bed and straddled him.

"Are you still wearing your blade and poisons, my viper?" Lys's warm hand slid up my leg and under the edge of my rumpled dress, making me tremble.

Heat rushed through my veins, my Berserker magic growling inside me. "I have no need of such trappings now." I tugged my gown off one shoulder. Desire was a haze over his eyes. "You are fully in my thrall."

He sat up, his fine stomach showing off his dedication to training, and he set his teeth against my bare shoulder. His breath heated my skin. "I am at your mercy."

I took his face in my hands and lifted my chest, showing off my assets. "Too bad I'm not known for that particular trait."

Growling, he wrapped his arms around me and flipped me to my back. He threw off his tunic and I reached up to run my palms down the lines and angles of his bare and glorious torso.

"I have no idea what I'm doing," I said, a laugh of joy and sauciness coloring my voice.

He smiled, showing his Fae fangs. "I don't either, but I've heard talk."

I laughed loudly. "Yes. A great amount of talk."

"We can figure it out. Don't you agree?"

I unlaced the silver bindings at the front of my gown. "We *are* fairly intelligent."

Lys braced a hand just under my breast and his chest moved in a deep breath. "Perhaps five minutes ago, but now…" His eyebrow lifted as I grinned.

Leaning forward, he brushed his lips over my collarbone and his hair fell forward, creating a curtain around us. I slipped my legs free and wrapped them around his waist. Propped up on one elbow, he allowed some of his weight to sink into me, and I delighted in the feel of his solid presence and his delicious scent. I met his lips with mine and desire shot like lightning down my body as his tongue brushed over mine. With his nose, he tipped my chin up, then proceeded to nibble his way down my throat and lower, tasting and licking his way across my body. My back arched. I bit back a gasp.

He looked up at me as he kissed my stomach, his sooty lashes dark against his gold and green eyes. "No holding back. I want every ounce of who you are, venom and all."

His tongue curled and flicked against me and I writhed in pleasure, fisting my hands in his hair. He drove himself upward and sucked on my upper lip before opening his mouth and licking my lower lip.

Humming with longing, I took a turn savoring the planes and angles of his powerful body, drawing my hands over his muscled chest and down his toned form, teasing him with my fingertips and tongue. He moaned and called my name, his hands bunching the sheets, his rings catching the firelight, and a curse slipping from his lips. Desire jolted through my blood like I was on fire in all the right ways.

I had never thought I would love and be loved like this. Free. Fully. And with a Fae king no less. But I knew I deserved this just as any other person did. Master had twisted me, but I had the power to fight my way free of that evil and I would never stop battling for myself, my heart, and my love.

We took our time through the night, Lys and I, pressing kisses to damp skin and finding new ways that our bodies fit. He found he could make me gasp with a certain snap of his hips. The way he squeezed his eyes shut and could hardly restrain himself thrilled me.

Between lovemaking, we shared secrets and stories about our lives and what we hoped for in the future. At some point, his eyes drifted shut and I followed him into the world of dreams.

The next morning, we lay on our sides. He was behind me, tracing a circle on my shoulder blade. My skin pebbled under his touch. The sun rose in the colored glass of the window and spread gold and scarlet over the bed curtains. The heat of his body behind me sent longing vibrating through me.

"Is this what you desire, my viper?" He pressed himself closer, his body flush with mine. I shuddered with want. "Why don't you first tell me about your training and how we can improve our warriors?" He held completely still, and it was exquisite torture.

"Lys, I—"

"We need to talk about this." His tone was scolding, but I knew he was teasing me. I loved it. "You will be queen tomorrow." He rolled his hips into me and my body hummed. He dragged his fingers over my waist and slid them down my stomach, his touch light.

I pinched his arm hard and grinned, enjoying the game. "Please, Lysanael…"

His hand slid lower and my heart beat frantically. "How many warriors should we have at the ready in case the human king decides he is a fool and wishes to attack?" he asked, his hot breath on my ear.

Heat raced across my stomach and pooled low in my belly. I reached over my shoulder and found his pointed ear, the cool gold of his earring, and the softness of his hair.

"Answer your king." His voice was low and thunderous.

I breathed too quickly. Old Ones save me, this Fae male would have me burst into flames before this was over. My head was light as air, but in a way that made me want to lose myself in the feeling. His hand shifted lower still and I moved against him.

"Every Fae warrior is worth five humans," I struggled to say. "Your army is large enough..." I couldn't continue; I could scarcely draw breath for how much I wanted him.

He rolled me to my back, threw my leg over his shoulder, then pressed his body down onto mine. His eyes glowed with need and his nostrils flared as his gaze brushed down my neck and chest and hips. Sparks ricocheted through me and a wave of desire crashed over me. Moving slowly over me, he whispered my name as I took hold of his broad shoulders and dug my fingers into the muscle there, the velvet skin. I breathed him in as he moved, easy at first, then more insistent, inside me. Pleasure cascaded over me as his body pressed into mine, and I let myself happily drown in sensation as the tension built.

"I love you." His lips graced the hollow of my throat. "I am yours."

I tugged his face to mine and kissed him, drawing my teeth over his lip. "I love you too."

Soon his pace increased and we dissolved into the pleasure of two souls united.

53

REVNA

A knock at the door woke me. I was strewn across Lys's chest. He kissed my head.

"Go away, please," I called out.

Lys chuckled, bumping me around. "I second that idea."

"A message for Lady Resaynia," a servant said.

I shot up. For me?

I untangled myself from the sheets and blankets, threw on a sleeping shift some servant must have left here for me before the wedding, and opened the door.

No one was there, but on the floor, a tiny scroll showed a black wax seal. My blood went cold as I bent to retrieve it.

"Is everything all right?" Lys said from bed.

"I don't know yet." I took the scroll into the chamber and shut the door. The seal showed a mountain ram—Raulian's sign. I snapped the wax and began to read.

· · ·

I hope you're alive. I hope this message gets to you if you are. They know about your freedom and your new union. All three puppet masters are in the keep and pulling strings for answers.

It was Raulian's hand and though he was being careful with his wording, I gathered the message's meaning. Master knew that I had somehow negated the death rune and that I had agreed to wed Lys. Both King Darrew and the Witch were at Isernwyrd, meeting with him. Were they plotting against me? Most assuredly. But I was no longer a slave. I was to be queen and I would see them bow.

Lys came up behind me and set a kiss on my shoulder through the shift's soft fabric. "What are you thinking?" he asked.

"That it is time to strike with my venom and watch my enemies fall."

❦

At the Caer Du stables, I rubbed Arkyn's chin then examined a tear he had in his wing from the battle with the Unseelie monsters on my wedding day. "You're healing nicely, but you're sure you can handle carrying Lys and me all the way to Saxonion?"

Arkyn huffed a breath against my cheek and licked my chin.

"I guess that means *yes*." I wiped my chin with the sleeve of my tunic.

I glanced behind me to see Lys discussing strategy with Neeria near the horses and the servants who were readying them. The Druid was finishing up his runes. He'd drawn a multitude of the magical symbols over the horses' flanks and chests, giving them strength, healing, and speed so they could attempt to keep up with Arkyn. A dozen Fae knights were already mounted and looking more than ready to ride into the Gwerhune. We were headed to Isernwyrd for full destruction. This was nearly as exciting as being behind closed doors with my Fae king.

The autumn wind had a real bite to it this morning, but the thick woolen cloak Malaynia had provided kept me plenty warm. I checked the girth holding the saddle in place, tugging the leather strap so it held more firmly, then I called to the others to get us going.

The Druid mounted a jet-black steed, Lys hopped onto Arkyn behind me, and Neeria climbed atop a sleek dun mare. The plan was to ride as fast to Isernwyrd as our varied mounts could handle. The Druid would target the Witch, Lys the king, and I would be focusing all my rage on Master. We would have the small contingent of Fae knights as support, of course. Neeria would use the description I'd given her to find Raulian and inform the Hunters of our loyalties, promises, and strategy if things went south. King Darrew would likely have a small retinue of knights with him, but perhaps if we moved quickly, we could win this without dealing with his entire army.

After days of travel through the dark and magical shadows of the Gwerhune, a crossing of the Veil, then the farmland and forest between the Border River and Isernwyrd, it was at last time for me to slake my thirst for revenge.

Below us, the Druid blasted open the castle's portcullis. Metal shrieked and Hunters called out warnings as the earth wizard's emerald-hued power shattered rock and sent two guards flying. Roots surged from the ground to catch them before they hit the ground. He had remembered my direction not to hurt any Hunters if we didn't have to.

Neeria and the other Fae knights trailed the Druid inside the castle. Flying low in the sky, I urged Arkyn through the thick morning fog and over the mossy, time-worn walls of Isernwyrd. Lys rode at my back, mace and sword drawn already.

Hunters aimed bows from the curtain wall and the partially destroyed gatehouse.

I waved and their arms slackened as they took in Arkyn and me. "We are here to liberate you!" I called, hoping they could understand my mission here.

Shouts rose and more Hunters ran into the courtyard below. Black-fletched arrows zipped past Arkyn's wings and our heads, but none hit their mark.

I grinned viciously. That was no accident. My fellow Hunters didn't miss. They must have guessed my plan or heard my words and were ready to support me regardless of how they viewed me personally. Perhaps Raulian had swayed them to be prepared for such an outcome.

I didn't see Raul anywhere. I had to keep my eyes out for him and move quickly or Master would snatch him up and use him to control me.

Leaning forward, I shouted against the wind and toward Arkyn's ear. "Bash right through Master's chambers." I tapped his scales to help direct him, but he snorted as if to say he fully understood our plan.

Lys set his lips on my ear. "Order me as you see fit. I long only to watch your venom strike."

Fire flashed through my veins and I briefly squeezed Lys's thigh with my free hand to thank him for being exactly who I needed.

Back talons first, Arkyn crashed through the roof of Master's living quarters. Rubble blasted over my head and Lys shouted a warning as a dagger zipped past my ear. I glanced through the shower of dust to see that oaf Cuthnor's ragged beard and tan skin. Of course that arsehead would support Master.

Arkyn flapped his wings and knocked a body to the ground amid the ruin of stone, wood, and plaster. Clouds of dust marred my view.

"Take down anyone who comes at us," I said to Lys. The Hunters would know what was afoot by now and if they didn't, well, I couldn't risk Lys's safety. This was already messy and it would only grow messier unless we acted quickly.

"As you wish." Lys jumped free of Arkyn's wings and launched himself at Cuthnor. His mace was a black slash in the plumes of destruction. Another shout rose and I knew Cuthnor had fallen. Good riddance.

I leaned over Arkyn's head to view the three who lay on the ground before us and smoothed my dragon's left ear, signaling him. He let out an ear-splitting, chest-cracking roar that had all three covering their faces and scrambling to get back.

Cloaked in pale dust, Lys grinned like the wonderful Unseelie demon he was. His wicked, fanged smile showed as he rained down justice on the human knights —those who supported King Darrew, the man who had killed my mother.

Dressed in scarlet, the king's retinue burst through the remnants of the sitting room's broken wall. Neeria, the Druid, and a few of our own Fae knights trailed them in. The clang of steel, the grunt of close combat, and the continued rain of rubble filled my ears. The Druid raised his palms and released a blast of emerald magic that knocked four human knights against the last standing wall.

Arkyn lowered himself and I climbed down to face one of the three, the only one who had found his feet.

Master smiled and smoothed his greasy gray hair

back. "My rebellious daughter has returned home. We can easily make a deal. If not, I can call out one word and drop Raulian and the rest. It's your choice."

Their death runes were still intact, so he wasn't bluffing. The Witch had crafted the runes so that Master could kill with one ancient word of power.

One of the other two figures shook themselves in the shadow of a partially collapsed side wall, then lunged at Arkyn. It was King Darrew.

The king's scarlet cloak fluttered as he whirled to avoid Arkyn's snapping sharp teeth, then he thrust his short sword toward the dragon's neck.

My blood shot fire through my body and I lunged to defend Arkyn, but he didn't need me. He knocked the fair-skinned man down with the flick of one wing, then forced him to the floor. He glanced at me as if for permission.

Darrew had wanted war. Bornien, the Druid, Lys, and I had discussed his motivations at length, noting the way he'd grown more and more greedy for resources that could only be found in the Realm of Lights. He had wanted to create chaos by having me kill Lys and then he was going to invade the Fae kingdom while they were distracted.

King Darrew needed to die.

I nodded grimly at Arkyn and he relieved the Saxonion ruler of his head.

A strangled sound came from Master's throat, and it

brought a smile to my face. He gripped his beating stick like it might save him. It would not.

The Witch came forward, her face coated in dust. Master eyed her, his gaze wide and panicked. They fought their features, obviously straining to mask their fear, but their trembling forms and tight-lipped frowns gave them away.

Master's face was pale as a corpse's. "Let us negotiate."

The Witch's gaze snapped from Arkyn to the Druid and Lys—who had successfully killed Darrew's knights —then she looked back at me. "I was never a willing participant in their plots," the Witch said.

I raised an eyebrow and hefted my sword, ready to be done with this. "Explain yourself."

The sounds of fighting behind me lessened and I knew Lys and the others had defeated the enemy for now. No more Hunters had appeared to fight and I wondered if they still lived or if Master had already whispered the ancient words needed to undo their lives.

Lys joined me with the Druid at his side. "Speak, Witch," Lys said. "Did you not place the runes on the Hunters? Did you not scheme with Darrew and this piece of filth to frame me for the murder of an innocent?"

The Witch's eerie owl-like gaze sent shivers down my spine. Her eyes were too big for her slim, wrinkled face. "I sheltered the princess. She resides in my forest at my home. I hid her when she ran from her father."

"Why did she run?" I asked. Was she lying?

"As you already know, the king is not a good man," she said.

Her tone and the rage in her eyes filled in the meaning hiding in her words. Images formed in my mind, gray but detailed. I shook as they faded. The Witch had shown me the princess's memories. Darrew had beaten his daughter.

"I protected her," the Witch continued, nodding as if she knew I had seen those memories. "When the king insisted on sending the Huntress after you," she said to Lys, "I did what I had to do to keep the princess safe. I couldn't have the king digging through my home and my trees, searching out his daughter after realizing I was not loyal to him. I prepared the Huntress for her mission, yes, but I did it unwillingly. I never wanted to place death runes either, but it was that or they would have sought out my son to cut him down. Kill me if you must. I certainly deserve it. I would do it all again to protect my boy, his family, and the innocent princess."

I never would have guessed the Witch had set the runes on us unwillingly, but looking back… *I loathe you and you loathe me,* I believe had been her words to Master when I went to her house with him to get the illusion potion.

The Druid waved his hand. A shimmering indigo light washed over the Witch. Her mouth fell open and light poured from her lips as she dropped to her knees. Emerald and blue light leaked from her fingertips, and the necklace at her throat, the one with three blue spirals, sparked like it was crafted of lightning.

"What are you doing?" I stepped forward. Was he killing her? Taking her power?

"I am examining the truth of what she is," the Druid said, his voice calm and almost friendly. "Do you order that I stop, Queen-in-Waiting?" A wind that affected no one else ruffled his stark white robes.

"No, go on. What do you see?"

"She speaks the truth." He lowered his hand, and his magic faded, leaving the Witch sitting on the ground, looking as normal as she ever could.

I traded a look with Lys, who inclined his head as if to say it was wholly my decision whether to kill the Witch or not.

"Unmake your death runes," I said to her, "and we may let you live."

She stood in one graceful motion then set her palms together and began whispering.

I faced Master's glare. The scar he'd received from me the first time he'd beaten me showed above his wrist as he gripped his stick. A shard of broken glass and a piece of plaster fell from his robes and the scent of marula oil wafted into my nose.

"You can't win this, Huntress." His words slithered across the room and into my ears. "You are mine to order. I created you. Without the Hunters, what are you? Nothing. You are nothing."

My stomach rolled. I gritted my teeth. Fingers damp and curled around my sword, I stepped closer.

A windstorm of memories assaulted me.

Strikes to my face. A tooth flying from my mouth to clatter across the floor of this chamber. The dull pain of healing ribs. Master's soft voice that promised food if I would only stand up and fight one more time.

I set my jaw and swallowed bile. Sweat dripped down my spine.

He was not going to treat me like that, or anyone like that, ever again.

Calling up my blood, I sent strength surging through my back, limbs, and even into my vision. I could see each pore on his face, a set of features as familiar as my own.

I strode forward and he pulled out a knife.

Arkyn squawked in warning. I kicked the blade from Master's grip easily, then shoved my foot into his belly. He landed roughly, exhaling and shouting a curse, but I didn't bother listening. I put my boot on his throat. He spit and thrashed, trying to threaten me, surely.

"You sharpened me," I said, my voice a stiletto blade, "honed me, and crafted me into the most dangerous of blades. Now, that edge will cut down you and your dark empire."

"I have him, you know." The loathsome worm pushed at my boot and his face went as red as a beet. "Raulian. His lover. Child."

Rage limned the edges of my vision in blood. "Where? Tell me now." I pressed my heel in harder.

He bucked his hips and gasped, sweat pouring from him like rain. I left off the pressure for a moment and he began sputtering, but another voice interrupted him.

"Oh no, he doesn't." Raulian sauntered into the room and saluted Arkyn.

Relief as bright as pain washed through me. I soaked in his familiar smile, the lean of his posture, and the victory in his eyes.

"He has no one and nothing," Raulian said.

Lys didn't seem to notice Raulian or the murmurings of the Witch. His gaze focused on Master. A vein in his temple throbbed and his knuckles were white on his mace. He wanted to annihilate Master, but he was holding himself back. Good. This was my job.

"You can't just kill a king," Master spat out. "His men will go to war with you. The Fae will be hunted. You will hang." His red-eyed gaze flew from me to Lys and back again.

Turning away, I smiled at my fellow Hunters. "Anyone else tired of hearing this arsehead's blathering?"

"I know I am." Raulian crossed his arms and glared death at Master.

Lys grinned, showing both fangs.

I leaned down and looked Master in the eye. "You deserve a long and terrible death, but I, unlike you, am strong enough to show mercy."

He struggled against my boot and the hate in his eyes made me feel strangely sad.

Lifting my boot, I drew my sword across his throat and ended the Hunters' suffering once and for all.

EPILOGUE

Revna

"Get me that hammer." I looked to Arkyn and nodded toward the tools on the small ledge two levels down.

The sound of saws, picks, and happy conversation filled the new settlement in Fjordbok, not five miles from where I made my promise to my mother and watched the life leave her eyes. We were building up a traditional cliff dwelling structure complete with individual chambers that looked out to the sea but also held cozy cave-like areas protected from the weather. Eleven floors had been constructed thus far and the vented kitchens and storage chambers deep inside the wall of earth were nearly finished as well.

We had flown on Arkyn, back and forth for months, from the Realm of Lights to Fjordbok to establish peace with the Saxonion princess's regent and to fulfill my mother's dying wish. There were only sixty-five Fjordbok natives here; sadly, none of my cousins had shown up yet. But more folk arrived every day. Some were half-Fjordbok blood and others had never had kin on this island. It didn't matter to my people. We welcomed all. More bodies made for an easier work load as we developed trade and reinvigorated the fishing industry.

Soon, I'd seek out my cousins as well as those with Berserker magic. There had to be a few with the power. I hoped so, at least. I planned to train them and they would become Fjordbok's generals in the future. For now, we relied on the princess and her regent's protection as well as the Fae army and assistance.

Bornien had followed Lys's every suggestion in the plan to do as I had dreamed my whole life. It was all coming true.

For you, Mother. I wiped a tear and kept on working, taking joy in my calloused hands and the echo of Raulian's noisy toddler playing with Gwyn on the beach below.

Lys stood at the edge of the cliff dwelling structure and looked down at the cold black sea. "I'll never get used to this. How in the name of the Old Ones do you ever relax enough to sleep?"

Every night we'd been here so far, we'd slept in

hammocks hung in the ice pines, the trees that grew wide and lush along the rocky coastline. "I would have thought someone who spends a good chunk of his day as a bird wouldn't be worried about heights."

He glanced at me over his shoulder and his nostrils flared, a sure sign my mate was displeased. "I can't sleep in my raven form unfortunately."

I chuckled and met Arkyn at the edge. The dragon snorted happily as he opened his mouth and released the hammer into my waiting hands. I finished nailing the spike along the ledge and waved at Lys to grab the netting. We stretched it across all five spikes to create a barrier just in case Gwyn came to visit our chamber and walked too close to the edge.

"Seems like a full wall would be a better choice," Lys muttered.

I poked him in the ribs. "You're mated to a Berserker now, King Lysanael. You had better steel yourself for more cliffside adventures."

His eyes widened. "You weren't serious about the ice climbing, were you? Please say no."

I laughed and laughed. Wiping a different type of tear away, I grabbed Lys from behind and set my cheek between his shoulder blades. He smelled divine. His hand snaked down my hip to my thigh and he leaned his head back to rest gently on mine.

"I never thought I would find such adventure in the human realm."

"Just you wait," I said. "I haven't even told you about the shark hunt."

"Queen Viper, you will surely be the death of me. It's been true since the day of our meeting."

"Do you regret raising this little snake from assassin to queen?" I slid around to his front and pressed myself into him, savoring the feel of his strong body and running my hands wherever I pleased.

A purr rumbled from his throat and vibrated through his chest into me. He slipped his hands under my thighs and lifted me up. I laced my legs around his waist and tried to kiss him, but he leaned back, raising an eyebrow.

"Queen Revna." His lips brushed over mine, hardly touching but sending waves of desire through me. "I do not regret a single moment with you."

"Even the poisoning? That had to be at least a little uncomfortable."

His thumb drew circles over the small of my back and he nipped my throat with his sharp Fae teeth. I wanted him now. On this floor. Immediately.

"I have payback in mind for that portion of our relationship." He walked to the back wall and pressed me against the cold stone, kneading his hips into me.

Pleasure sparked across my skin and shivers rode down the backs of my legs. I kissed him hard. His tongue slipped over my bottom lip. Bracing himself with one arm on the wall, he unbuckled his weapons belt and tugged his trousers down. With a roughness I didn't mind, he rucked up my dress and soon his heat found mine.

He stilled then, his forehead on mine, his breath coming in gasps. My pulse beat low in my body like an insistent drum. I shivered with want as a feeling like hot honey poured over me. Leaning down, he took the neckline of my dress in his teeth and lowered the fabric. His mouth came down on me and a moan escaped me. I shoved my fingers into his tousled knot of hair and felt the tips of his Fae ears brush my palms. I drew my nails over one and felt him tremble.

"What was that about payback?" I teased.

He chuckled darkly into my neck, then began moving ever so slowly, his hands braced on the wall on either side of my head. The rock was as cold as ice on my back, but our heat provided more than enough warmth. My body demanded more, my heart pounded, and I rolled my hips, asking physically for what I wanted.

He tsked me and looked through his obsidian lashes. "I am a wicked Fae king and I will do as I please."

His hips thrust once, and satisfaction washed down me in waves. Pleasure blurred my view of his handsome face and deep green and gold slitted eyes.

With a quick movement, I set a foot on the wall and pushed lightly, latching onto him and lifting up. He gasped, his head falling back as his cheeks flushed with color.

"You can try," I whispered into his ear as he dropped back onto the wool sack. "But I tend to get what I want."

I claimed him exactly as I wanted to then, not taking any more of his teasing arrogance, and instead, seizing what was mine. Riotous pleasure and joy gripped us, our bodies fated to fit perfectly.

"My viper," he rasped out, his eyes shut and the veins in his neck standing out.

After, he flipped us over and held me tightly until the stars of my homeland winked over the ocean.

Whether here or in the Realm of Lights, in Lys's arms, I was finally at home.

Readers,

Thank you so much for diving into this new world with me! I hope you'll continue the adventure with another book in the Realm of Dragons and Fae *world,* A Thief and Her Pirate King *(Spring 2022). Lina is a human desperate to escape an arranged marriage and Zavi is a half-Fae pirate king who might just be the perfect rebellious male to take her away. But Zavi has a secret that means death for at least one of them...*

If you'd like to read a free prequel to Revna and Arkyn's relationship, join my newsletter at https://www.alishaklapheke.com/free-prequel-1 today!

Thanks for being fabulous,
Alisha

AFTERWORD

A little about The Fae King's Assassin…

I have loved Fae stories ever since I first read *The Cruel Prince* by Holly Black. Fascinated by darkly magical settings and dangerous, beautiful beings, I wrote The Fae King's Assassin for every reader who, like me, is always seeking a portal to the Fae realm.

Both Brittany, France, and early England inspired the settings for this book. I have ancestors from both places and enjoyed researching the architecture and customs of both places, although I went off the rails and designed the world how I wanted. You can see some French influence in the castle of Caer Du and its maze and Isernwyrd in Saxonion brings us back to 13th century structures in England. Yes, I am a nerd through and through.

Two media sources influenced the building of Arkyn's character—*How to Train Your Dragon* by

Cressida Cowell and *His Majesty's Dragon*, a book by the talented Naomi Novik. Toothless captured my heart long ago with his cat-like behavior and loyal soul. Temeraire (the dragon in *His Majesty's Dragon*) also had me cheering when I read that series. Temeraire's relationship with his human touched me and I wanted to echo that in this novel.

ACKNOWLEDGMENTS

As we all know by now, creating a book takes a village. Thank you to Rose Griot (IG: rose.the.book.griot) for the name of the Fae kingdom, the Realm of Lights. Thank you to my Dragon Divas—Kelly, Ali, Rachel, Megan, and Erin—my Turtles, the Shield Wall, my editor, Laura Josephson, my Typo Hunters, the Uncommon Crew, the Dragon Den Facebook group, and my family, especially my amazing husband, Daniel. Also, thank you, readers, for indulging my obsession with all things Fae. I couldn't do this without you all!

ALSO BY ALISHA KLAPHEKE

Enchanting the Elven Mage

Stolen by the Shadow King

The Edinburgh Seer

Full List of Titles

Kingdoms of Lore Series

(Standalone series—new couple in each one but earlier couples are in most of the books)

Enchanting the Elven Mage

Enchanting the Fae Prince

Enchanting the Dragon Lord

Enchanting the Dryad Prince

Kingdoms of Lore: Underworld Duology

Stolen by the Shadow King

Rise of the Fire Queen

Dragons Rising Series

Fate of Dragons

Band of Breakers

Queen of Seas

Sword of Oak

Magic of Lore

Realm of Dragons and Fae

The Fae King's Assassin

A Thief and Her Pirate King (late spring 2023)

Bound by Dragons (summer 2023)

The Edinburgh Seer Trilogy

The Edinburgh Seer

The Edinburgh Heir

The Edinburgh Fate

Uncommon World / Queens of Steel and Starlight

Waters of Salt and Sin

Fever

Plains of Sand and Steel

Forest of Silver and Secrets

Rune Kingdom (standalone in same world)

Yew Queen Trilogy

(spicy urban paranormal portal romance under pen name of
Eve A. Hunt)

Fae Curse

Fae World

Fae Spell

Printed in Great Britain
by Amazon

42942256R00233